# Making the Tunisian Resurgence

Mahmoud Sami Nabi

# Making the Tunisian Resurgence

palgrave
macmillan

Mahmoud Sami Nabi
LEGI-Tunisia Polytechnic School and FSEG Nabeul
University of Carthage
Tunis, Tunisia

ISBN 978-981-13-3770-3 ISBN 978-981-13-3771-0 (eBook)
https://doi.org/10.1007/978-981-13-3771-0

Library of Congress Control Number: 2018967953



This Palgrave Macmillan imprint is published by the registered company Springer Nature Singapore Pte Ltd.
The registered company address is: 152 Beach Road, #21-01/04 Gateway East, Singapore 189721, Singapore

*To the Tunisians across time, striving for justice, peace and dignity,*
*To my parents, the light of identity shining on modernity,*
*To my wife and my daughters, the gifts from the Almighty,*
*To my stepparents and all my family,*
*To my friends in Monastir, Tunis and globally,*
*To my colleagues and students in the university,*
*To all my teachers and professors since the primary.*

# Foreword

Mahmoud Sami Nabi offers us a large and ambitious fresco, drawing the directive lines for an inclusive and sustainable development of Tunisia. He conducts rigorous diagnoses of the current periods before and after the Revolution, as well as of the Tunisian economy and its multiple disequilibria. The author analyzes the necessary dimensions for the recovery of the country and its insertion in an inclusive development path: unlocking energies, efficient and sound public policies, rebuilding the social contract linking the state to the social stakeholders, institutional reforms and creativity, innovative modes of financing, smart integration in the globalization and adoption of the knowledge economy as a development platform guaranteeing a sharable prosperity.

Nabi allies continually a subtle analysis of issues and challenges with justified suggestions of mechanisms and instruments for their resolution. Obviously, some of these analyses and proposals might generate critiques and controversies and possibly divergences. Yet, this is the sign, the proof of their interest and their substantial contribution to a debate leading to the social and economic resurgence of the country, at a time where the multiple crises mining it, are requiring urgent solutions.

Tunis, Tunisia
19 November 2017

Tahar Abdessalem

# Preface

"*If the people one day will to live, then destiny must respond, the night must disappear and the chain must break.*" This famous verse was written by the Tunisian national poet Aboul-Qacem Echebbi (1909–1934) in his poem *Will to Live*. At that time, Tunisia was under the French colonization. It is now part of the country's national anthem and symbolizes the willingness of Tunisians to defeat oppression. As the country is emerging from its "revolution for dignity" (December 2010–January 2011), Tunisians are still aspiring to a modern and developed country.

One of the triggering factors of Tunisia's "revolution for dignity" is the unequal access of citizens to the socioeconomic opportunities. The Tunisian economy is not inclusive. The economic opportunities are not available to citizens on the basis of their competencies, ideas or initiatives but influenced by the wealth of their families and their social and political connections. Five years after the revolution, social protests emerged again in many disadvantaged regions of the country fueled by the deterioration of people's daily living conditions. More recent ones triggered successively in January 2016 and April 2017 claiming for credible and concrete public policies in order to tackle the chronic unemployment, especially among the youth, and the unequal access to economic opportunities.

The failure of Tunisia in generating an inclusive economic system is the result of many factors among which are the extractive political regime under the dictatorship and the underdeveloped institutional environment. But even in developed countries where institutions are developed, the economic system is failing in generating inclusive growth. There are suggestions that advocate the inclusion of ethical dimensions and defend a more active social role of the state within the free market economy. I believe that the debate on the type of the economic system shall not take place on theoretical grounds. Instead, we have to conceive an integrated development strategy encompassing all the dimensions of the society in order to unlock the dynamism, the creativity and the solidarity of the individuals. This naturally requires the exploration of new mechanisms and institutional changes to bring inclusiveness, social justice and sustainability to the economic system. The exercise is difficult in a transition period where a country like Tunisia is still exposed to threats of violence, social chaos, spread of corruption, political instability and lack of trust in the political elite. It is even more difficult in a post-revolution phase where latent divergences among citizens are suddenly emerging. These divergences are deeply anchored in the society and geographically differentiated. They are intimately related to the history of the country and to the position of religion in the society. Therefore, achieving a national identity respectful of individuals' opinions and ensuring social cohesion is becoming an extremely important pillar of the Tunisian development path.

From an economic policy-design perspective, the difficulty of the Tunisian context is substantial. Despite its small population, the economic problems of Tunisia are accentuated by the specificity of the political transition period. The enforcement of law is weakening, corruption is spreading and corporatism is influencing the design of the economic policies. Hence, no economic solution for Tunisia will emerge without the openness to the multidimensional aspects of the society. Besides, the traditional macroeconomic policies are not sufficient. It shall be complemented by nonconventional mechanisms and instruments enabling public institutions to play their strategic role in complementarity with the private sector.

My aim in this book is to investigate the current socioeconomic issues and challenges facing Tunisia and to suggest mechanisms and instruments for their resolution. Therefore, this book is not of pure economic analysis. I believe, like many economists,[1] that focusing on economic issues solely

[1] Ronald Coase affirms that economists shall reorient the field of economics to the study of man as he is and the economic system as it actually exists, taking into consideration the cultural, institutional and organizational diversities (Ronald Coase, 2012). Ronald Coase (2012) "Saving Economics from the Economists," December 2012, Harvard Business Review.

is far from being sufficient to conceive a development strategy. At the opposite, we have to explore the multidimensional aspects of the society. In the first chapter, I analyze the roots of the revolution and the post-revolution situation of the country from a political sociology perspective. I particularly investigate if the country is becoming more cohesive after the revolution and what are the main challenges it faces from this perspective. Chapter 2 is dedicated to a detailed diagnosis of the Tunisian economy before and after the revolution. I particularly focus on the various binding constraints preventing it from escaping the middle-income trap. In Chap. 3, I present the current economic reforms' agenda and pinpoint the institutional bottlenecks that are preventing the successive governments from escaping the post-revolution vicious circle.

In Chap. 4, I explore the pillars of an inclusive development strategy that a country like Tunisia shall pursue. I particularly examine three multidimensional approaches of change and development. First, I present Kaplan and Freeman's (2015) approach for a successful inclusive reform during a political transition. Then, I examine the multidimensional development theory of the Tunisian philosopher Abderrahmane Ibn Khaldun. Finally, I look at the multidimensional development paradigm of the laureate of the Nobel Prize in economics, Joseph Stiglitz. I dedicate special sections at the end of this chapter to the building of inclusive institutions and the reinvention of leadership on the institutional ground, in order for Tunisia to progress on the path of socioeconomic transformation toward a modern and inclusive country. This institutional dimension is crucial to Tunisia which shall conceive its development strategy taking into account its strengths and weaknesses on a multidimensional space. This is the reason why I assign an important place in this chapter to the reengineering of institutions and to the role of leadership in the country's transformation process.

In Chap. 5, I continue the exercise of developing an integrated inclusive development strategy that would unlock Tunisia's economic potential. I particularly emphasize (1) the need to modernize the Tunisian state and reengineering its role, (2) the importance to develop a new social contract, (3) the urgency to immunize the Tunisian economy against the political instability, (4) why a pluralistic approach of economic development is timely, (5) how urgent is reforming the Tunisian economy to make it open, fair and more productive, (6) why the economy needs to modernize its judicial and property rights systems and finally, (7) how important is the positive disruption of the financial system.

The economic transformation of Tunisia requires the activation of new financial channels beyond the traditional ones in order to raise the necessary financial resources. As noted by the Asian Development Bank, the governments shall explore diverse sources of finance (public and private, domestic and international) and combine it coherently around shared agendas (ADB, 2015).[2] My intention in Chap. 6 is to shed light on a variety of nontraditional mechanisms and instruments to mobilize financial resources. I begin by exposing the benefits of various mechanisms of securitization including an original mechanism I tailored for the Tunisian context. Then, I defend the opportunity to develop equity finance, crowdfunding and trade finance. In a third section, I suggest a nonconventional monetary policy based on targeted quantitative easing (TQE) coupled with securitization. I dedicate a special section to the role of participatory banks in improving access to finance and the potential of coupling cooperatives and microfinance in generating jobs for youth. Finally, I motivate the opportunity to utilize an emerging financial instrument at the international level, the Social Impact Bonds, to unlock the philanthropic potential of Tunisia and channel it to support governmental social programs.

Tunisia is already connected to the global economy through many regional and bilateral free trade agreements, hosting international firms, and has been for a longtime one of the main touristic destinations in the Mediterranean basin. Yet, one of the main drivers of a successful economic transformation of Tunisia shall be an intelligently better integration into the global economy. This dimension is analyzed in Chap. 7, where I explore how Tunisia shall enhance methodically its integration into the global economy. I recall the "flying geese" catching-up process that characterized the development strategies of East Asia and motivate the opportunity for Tunisia to inspire from it, while conceiving its proper process coupled with a well-tailored industrial policy. An important place is also given in this chapter to the role of the state in facilitating the integration of the Tunisian small and medium enterprises (SMEs) in the global value chains. A second important dimension that Tunisia shall consider in relation to its integration into the global economy is the external financial liberalization. I present the current situation of the capital account

[2] ADB (2015) "Beyond the MDGs: Technology, Finance and Statistics to Unlock Sustainable Development in Asia Pacific," News Release, 28 May 2015.

liberalization and emphasize the importance of a good sequencing of the next phases of this process, as well as its pace.

If there is one dream that shall unify Tunisians and catalyze their energy is to transform their country into a knowledge-based economy. Tunisia's development strategy shall set as vision to be "*a knowledge-based economy*" by 2030. In this regard, it is clear that the state has to play an active role in concretizing this vision. The state shall catalyze the drivers of a deep socioeconomic transformation placing knowledge and innovation at the heart of the society. Such a transformation cannot be led by the private sector and markets solely. There is room for intensive public investment to build the required ecosystem (institutions, incentives, infrastructure, national programs, etc.) The speed of transforming Tunisia into a knowledge-based economy will depend on the effectiveness of the state's strategy in positioning *knowledge* at the core of the socioeconomic dynamic of Tunisia.

In the last chapter of this book, I begin by discussing the drivers of a knowledge economy. Then I show that Tunisia has no choice but to adopt an ICT[3]-based strategy for digital capital accumulation. The importance and the manner to improve the ecosystem of education, innovation and research are presented in a separate section. I dedicate a section to motivate the importance for Tunisia to benefit from the global opportunities in the IT-enabled services and the data science fields. Finally, I urge the policy makers to accelerate the digitalization of the public administration and to incentivize the state-owned and private companies to start their digital transformation. It goes without saying that many important development issues are not analyzed in this book. Three issues are particularly important for Tunisia: modernizing its agriculture, securing its energy supply and its water resources. All these dimensions are worthwhile to be considered along a green and sustainable vision of the Tunisian economy.

Tunis, Tunisia — Mahmoud Sami Nabi

[3] Information and Communication Technologies.

# Acknowledgments

I would like to thank Prof. Tahar Abdessalem for his comments and for accepting to write the foreword. I also thank Prof. Mongi Boughzala and Dr. Oualid Missaoui for their helpful comments. I could not have completed this book without the encouragements of my beloved mother and wife with whom I had permanently rich discussions on multiple subjects related to the past, present and future of Tunisia. I am deeply grateful to them. I much appreciate the comments and suggestions of two anonymous referees. Naturally, I am responsible for any remaining errors and shortcomings.

# Contents

# List of Figures

# List of Tables

CHAPTER 1

# The Revolution and the Post-Revolution Political Arena

## 1.1 The Roots of the Revolution

Tunisia achieved an average economic growth rate of 4.75% during the period 1990–2010. *Given this relatively good macroeconomic performance, it is legitimate to delve into the roots of the revolution of December 2010–January 2011.*

The benefits of the economic growth were not shared across the various regions and social classes. In particular, the Tunisian economy was not able to create sufficient jobs for the youth, to reduce regional disparities and to limit the proliferation of the informal sector. From a political economy perspective, the authoritarian bargain between the regime and the society became gradually more and more fragile. For a long period, the legitimacy of Ben Ali's regime was based on the economic, social and security gains. However, its legitimacy eroded when the losers began to outnumber the winners (Achy, 2011). Since the early 2000s, the perception of the regime as an immoral authority increased among the population as the result of illegal diversion of goods, corrupted bureaucracy and crony capitalism (Hibou, 2011). The first serious sign of the dictatorship's erosion was the revolt in the south mining region of 2008.[1] However, the roots of the Tunisian "Dignity revolution" were not only economic but encompassed a general feeling of indignity and degrading of the collective

[1] It began in the small town of *Redeyef* and was violently repressed.



M. S. Nabi, *Making the Tunisian Resurgence*,
https://doi.org/10.1007/978-981-13-3771-0_1

self-image. According to Hibou (2011), the uprising that followed the self-immolation of the street vendor *Mohamed Bouazizi* (on 17 December 2010), in the inner governorate *Sidi Bouzid*, was the expression of a social recognition demand fueled by a sense of collective self-respect recovery. The slogan "*Labor, Freedom, National Dignity*" expresses clearly the nature of this revolution, which ended the regime of Ben Ali on 14 January 2011. Initially triggered by a few thousands of people (unemployed graduates, young bloggers and Internet surfers), the revolutionary crowds were progressively escalating, especially after the appeals of the *General Union of Tunisian Workers* (UGTT), the *Lawyers' Bar*, the *Association of Tunisian judges*, the *Tunisian League of Human Rights* and other political parties and organizations. Gherib (2012) notes that the compromising relationship between the state and the UGTT exploded during the revolution. He considers that this volte-face resulted from the pressure exercised by the union workers over their elite. Whatever the internal and external factors that contributed to the trigger of the Tunisian revolution, it represents, as noted by Yadh Ben Achour, "a radical change in 'mentalities' and in the 'civic spirit'". This is because it was based on the ideas of liberty and of political pluralism, of the dignity of man and of social justice, and called for the integrity in the administration of public affairs (Ben Achour, 2012).

## 1.2 The Post-Revolution Political Arena

### *1.2.1 The Political Scene After the 2011 Elections*

By late January 2011, an interim government was formed while the opinion of the Tunisians diverged regarding the democratic transition process. A first current advocated an incremental change strategy. A second opinion defended a rupture with the existing political system and the rebuilding of its institutions. Given the extreme tension at that time, it was fortunate for the country that all the opponent political opinions converged toward the establishment of a political road map under the coordination of the *Political Reform Commission* headed by *Yadh Ben Achour*.[2] In March 2011, the constitution of 1959 was suspended and a new constitution was expected to be written by a Constituent Assembly to be elected by October 2011. The interim Government organized a national free and

[2] I have expressed this point of view in February 2011 in Nabi (2011).

fair election of the Constituent Assembly with the participation of approximately 52% of the 8.2 million registered voters. The Islamist party *al-Nahdha* obtained 1.5 million votes and a relative majority of the seats (41%). It formed a governmental coalition with two secular-oriented parties. A large fraction of the society had a deep suspicion of al-Nahdha's credible engagement in the democratic game. It feared that it will "re-orient" the country toward more conservatism at the expense of women's rights (Marks, 2014). Meanwhile, the popularity of al-Nahdha among a large part of the public opinion was due not only to its resistance to the dictatorship but also to its reconciling message between Islam and democracy (Arieff, 2012). Another factor that could explain the victory of the Islamist party is the fact that the elections campaign was deeply focused on the religious question. A large fraction of the population who voted for al-Nahdha feared the "threat" of the secularist parties (Ben Achour, 2012). Alexis Arieff notes that the strategy of the secularist parties that consisted in opposing the Islamists may have backfired among the Tunisians hoping for the reconciliation between democracy and their Arab/Muslim identity (Arieff, 2012).

### *1.2.2 The Difficult Gestation and Adoption of the New Constitution*

The new constitution was expected to be developed in one year but was finally adopted on 27 January 2014. The forming process slowed down mainly due to the ideological divide between al-Nahdha and the secularist parties. Ben Achour (2012) notes that the debate revolved around three focal points:

1. The relationship between Shari'a and the positive law
2. Women's rights and gender equality
3. The freedom of conscience, of thought and of expression

Tunisians are deeply religious but are also attached to the separation of the political and religious spheres (Dhif, 2015). This explains the origin of the important pressure placed on al-Nahdha by the civil society and the secular parties of the opposition throughout the constitutional drafting process. This pressure has led to compromising on the abovementioned focal points. The protests came also from the Salafist camp, which defended Shari'a as a basis for legislation and undertook violent actions as part of its demonstrations. Regarding the presence of Islam in the constitution, Rached Ghannouchi—leader and co-founder of al-Nahdha—announced on 25 March 2012 that the first article of the 1959 constitution was sufficient. The constitution-making process was put at risk after the assassination of two political leaders from the opposition: Chokri Belaïd on 6 February 2013 and the assembly's member Mohamed Brahmi on 25 July 2013. During the summer of 2013, the protests against al-Nahdha and the Troika government intensified. This movement paved the way for the quartet[3] to initiate a national dialogue in order to accelerate the reaching of a consensus over the political road map and to end the transition period. In recognition to that role the quartet was awarded the Nobel Peace Prize in 2015, more precisely "for its decisive contribution to the building of a pluralistic democracy in Tunisia in the wake of the Jasmine Revolution of 2011" (Nobel Prize Committee[4]). As a result of this dialogue, al-Nahdha withdrew from the government. An independent technocratic government was nominated to rule the country until the legislative and presidential elections of October–December 2014. Finally, the new constitution was adopted consensually in January 2014. The principles, values and mechanisms embedded in it guarantee the respect of human rights and the creation of counterpower institutions that the country needs in order to enforce the rule of law and freedom.

### 1.2.3 The Political Scene After the 2014 Elections

In the legislative elections of October 2014, the secular party Nidaa Tounes gained the majority of votes with 86 seats out of 217 (37.56%) before al-Nahdha with 69 seats (27.79%). In December 2014, Mohamed Beji Caid Essebsi, the founder of Nidaa Tounes, won the presidential elections during the second round with 55.68% of votes ahead of the incumbent Mohamed Moncef Marzouki with 44.32%. The elections of 2014 constituted a major step in the democratic transition process of the country. One of its most important features is that an Islamist party gave

[3] The quartet encompassed the *General Union of Tunisian Workers* (UGTT), the *Tunisian Confederation of Industry, Trade and Handicrafts* (UTICA), the *Tunisian Human Rights League* and the *Order of Lawyers*. The quartet won the 2015 Nobel peace prize for its role in the success of the political transition process in Tunisia.

[4] https://www.nobelprize.org/nobel_prizes/peace/laureates/2015/tndq-facts.html.

up power gracefully. This first free election increased the confidence about the compatibility of Islam and democracy without settling, however, the debate over political Islam or ending the fears from a tactical attitude of al-Nahdha (Boukhars, 2015). Meanwhile, the votes revealed the political divide of the country. As shown in Figs. 1.1 and 1.2, the northern and coastal governorates voted for Nidaa Tounes and Beji Caid

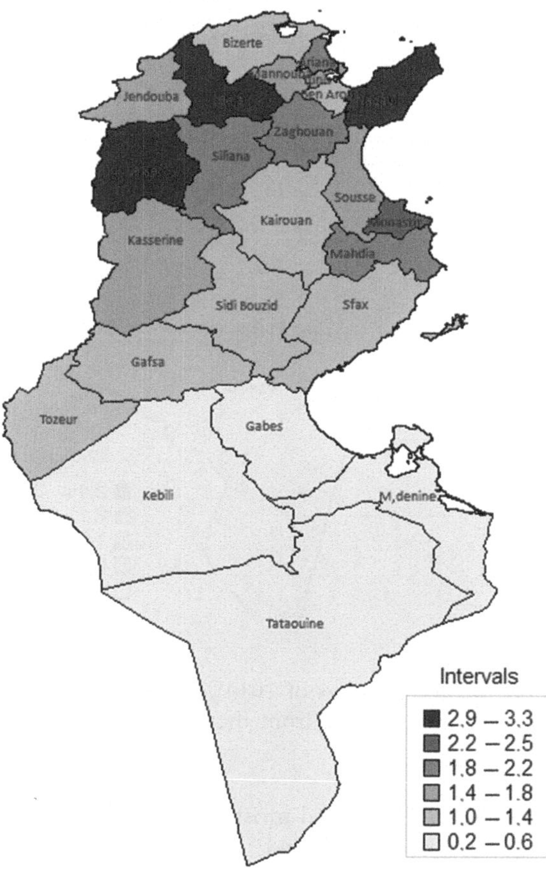


**Fig. 1.1** The legislative elections of 2014: intensity of votes to Nidaa Tounes relative to al-Nahdha (Source: Data from the Independent High Authority for Elections)

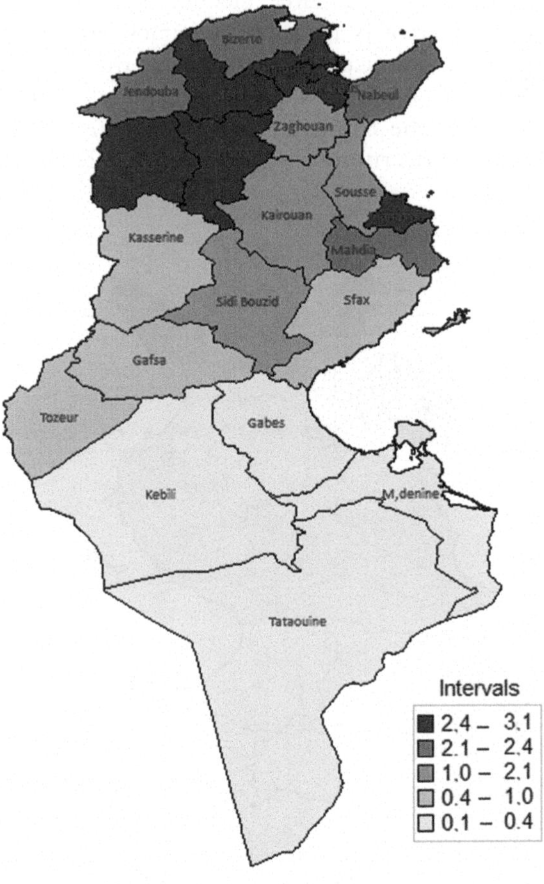


**Fig. 1.2** The presidential elections of 2014: intensity of votes to Caid Essebsi relative to Marzouki (Source: Data from the Independent High Authority for Elections)

Essebsi, whereas the southern and most of the inner governorates voted for al-Nahdha and Moncef Marzouki.[5]

[5] Beyond the fact that he created the secular party Nidaa Tounes to equilibrate the political arena, Beji Caid Essebsi belongs to a Bourgeois family from Tunis. He is considered as a pupil of Bourguiba having served as his minister for many years. Moncef Marzouki was a

Therefore, it might be inferred that the country is divided between the north coast and the south inner regions vis-à-vis the reflection of the Islamic identity and the rupture with a postindependence political system, considered by a fraction of the population as the origin of unequal access to the socioeconomic opportunities. After the elections, Nidaa Tounes and al-Nahdha formed a governmental coalition with two other secular parties. This was rather a political constraint imposed by the results of the legislative elections (none of the parties had the absolute majority). Monaldi et al. (2006) note that the existence of few relevant political players and repeated interaction among them might generate long-term cooperation and effective, coherent and stable public policies.[6]

In the Tunisian case, the rapprochement between Nidaa Tounes and al-Nahdha is certainly contributing to calming the ideological opposition in the country. However, it is criticized for generating difficulties in the decision-making process and inefficiency in the governmental coordination. It is also criticized for being the source of difficulties that prevent the adoption of a development vision and a strategy, and that slow down the undertaking of urgent and necessary economic reforms.[7] This rapprochement has also disappointed a large fraction of Nidaa Tounes voters and contributed to its division in two camps. This is not surprising as al-Nahdha was considered by a fraction of al-Nidaa's voters as a retrograde group of incompetent outsiders that try to import Ikhwani Islamism from the east to the Tunisian indigenous culture (Marks, 2014).

Many observers and analysts are recognizing the evolution of the political ideas and referential of al-Nahdha. Ben Achour (2012) calls this evolution "acculturation", noting the positive notion of "procedural secularism" used by Rached Ghannouchi, who opposed it to "integral secularism" (considered as antagonist to the religion). Other secularists consider this

human rights activist and one of the opposition figures under the dictatorship. Supported by al-Nahdha within the Troika coalition, he was elected as president by the Constituent Assembly in December 2011. His father was a supporter of Salah Ben Youssef and an opponent of Bourguiba.

[6] This was the case of Venezuela between 1958 and 1988 characterized by an institutionalized cooperative process. However, they note that the period from 1989 to 2004 was characterized by the decline of the political cooperation and the polarization of the actors.

[7] Social protests were renewed in January 2016 propagating from Kasserine to many southern and inner regions of the country, blaming the government to have no clear vision on how to tackle the unemployment problem.

evolution as a sign of divorce of al-Nahdha, under the pressure of the pluralistic environment, from its ideological principles. They argue that Islamists are obliged to surpass political Islam and adopt a new language and politics coherent with rights, plurality and civil state (Boukhars, 2015). Marks (2014) notes that the evolution of al-Nahdha is the result of a long historical process of deep political learning recently informed by the Egyptian coup of 2013. In 2011, she conducted interviews with more than 80 persons from al-Nahdha (leaders, grassroots members and party supporters) and noted that the vast majority considered Turkey's AK Parti and the German Christian Democrats as the most relevant political parties to al-Nahdha's model. The combination of piety, prosperity and democratic credibility was the commonly advocated feature (Marks, 2014).

## 1.3 The Emergence of a More Cohesive Country?

### *1.3.1 Social Cohesion After the Revolution*

The Tunisian revolution was initiated by the crowd with an important role of the social media in propagating the uprisings across the different regions of the country. During the revolution and the first weeks following the overthrow of the dictatorship, Tunisians showed a sense of national cohesion. In February 2011, Joseph Stiglitz noted that Tunisia must strive to maintain that sense of cohesion. For that to be realized, he emphasized the importance of transparency, tolerance and economic and political inclusiveness (Stiglitz, 2011). Contrarily to the postindependence period, there was no political leadership benefiting from the legitimacy of the historic event and inspiring the confidence of all the Tunisians. *In the absence of such a political leadership, does the revolution dynamic lead to a sustained cohesion of the Tunisian society?*

A cohesive society is a prerequisite for building efficient political and public institutions which could conceive and implement socioeconomic alternative solutions, respecting a shared identity of the society without rejecting the unavoidable globalization and its benefits (Verhelst, 2000). Social cohesion is a continuous process targeting the equal access of all the citizens to socioeconomic opportunities, resulting in the reduction of wealth and income disparities. This process cannot take place without engaging the citizens in a common national project based on shared values (Maxwell, 1996). Easterly et al. (2006) define social cohesion in opposition to the degree of social and economic divisions (in terms of ethnicity, political party, caste, language, income, etc.) within society. They argue that in the absence of a common identity, opportunistic politicians tend to exploit ethnic differences to build up their power base. Once an ethnic group is politically mobilized by one opportunistic politician, other groups will be according to opposite ethnic lines that exacerbate the social division (Easterly et al., 2006, 14). Meanwhile, they do not exclude the possibility that some politicians contribute to unify fractionalized people and to build good institutions, despite the average tendency to divide and rule. A social cohesive country is not only less vulnerable to conflicts and divisions but also takes advantage from its diversity to build a common identity. As social cohesion increases, institutions become more inclusive, leading in turn to more cohesion (Easterly et al., 2006). In technical words, Easterly et al. (2006) find evidence of a positive bidirectional relationship between the degree of social cohesion and the quality of the political institutions. The quality of political institutions in turn affects the type of economic reforms (Fig. 1.3). If social cohesion is lacking, it is likely that political institutions will be supportive of economic policies that benefit the most representative classes solely.

Thus, social cohesion and inclusive political institutions are critical for building the confidence and patience that policymakers need to implement costly short-term reforms with expected long-term gains (Easterly et al., 2006, 14). As noted by Kaplan and Freeman (2015), this is particularly crucial during the long and difficult process of reorienting a country after extensive repression or conflict, and even more important when the country faces threats of violence, exclusionary behavior, administrative chaos, predatory actors and drops in investment. This is the case of Tunisia which is classified by Kaplan and Freeman (2015) among the deeply divided societies needing a more inclusive state and society.

**Fig. 1.3** The relationship between social cohesion, institutions and development

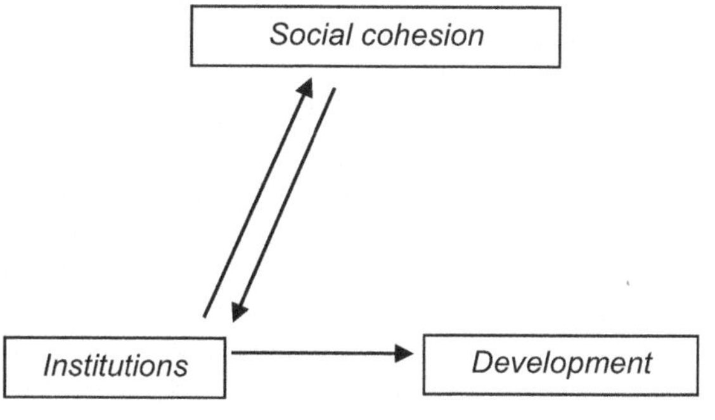

The institutional dimension was not absent in the post-revolution path of Tunisia. Many institutions emerged and others obtained more autonomous status progressively. These institutions are assigned various crucial tasks such as the management of the political elections, the judiciary system, the fight against corruption, the regulation of the media and the telecommunication sectors. However, many institutions still need to gain the confidence of the public by improving their effectiveness while others shall be redesigned. The most serious deficiencies concern the insufficient inclusiveness of the political institutions. There are competing political parties opposing mainly on the ideological ground, with timid and insufficient signals about their willingness to build inclusive institutions, modernizing the state and conducting the economic transformation of the country.

Despite the progress on the political side, the economic welfare of the Tunisian's middle class is deteriorating. The lack of a strong political leadership deprives the country from rapidly reaching a national consensus on the implementation of the necessary economic reforms. Meanwhile, social links progressively crumbled during the political transition, which is characterized by recurrent strikes and sit-ins (impacting the activities of many firms and deteriorating the investment climate) and the dilution of the state's authority. Mohamed Ennaceur notes that the social unease is endogenous to the revolutionary process itself, and culminated with the failure of the state in playing its role as regulator of the development dynamic and guarantor of social cohesion (Leaders News, 2011). In April 2017, young people protested in the region of Tataouine asking for a new type of development policies. Some of them claimed for the right to benefit from 20% of the revenues of the oil extracted from their region. This signals the crumbling confidence in the ability of the state to fulfill its role in alleviating the constraints impeding the development of their region. It also reveals that the journey toward a more cohesive society is still long. Tunisia seems to be at the crossroads of its civilizational path needing a strong leadership which could conduct its multidimensional transformation. Time will testimony if the Tunisian transition will succeed or fall short of expectations. As argued by Kaplan and Freeman (2015), success requires that political, social and business leaders forge coalitions, establish legitimate processes and build inclusive institutions which reassemble a divided society.

### *1.3.2 Has Tunisia Resolved the Modernity-Identity Equation?*

Tunisia is representing an interesting example of a developing country that tries to marry its belonging to the Muslim countries with the adhesion to a democracy regime. *To what extent is the Tunisian society succeeding in achieving this marriage?*

Since the early days of independence, the Tunisian elite was aware of the sensitivity of the religious issues and the importance to resolve the modernity-identity dilemma. For instance, in April 1956, the Tunisian philosopher Mahjoub Ben Miled (1916–2000) qualified the "mentality dualism" in Tunisia as the most important impediment to its progress. He noted that "*the technical, industrial and financial difficulties could be resolved through capacity building. However, the 'mentality problem' is more difficult and delicate to resolve ... and constitutes the main risk which threatens our recent independence*" (Ben Miled, 1956, 14). He argued that Tunisia shall find its balanced path between its Eastern and Western connections in order to constitute a modern mentality capable of understanding and benefiting from the Islamic thinking philosophy. I think that the solution to the modernity-identity equation was conceived by the postindependence Tunisian elite in an ad hoc manner rather than resulting from an endogenous and inclusive process encompassing all the spectrum of the intellectual elite.[8]

The emergence of a social and political consensus about the place of religion in the Tunisian modernization path was not possible in the context of the authoritarian political context. To the contrary, the oppressive political regime generated aggressive confrontations between opponent visions of the society (leftist and Arab nationalist versus Islamist) whose effects continue to feed today's political interaction in the country. This has naturally led to an instable socioeconomic situation where the affinity

[8] The control of the religious sphere by the state was certainly an important factor which limited the credibility of *al-Zituna's* scholars. As recently recognized by its cofounder *Hmida Enneifer*, the *Islamic Tendency Movement* had an insufficient awareness of the deep anchor of the Islamic values in the Tunisian society. He recently noted that the majority of the ruling party's elite emphasized, at the occasion of a meeting in 1967, the coherence between modernity and Islamic identity. Meanwhile, he recognizes that there was a minority which argued that Islam should not be considered beyond the individual religious sphere (Enneifer, 2011).

with religion and piety could be an accusation per se.[9] According to Ben Achour (2012), this polarization is persistent at the very heart of intellectual, cultural and political life and is reflected by antagonist notions around pairs like modernist/religious, scientific/theocratic, secular/conservative and so on.[10] Therefore, one might argue that the divergence from Khayr al-Din's reforming approach to modernity—conceived in symbiosis with the Tunisian identity[11]—is rooted in the political interactions which began at the dawn of the independence. It began with the Bourguiba-Ben Youssef conflict and was fueled by the authoritarian regime and the state's control over religion. The establishment of a modern state in the continuity of Khayr al-Din's ideal would have saved Tunisia the negative consequences of the dualism between modernity and identity to which many

[9] That was the case of *Mokhtar Latiri* (1926–2007) who graduated from *Ecole Polytechnique* (France) in 1949 and founded the first Tunisian engineering school (ENIT) in 1968. Si Moktar was one of the most brilliant and influential engineers of the country and a close adviser of *Bourguiba*. He was reproached on his piety as if it was shameful disease after the construction of a mosque within ENIT. He noted that "*some have even accused me of complaisance with Islamism*" (Ghorbel, 2006). This reaction clearly illustrates the polarization of the Tunisian society even at the elite level.

[10] In this regard, I consider that the sociopolitical interactions subsequent to the revolution shall be perceived as a difficult catching-up process of the stamped debate (on the place of religion in the society in particular) under the coercive political system. *Yadh Ben Achour* affirms that "*[t]he implicit contradictions were sustained under the dictatorship. … Today, we have two societies each one observing the other. … The constitution of 2014 clarified this duality and the referential contradiction*" (Ben Achour, 2015).

[11] After a four-year tenure in Europe (in Paris from 1853 to 1857), Khayr al-Din wrote his book *Aqwam al-Masalik fi Ma'rifat Ahwal al-Mamalik* (The Surest Path to Knowledge Concerning the Conditions of Countries) in 1867. He developed a detailed vision to reform Tunisia based on the following principles:

1. Progress is not possible without justice and freedom, both being inherent pillars of Islam.
2. Islamic prescriptions do not forbid getting inspired from the West's practices related to development and civism.
3. Muslim countries wishing to exit underdevelopment have to undertake institutional reforms in the political, administrative and socioeconomic spheres.
4. Refusing progress and reforms is a sort of treason to the nation.

Abdul Azim Islahi notes that Khayr al-Din "*discussed in this book the economic superiority of the West and offered a practical guide for Tunisia to improve its economic and political system. The book is enough to give him a place in the revival movement of the nineteenth century*" (Islahi, 2015, 3).

Muslim countries continue to be exposed since the nineteenth century.[12] I believe that Tunisia is reaching a historical stage where Islam shall not be the center of ideological competition between the political parties. On the contrary, the moral force of Islam (mainly its stress on justice, brotherhood of mankind and tolerance) shall unify Tunisians in their search for socioeconomic solutions favoring social justice and the equality of opportunities. To this end they have to develop the pillars of their culture[13] based on a modern mentality benefiting from the moral force inherent to the Islamic thinking philosophy. Indeed, any project of socioeconomic development requires shaping a common vision and drawing energy from the spiritual and humanist convictions of the population. This cultural driver is necessary for a coordinated, fair and democratic action (Malitza, 1976). That is why we need culture in rediscovering the meaning of our individual and collective lives and building social cohesion.

It is hopefully that the new constitution of Tunisia reflects the emergence of a social and political consensus about the place of religion in the society. Yet, the constitutional edifice adopted in January 2014 after more than two years of intense interactions between the political parties and the civil society should be implemented in practice in order to catalyze the collective efforts toward the modernization process of the country. This would disconnect religion from interfering with the political parties' competition. Islam as a common religion of the quasi-all Tunisians shall be considered as a non-exclusive river inspiring the search of socioeconomic solutions.

[12] The advocates of this opinion might recall that the Tunisian Reform movement of *Khayr al-Din* was supported by enlightened scholars from *al-Zituna* such as *Cheikh Salem Bouhajeb* (1827–1924) and *Cheikh Mohamed Beyram al-Khames* (1840–1889) (Haddad, 2011). I think that the intellectual legitimacy of *Cheikh al-Fadhel Ben Achour* and others, coupled with their contribution to the national movement, would have played a pivotal role in that process. At the opposite, one might argue that the necessary conditions for this ideal project to be feasible were inexistent, namely, from the religious side. Charfi (2005) argues that the majority of the religious scholars were prisoners of ancients' theses after the closure of the reflective effort process.

[13] Culture corresponds to the reflection of a population's values, where preferences are expressed and ordered. The word "culture" is generally scented with improvement and social progress, both of them being linked to the concept of development (Parra and Moulaert, 2011). Populations need culture to self-affirm and maintain their unity. Indeed, the self-affirmation in the cultural domain corresponds to independence and sovereignty in the political domain. In this context, culture is deeper than the definition which restricts it to the entertainment activities.

## References

Achy, L. (2011) "Tunisia's economic challenges," The Carnegie Papers, Carnegie Middle East Center, December 2011.

Arieff, A. (2012) "Political transition in Tunisia," Congressional Research Service.

Ben Achour, Y. (2012) "Religion, revolution, and constitution: The case of Tunisia," Lecture at the Center for Middle Eastern Studies, Harvard University, 17 September 2012.

Ben Achour, Y. (2015) "La constitution tunisienne permet au musulman de sortir de sa religion!" Interview in www.espacemanager.com.

Ben Miled, M. (1956) "Tunisia between the East and the West," lecture in April 11, 1956, Tunis. Tunisian Society of Art Printing.

Boukhars, A. (2015) "The reckoning Tunisia's perilous path to democratic stability," Carnegie Endowment for International Peace.

Charfi, M. (2005) "Islam and liberty: The historical misunderstanding," Albin Michel, Paris, 1998, Zed Books, London and New York.

Dhif, K. (2015) "'Tunisian exception' teaches democratic lessons" interview of Yadh Ben Achour, www.swissinfo.ch/eng/global-forum-in-tunis_-tunisian-exception%2D%2Dteaches-democratic-lessons/41426492?ns_mchannel=rss.

Easterly, W., J. Ritzan and M. Woolcock (2006) "Social cohesion, institutions, and growth," Economics and Politics, Vol. 18, No. 2, July 2006, 103–120.

Enneifer, E. (2011) "A testimony on the founding years," in "From the control of Ben Ali to the Jasmin revolution: The political Islam in Tunisia" (in Arab), Almesbar Studies and Research Centre, Dubai, UAE.

Gherib, B. (2012) "The political economy of the Tunisian revolution: Social groups versus crony capitalism," Revue Tiers Monde, No. 212, 2012/4.

Ghorbel, S. (2006) "Mokhtar Latiri," http://www.jeuneafrique.com/132277/archives-thematique/mokhtar-latiri/.

Haddad, M. (2011) "Political Islam in Tunisia after the Jasmin Revolution," in "From the Control of Ben Ali to the Jasmin Revolution: The Political Islam in Tunisia" (in Arab), Almesbar Studies and Research Centre, Dubai, UAE.

Hibou, B. (2011) "The Tunisian Revolution did not come out of nowhere," Interview with Sadri Khiari, April 2011, www.pambazuka.net/en/category.php/features/73574.

Islahi, A. A. (2015) "Ibn Khaldun's theory of taxation and its relevance," Turkish Journal of Islamic Economics, Vol. 2, No. 2.

Kaplan, S. and M. Freeman (2015) "Inclusive transitions framework," Institute for Integrated Transitions, July 2015.

Leaders News (2011) "Les grèves et les sit in: la médication de Mohamed Ennaceur," Leaders NEWS, 9 December 2011.

Malitza, M. (1976) "L'intégration de la culture dans le nouvel ordre" in La culture est inséparable du processus de développement économique et social, Cultures, Vol. III, N° 4, 101–110.

Marks, M. (2014) "Convince, coerce, or compromise? Ennahda's approach to Tunisia's constitution," Brookings Doha Center Publications, Analysis Paper, No. 30, The Brookings Doha Center.

Maxwell, J. (1996) "Social dimensions of economic growth," Eric John Hanson Memorial Lecture Series, Vol. 8, University of Alberta.

Monaldi, F., R. A. González de Pacheco, R. Obuchi and M. Penfold (2006) "Political institutions, policymaking processes, and policy outcomes in Venezuela," Research Network Working Paper No. R-507.

Nabi, M. S. (2011) "L'intelligence des Tunisiens, leur lucidité et leur solidarité leur permettront d'inventer leur propre chemin démocratique," Leaders.com, opinions, 25 February 2011.

Parra, C. and F. Moulaert (2011) "La nature de la durabilité sociale: vers une lecture socioculturelle du développement territorial durable," Développement durable et territoires Vol. 2, No. 2, "Culture et développement durable: vers quel ordre social?".

Stiglitz, J. E. (2011) "The Tunisian catalyst," Project Syndicate, 4 February 2011.

Verhelst T. (2000) "Mondialisation, culture et spiritualité," Cultures et Développement.

CHAPTER 2

# Diagnosing the Tunisian Economy

## 2.1 In Progress Toward More Inclusive Human Development

Tunisia belongs to the lower-middle-income countries with a gross national income (GNI) per capita (based on Atlas Method current US$) of 3690 in 2016. More than 30% of Tunisia's land surface is covered by the Saharan desert, about 65% by agricultural land, while the forest area covers 6.7%. It has a population of around 11.2 million (2015) of which almost two-thirds live in the urban areas (Fig. 2.1). The country has carried out family planning since 1966 in order to control the population growth. The average annual rate of population change equaled 1.5% in 2014 and the fertility rate increased from 2.03 in 2006 to 2.5 in 2014. Tunisia's demography is characterized by a majority of people aged 15–59 years. Indeed, 15.05% of the population is aged between 15 and 24 years and 44.52% aged between 25 and 54 years (2016). The proportion of people aged 65 years and over is 8.2%. The life expectancy of women is 78.5 and that of men is 73.8 years (2014). The country progressed toward the achievement of the Millennium Development Goals (MDGs) at the national level despite the fact that the rural and inner regions have not equally benefited from this progress[1] (Fig. 2.2).

[1] For more details, see the report African Union Commission, UNECA, AfDB and UNDP (2013) "*Food security in Africa: Issues, challenges and lessons*", MDG Report 2013, Assessing Progress in Africa toward the Millennium Development Goals.



M. S. Nabi, *Making the Tunisian Resurgence*,
https://doi.org/10.1007/978-981-13-3771-0_2

Figure 2.3 shows that Tunisia and Turkey shared similar path of the Human Development Indicator (HDI) until 2009. While the Turkish HDI accelerated since 2010 reaching 0.76, in 2015 the HDI of Tunisia stagnated at around 0.72. The rate of poverty in Tunisia decreased at the national level from 23.1% in 2005 to 15.2 in 2015.

It is however much higher in non-municipal zones where it reached 26% in 2015. The proportion of Tunisians living in extreme poverty (less than US$1.9 a day) decreased from 7.4% in 2005 to 2.9% in 2015, but is

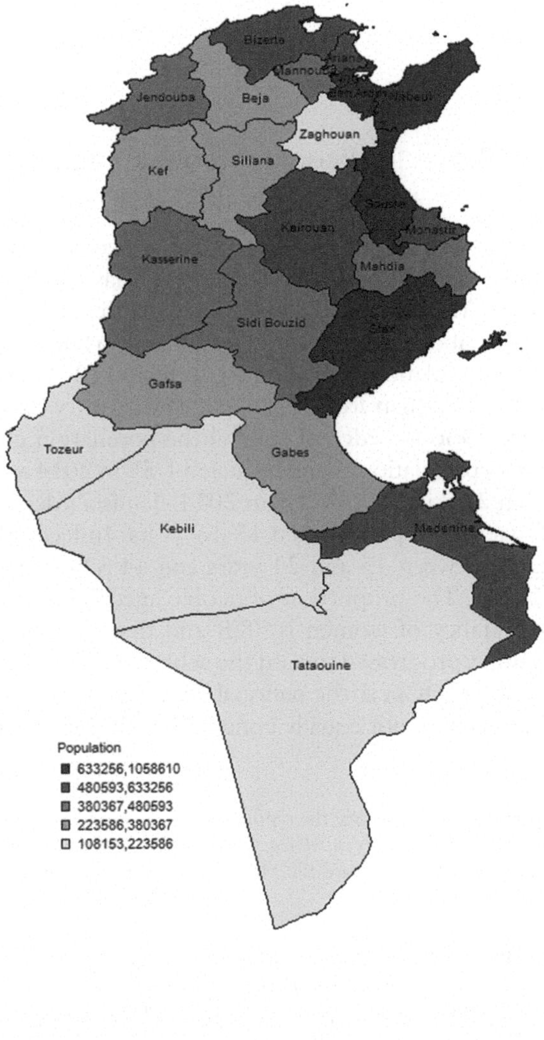


**Fig. 2.1** Geographical distribution of the Tunisian population (2014) (Source: Data from the National Institute of Statistics (INS))

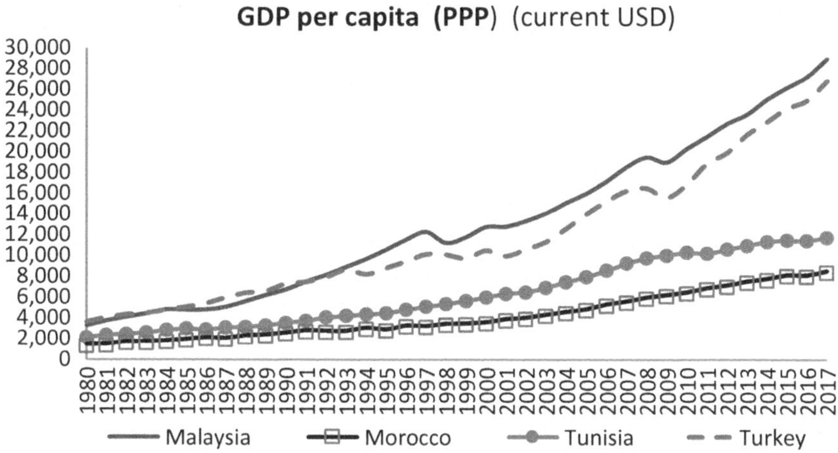


**Fig. 2.2** Evolution of Tunisian's GDP per capita (PPP current $US) in comparison with other upper-middle-income countries (Source: World Economic Outlook and World Development Indicators (estimates for 2016 for Tunisia and Morocco))

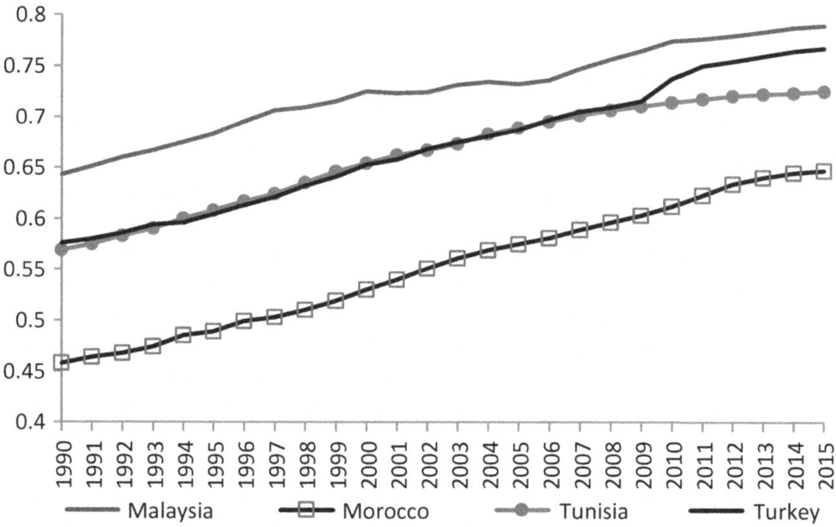


**Fig. 2.3** Regional and national trends in the Human Development Index 1990–2015 (Source: Data retrieved from the UNDP database)

still relatively high in non-municipal zones (6.6% in 2015 and 15.5% in 2005).[2] The increase of the living costs after 2011 could be inferred from the ages of the newly married. Indeed, the percentage of women who married before 29 years of age decreased from 69.1% in 2011 to 62.6%. In 2015, this effect is much more perceivable among men whose married proportion before 29 years decreased from 35.8% to 25.6%. In addition to that, the rate of divorce per marriage has regained in 2015 the level 13.8% of 2011 exceeding the 12.4% of 2012. Another negative socioeconomic fact in Tunisia is the high number of road traffic deaths (2679 in 2013) with a death rate (per 100,000 population) of 24.4.[3]

## 2.2 A Diversified and Dual Economy … Enthralled in the "Middle-Income" Trap

### 2.2.1 *A Dualistic and Non-Inclusive Economy*

The economic growth was mainly driven by the low cost of labor in the export-oriented sector. This sector is concentrated in low value-added and assembly activities exporting for the European countries. The productivity of the offshore sector improved as a result of the successive reforms that started in the early 1970s but also due its exposure to international trade. This was not the case with the onshore sector. According to the World Bank (2008), the productivity gap between Tunisia and the European Union in sectors exposed to international trade was estimated at 27%, much lower than the 67% gap for the remaining sectors. Since 2010, the World Bank emphasized in its report "*Towards Innovation-driven Growth*" the failure of the Tunisian economy to reallocate its production resources to high-return activities and escape the low-productivity conundrum. The relatively low rate of gross domestic product (GDP) growth and insufficient and low-quality job creation were symptomatic of this failure. In addition to the dual nature of the Tunisian economy in terms of onshore/offshore sectors, it is dualistic in terms of geographic localization of the economic activities. Most of the private investment and the public infrastructure are located in the urban and coastal regions (see Fig. 2.4).

[2] Tunisian National Institute of Statistics.

[3] Global Health Observatory data repository (2013). The death rates in other countries are Turkey (8.9), Morocco (20.8) and Malaysia (24).

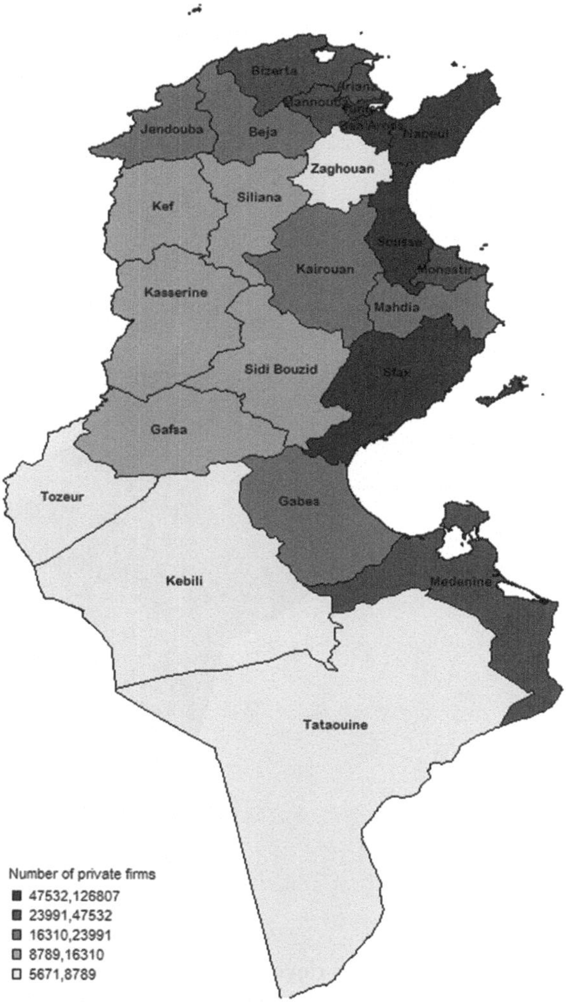


**Fig. 2.4** Number of private firms by governorate in 2014 (Source: Data from Ministry of Development and International Cooperation and the National Institute of Statistics (INS))

**Fig. 2.5** Regional development indicator of Tunisia in 2012 (Source: Data from Ministry of Development and International Cooperation and the National Institute of Statistics (INS))

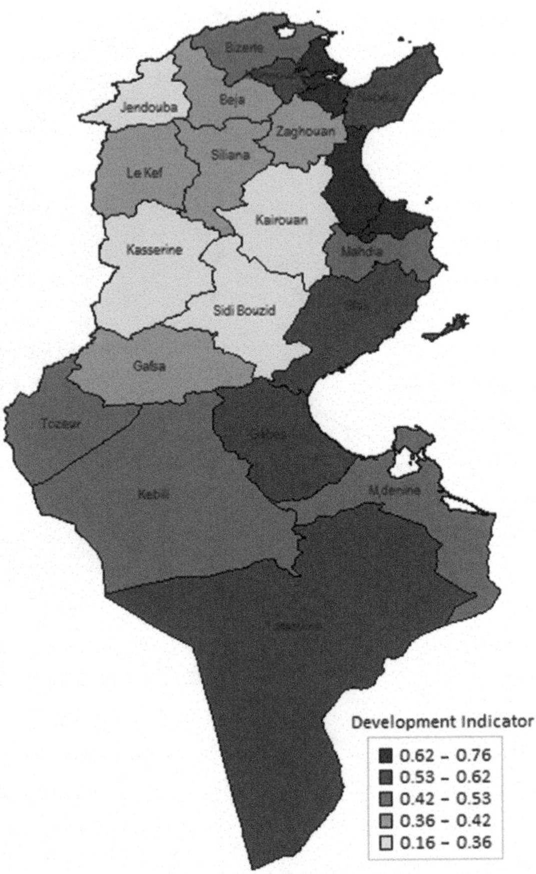


The non-inclusive economic development dynamic is also reflected in the widening of income inequality between the inner and the coastal regions of the country (see Fig. 2.5 reflecting the divergence captured by the regional development indicator). According to INS (2012), the GINI index measuring the inequality of income between the regions increased from 11.4% in 2000 to 13.3% in 2005 before decreasing to 12.6% in 2010.

### 2.2.2 *The Private, Public and Informal Sectors*

The state played an active role in the economic development of Tunisia. It favored the emergence of an export-oriented (offshore) sector at the beginning of the 1970s. It has also accompanied the raising of the Tunisian capitalism and industry by protecting the domestic-oriented sector. The state has also developed the infrastructure and basic utilities and services in many regions but mainly in the coastal areas where tourism and textile sectors have been dynamic. As noted by the World Bank's report "*The Unfinished revolution: Bringing opportunity, good jobs and greater wealth to all Tunisians*" released in 2014, this public sector-led development model enabled the country to experience increased prosperity and rapid poverty reduction.

The private sector contributes to around 68% of total employment, 72% of exports and 63% of GDP. Among the 3,417,600 active individuals there are approximately 671,048 employees in the public sector. The private sector is experiencing increased transactions costs due to the deterioration of the business environment and its exposure to a galloping informal sector. According to a study conducted by the UTICA and the Institute of Liberty and Democracy in 2012, 85% of the enterprises are extralegal. Ayadi et al. (2013) estimate the size of the informal economy to 30% in 2010 and 38% in 2013.[4] The ICC (2013) report of the International Crisis Group emphasizes the emergent and serious challenge of the informal cross-border trade. It notes that the government faces a difficult trade-off. On the one hand, the informal cross-border trade acts as a safety valve, contributing to maintain social peace in the disadvantaged regions. On the other hand, it is becoming the channel of arms and drugs trade by new actors (ICC, 2013).

As for the Tunisian public sector, it expanded after 2011 through the continuous hiring of around 20,000 new employees annually, and the consecutive wage increases which are indexed on inflation instead of

[4] ILO (2015) estimates the share of non-agricultural informal employment in the total employment of Tunisia to be 50.6%. Ben Cheikh (2013) estimates it to be 30%. Buehn and Schneider (2009) estimate the informal economy of Tunisia to be 39.5% of GDP in 2006 (the average for the 76 developing countries is 35.5%).

productivity.[5] Consequently, the wage bill in the public sector increased sustainably after 2011 (from 10% in 2010 to around 15% of the GDP and 75% of the government's receipts in 2016). Meanwhile, has contributed to accentuating the inefficiency of the public sector (state-owned enterprises and the administration) is increasing. Kouki (2017) estimates the total cost of non-quality in the public sector to 4500 million Tunisian Dinar (TND), which represents 74% of one-year external financing. The Tunisian public sector comprises 102 state-owned enterprises (SOEs) that account for 9.5% of the GDP in 2014. It suffers from weak governance and monitoring and constitutes a huge burden on the government.[6] In 2014, the amount of subsidy it received equaled 7.5% of the GDP. The external debt guaranteed by the government amounted to 12% of the GDP in 2015, while the domestic debt represents 5% of the GDP.[7] Morsay et al. (2017) note that the Tunisian SOEs are characterized by weak transparency, accounting, reporting, budgeting, ownership, executive boards and efficiency. They also pinpoint the absence of links between the transfers from the Ministry of Finance and the achievement of their performance targets. The presidency of the government is developing a reform strategy to restructure the SOEs and endow them with a modern governance framework. Still this reform strategy lacks the adhesion of the labor union UGTT.

[5] The current president of the Parliament *Mohamed Ennaceur* noted in 2011—when he was in charge of the ministry of social affairs—that "*the wage increasing shall not result from power relationship, but from the productivity indexed on the purchasing power, taking in account the competition of the enterprise and its sustainability*" (Leaders News, 2011). He regretted the disappearance of the division "Productivity and wage norms" within the ministry and noted the inexistence of an instrument to measure the evolution of the productivity.

[6] In my graduation project from *Tunisia Polytechnic School* (Nabi, 1998), I recommended the creation of a national authority mandated of monitoring the governance of the state-owned enterprises. In Nabi (1998), I analyzed the utilization by five state-owned enterprises of a methodology (called "Surplus Accounts Method") for the calculus of the annual change in their total factor productivity (TFP). I identified many imperfections and made some recommendations in order to correctly use that methodology. Unfortunately, it seems that the method is no more applied and there is no more production of annual reports analyzing the evolution of the TFP. I believe that it is important to revive the production of the TFP reports using the Surplus Account Method and other monitoring tools. Such reports are very useful during wage negotiations.

[7] The statistics are gathered from Tunisian Government (2018), "Livre Blanc: Rapport de synthèse sur la réforme des entreprises publiques en Tunisie", March 2018, www.reformes.gov.tn.

### 2.2.3 *The Sectoral Composition of the Economy*

The structure of the economy is dominated by services whose value-added share in GDP increased from 58.4% in 2000 to 62.3% in 2015. During the same period, the share of agriculture declined from 12.4% to 10.9%. The share of the manufacturing industries had also diminished from 18.4% to 16.4% for the same period. Within the services sector the most dynamic contributors to growth were the telecom services, the financial services, the transport services, real estate and trade. The mechanical and electrical industries grew rapidly, increasing their share in the manufacturing value-added from 27.5% in 2000 to 51.2% in 2015. The opposite pace happened for the textile and clothing sector, whose share in the manufacturing value-added declined from 46.9% in 2000 to 26.3% in 2015. Table 2.1 shows that most of the sectors were largely impacted by the revolution of 2011 except the telecommunication, the oil refining and the public administration and associations. The good signal emerges from the knowledge-intensive subsectors which are increasing their contribution to the economic activity. According to ITCEQ (2016), the total share of the value-added of "advisory and software", "paper and cardboard industry", "pharmaceutical industry", "services to firms" and "telecommunication" increased from 15.1% in 2008 to 17% in 2012.

**Table 2.1** The sectoral growth before and after the revolution

| *Growth of the added value* | *2005–2010 (%)* | *2011–2014 (%)* |
|---|---|---|
| Telecommunication | 17.2 | 13.2 |
| Mechanical electrical and metallurgical industries | 9.1 | 1.2 |
| Financial services | 8.5 | 3.4 |
| Public administration and associations | 5.2 | 5.6 |
| Transport services | 5.2 | −1.4 |
| Real state | 5.0 | 1.0 |
| Trade | 4.8 | 2.9 |
| Electricity, gas and water | 3.8 | 3.6 |
| Hotels and catering services | 3.7 | −1.9 |
| Agri-food industries | 3.6 | 1.9 |
| Extraction | 2.3 | −8.3 |
| Chemical industries | 1.1 | −5.2 |
| Mines | 0.5 | −5.5 |
| Textile, clothing and leather industries | 0.3 | −1.2 |
| Oil refining | 0.2 | 37.2 |
| Agriculture and fishing | 0.1 | 3.7 |

Source: Data from the National Institute of Statistics

According to the National Institute of Statistics of Tunisia, there are 711,442 active firms in the country among which 98.2% are employing less than 10 employees (year 2015). The economy comprises around 12,140 firms having more than 10 employees. In 2017, there were 3844 firms active in manufacturing with 1055 fully export oriented. They mainly belong to the agri-food industry (975), textile and clothing (959), electronic, electromechanical and electrical industries (595). In the same year, 2842 firms were active in services, with 1066 being fully export and 25.8% of it being active in the ICT. The electronic, electromechanical and electrical sector benefited from governmental support in the 1990s. It now provides principally semi-finished (such as cables, electrical distribution materials, batteries) but also finished components (embedded electronics for industrial use in the automobile, aeronautic and medical sectors, aeronautical wiring equipment and aeronautic systems) mainly to European clients in the auto and aeronautics industries.[8]

According to a recent report by the Telecom Regulation Agency, 85% of the clients of the fixed telephony, Box data and ADSL Internet are located in the coastal regions. It is clear from the Global Information Technology Report 2016 that Tunisia has to improve many dimensions of the ICT sector's ecosystem in order to be globally competitive. The country was ranked 81st in the Network Readiness Index (31st for Malaysia, 47th for Turkey and 78th for Morocco). Figure 2.6 shows the low scores assigned to the "social impact", "economic impact", "government usage", "business usage", "individual usage" and "skills". These are the symptoms of low integration of the ICT in the Tunisian economy. Therefore, the country has a huge growth potential if it can make ICT the driver of transformation of its economic system.

### 2.2.4 *Investment and Entrepreneurship*

The gross fixed capital formation (in % of GDP) in Tunisia decreased from 25.6% in 2010 to 19.6% in 2016 with only around 64% as private investment.[9] This level is inferior to that prevailing in most comparable countries (e.g. in Morocco it represents 33% of GDP and 26.8% is the average in the lower-

[8] This resulted from the dynamism of Tunisian companies like Coficab group and Chakira Cables which have become regional players in Africa. It also resulted from foreign companies like STMicroelectronics entering the market and growing since the 1990s. Tunisia is now a preferential EU partner and belongs to the top ten bundles and cables exporting countries (Whiteshield Partners, 2012).

[9] National Institute of Statistics and ITCEQ.

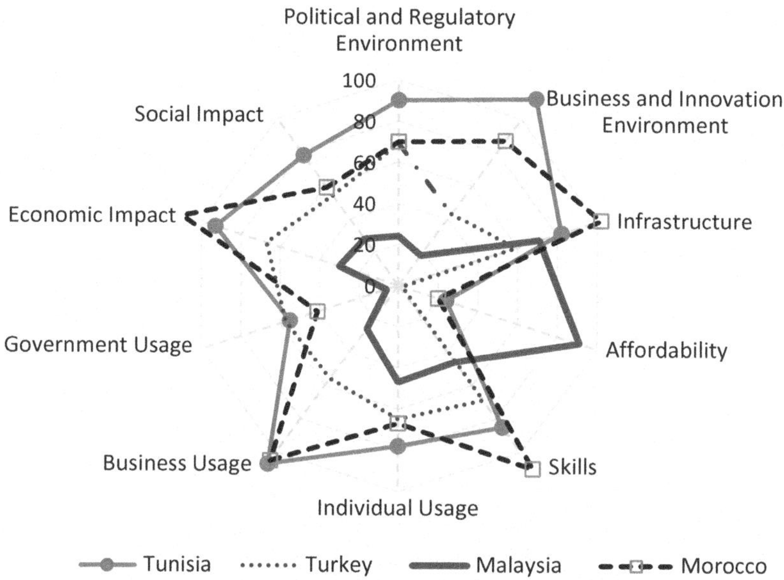


**Fig. 2.6** The networked readiness index in Tunisia and other developing countries (Source: Data from Global Information Technology Report 2016)

middle-income countries). The private investment declined in manufacturing (11% in 2016) and agriculture (7.8% in 2016) and is concentrated in low-value-added and low job-intensity sectors such as real estate. Besides, it is mainly located in the urban and coastal regions of the country.

The slowdown of the private investment is symptomatic of the "wait and see" behavior of the Tunisian investors during the political transition period characterized by the deterioration of the business environment and the recurrent sit-ins. Simultaneously, the rate of saving in percentage of GDP declined from 20.9% in 2010 to around 9% in 2016.[10] This huge decline in saving is an additional constraint on the national investment.

Figure 2.7 clearly shows the widening of the financial gap between investment and saving, obliging the country to count on external financing. An opposite tendency could be inferred from the Doing Business data (Fig. 2.8)

[10] It should be noted here that saving interest rate (fixed by the Central Bank of Tunisia) decreased from 6.87% in 1996 to 4% in June 2017 with an average of 2.82% during the period December 2010–December 2016.

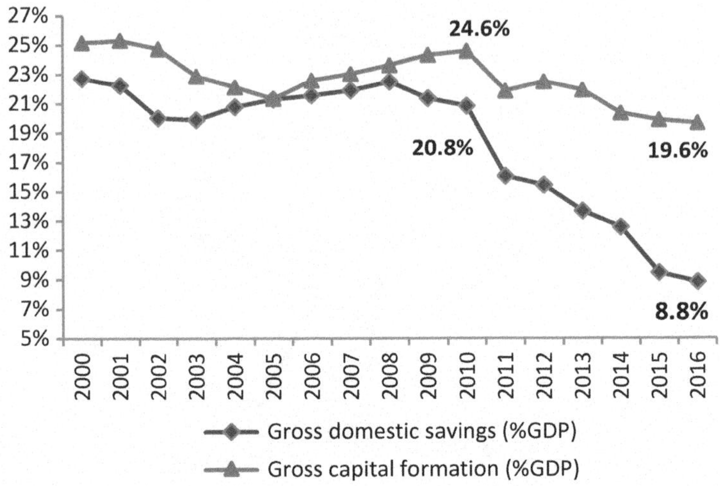


**Fig. 2.7** Gross domestic savings and gross capital formation (2000–2015, % of GDP) (Source: Data from the National Institute of Statistics (INS))

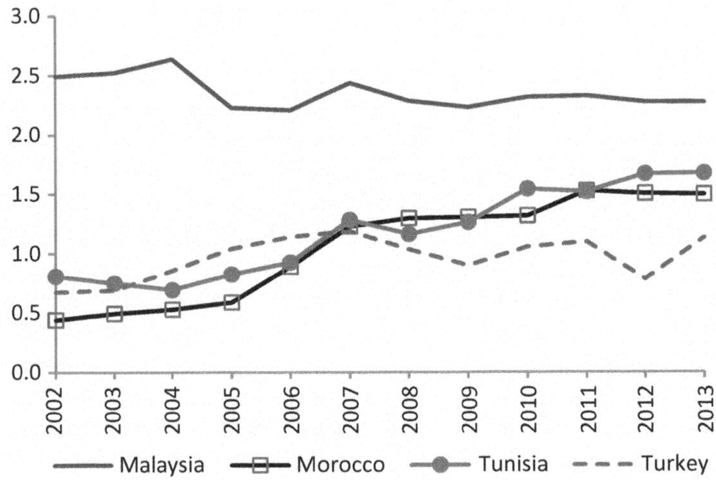


**Fig. 2.8** New entry rate for Tunisia and other countries (Source: Data from Doing Business database)

showing a higher rate of new firms' creation in Tunisia passing from 1.54 in 2002 to 1.67 in 2013. This evolution might reflect more entrepreneurship willingness among the university graduates in reaction to the lack of job opportunities that match their expectations.

## 2.3 Weak Business Environment

The Tunisian economy had become gradually marked by crony capitalism. The economic liberalization that was undertaken by the country at the end of the 1980s in a weak institutional environment exacerbated rent extraction. The economic policies intended to develop a free market economy had at the opposite undermined the entry of new firms, limited innovation and generated low investment in activities oriented to the domestic market. The weak institutional environment materialized under multiple forms: (1) discretion in the application of laws and regulations, (2) inefficiency of the public procurement processes, (3) manipulation of the privatization for the benefit of politically connected groups, (4) declassification of public land and assets and (5) improper use of public banks.

Given this weak business environment, it is not surprising that the Tunisian economy is suffering from low level of private investment. The country was assessed as being a "mostly unfree" economy in the 2017 Index of Economic Freedom (ranked 123 among 180 countries whereas Malaysia, Morocco and Turkey were ranked 27, 86 and 60 respectively, Fig. 2.9). Robalino et al. (2015) note the importance of enhancing competition to enable the entry of new firms and to promote the growth of the most productive ones. The Tunisian onshore environment suffers from severe distortions impeding the competition and the process of creative destruction. It resulted in a closed economy dominated by the statutory monopolies and the inability of good firms to grow and improve the overall productivity (Robalino et al., 2015). The authors have also made responsible the heavy state regulation which is impeding the performance of the Tunisian private sector and the entire economy. This heavy regulation is contributing to the exclusion of potential entrepreneurs who lack connections to politicians and to the administration. They conclude that inefficiency and rent extraction by cronies in the onshore economy is threatening the competitiveness of the offshore sector as well. The latter, as we have seen, remains concentrated in low-value-added and assembly-type activities. The Doing Business and the Global Competitiveness reports as well as the Governance indicators are useful to assess the type of barriers impeding the efficient operation of markets.

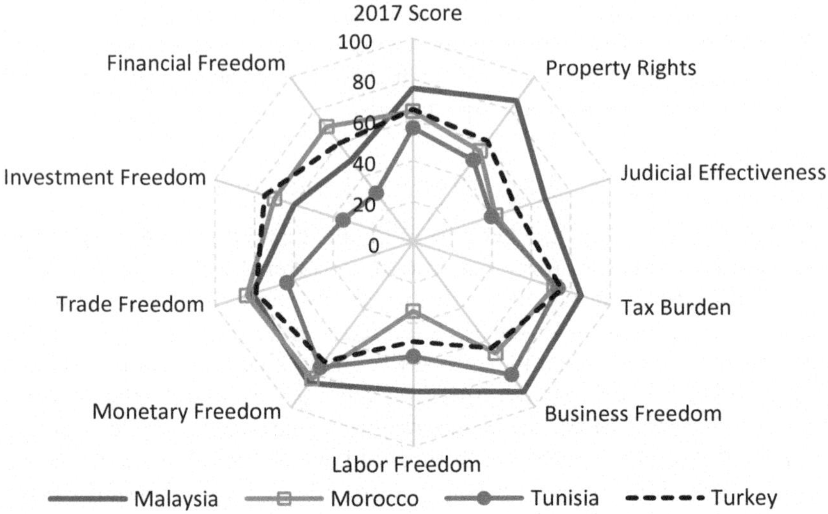


**Fig. 2.9** Economic freedom scores (2017) (Source: Data from the economic Freedom Index Database)

The Doing Business indicators (2017) show that the main axes that the country needs to improve are "protecting investors", "paying taxes" and "starting a business" (Fig. 2.10). On the "ease of doing business", Tunisia is ranked 69th among 189 countries in the Doing Business 2010 report. In the 2017 report it is ranked 77th.

The Global Competitiveness Report 2014–2015 shows that Tunisia is badly ranked according to most of the pillars, namely, "labor market efficiency", "financial market development", "good market efficiency" and "macroeconomic environment" (Fig. 2.11). However, its rank in the pillar "health and primary education" shows a better performance than Turkey and Morocco. Its rank in "higher education and training" is also positioning it ahead by 31 places over Morocco.

Figure 2.12 shows that, in regard to the Governance and Institutional Development scores of 2015, Tunisia outperforms Malaysia, Morocco and Turkey in the pillar "voice and accountability". However, the "political instability" and "regulatory quality" are undermining its economy.

Figure 2.13 shows clearly the deterioration of most of the governance indicators after 2011. The exception was clearly the "voice and accountability" as a result of the democratization process. The "rule of law" improved

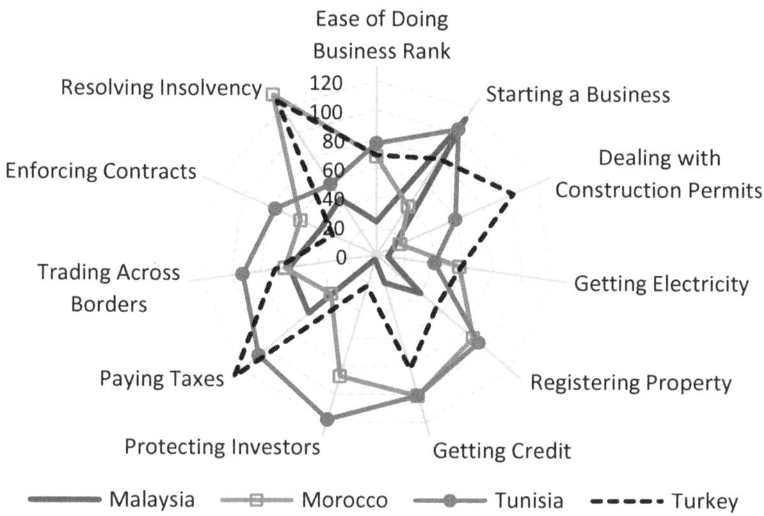


**Fig. 2.10** Doing Business indicators rank out of 190 economies (Source: Data from the Doing Business 2017)

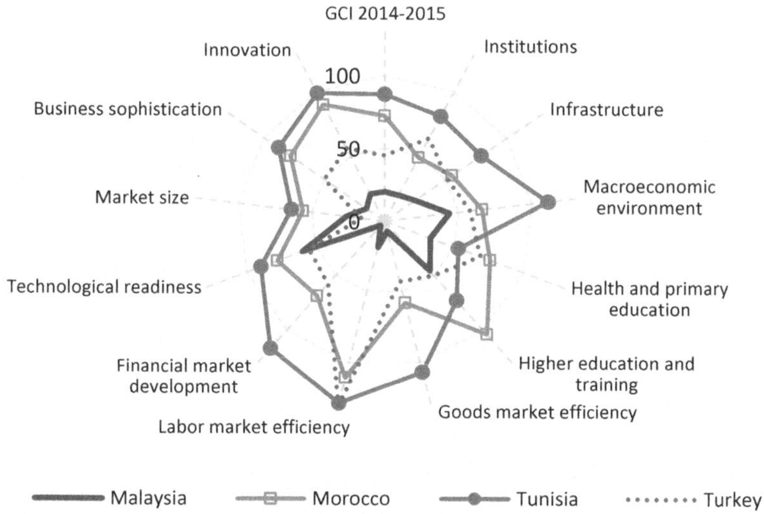


**Fig. 2.11** Global Competitiveness Index (rank out of 151) (Source: Data from the Global Competitiveness Report 2014–2015)

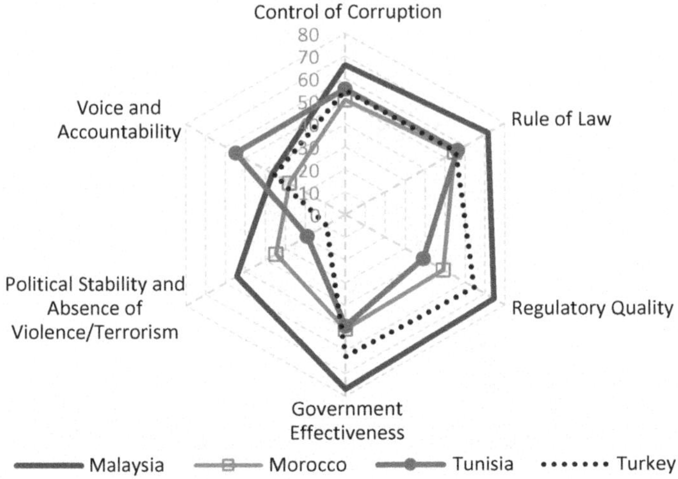


**Fig. 2.12** Governance and institutional development (rank in 2015 out of 200 countries) (ranges from 0 (lowest) to 100 (highest) rank) (Source: Data from the Worldwide Governance Indicators, 2016 update)

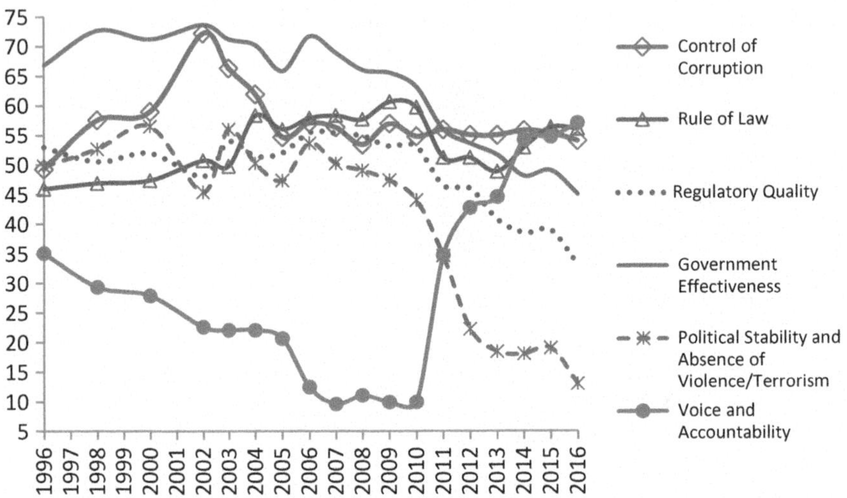


**Fig. 2.13** The Tunisian governance indicators (1996–2016) (ranges from 0 (lowest) to 100 (highest) rank) (Source: Data from the Worldwide Governance Indicators, 2016 update)

since 2014 after reaching its worst rank in 2013, whereas no clear improvement is registered in relation to the corruption level. Despite these negative perspectives, Tunisia is progressing in regard to the institutional building. This is exemplified by the new law of the *Central Bank of Tunisia* adopted in 2016 which guarantees its autonomy from the executive. Another signal is the willingness to enforce the Tunisian legal framework in relation to the fight against corruption and reducing its gap with international standards. This tendency began in 2011 with the creation of the Tunisia National Anti-Graft Instance (*Instance Nationale de Lutte Contre la Corruption*). More recently, in February 2017, the parliament adopted an anti-corruption law. In July 2017, the parliament voted the general law of the independent institutional instances,[11] organizing their legal status, financial autonomy, organization and so on. Yet, additional progress is needed in order to fight corruption that expanded after the revolution.

## 2.4 Education, Research, Innovation and Knowledge Economy

### *2.4.1 Education*

Since its independence in 1956, Tunisia invested intensively in universal education and human capital. Public spending on education varied from around 5% to 6.8% of GDP, allowing the country to universalize education and to increase adult literacy rate. The latter increased from 52.9% in 1994 to 79.1% in 2010. Boughzala and Hamdi (2014) note that even the poorest rural regions have benefited since independence from several government programs in education. They argue that the democratization of access to education contributed to raising the level of awareness about regional disparities and the economic gap between rural and urban areas. The country has already achieved the second MDG related to the achievement of universal primary education. Figure 2.14 shows that the average public

[11] Many independent constitutional bodies planned in 2014 have been created: The Elections Commission, the Audio-Visual Communication Commission, the Human Rights Commission and The Good Governance and Anti-Corruption Commission. The Commission for Sustainable Development and the Rights of Future Generations has not been created yet. The most urgent task today is establishing the new Constitutional Court, the most important pillar in the checks and balances system of a democracy.

spending on education as percentage of GDP was 6.3% during the period 1990–2012, exceeding the average spending of Malaysia (5.9%), Morocco (4.9%) and Turkey (3%) during the same period.

Despite this higher public spending on education the results obtained in terms of average years of schooling are much lower than those of Malaysia and not too much different from those of Turkey. In 2010, the average years of total schooling in Tunisia equaled 7.3 years, lower than the average of Malaysia (10.1 years) mainly due to lower average of years in secondary schooling. Tunisia shares with Malaysia the same average years of tertiary schooling (0.4) which is higher than that of Morocco (0.3) and Turkey (0.3) (Fig. 2.15). The importance of education for economic growth is recognized and empirically established. However, it is also known that the number of years of schooling is not sufficient to reveal the quality of education. Only 46% of the Tunisian students enrolled in "primary through end of secondary school" reached basic literacy in cognitive skills. Figure 2.16 shows that the performance of Tunisians is lower than their Malaysian and Turkish peers in international tests in the related disciplines, but higher than their Moroccan peers. In terms of equal access to education, Tunisia was ranked among the lowest countries with an Education GINI index of 0.92 in 1960. The efforts of the state since the 1960s contributed to relatively better access to education. Indeed, Tunisia is ranked 17th in terms of relative progression with an education GINI coefficient of around 0.43 in 2010. However, in absolute measure of access to education, Tunisia is ranked 43rd (ITCEQ, 2016).

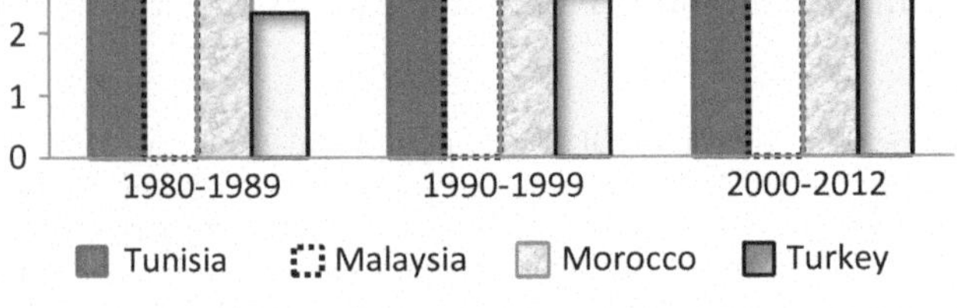


**Fig. 2.14** Average public spending on education (in % GDP) (Source: Calculus of the author based on data from the World Development Indicators)

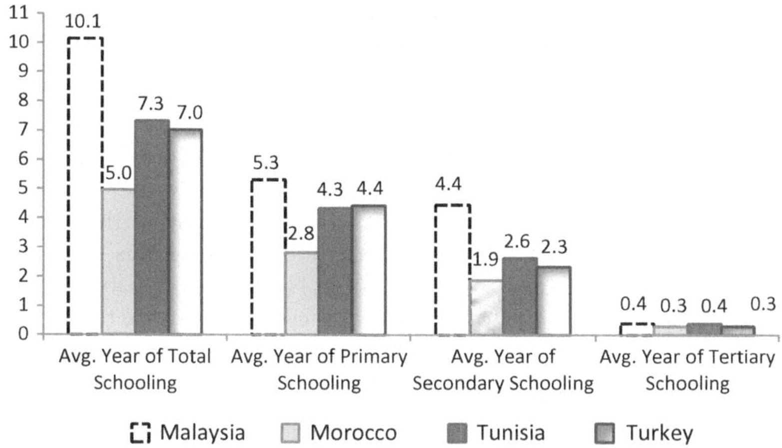


**Fig. 2.15** Average years of schooling (Source: Data from the Barro-Lee's (2013) Educational Attainment Dataset)

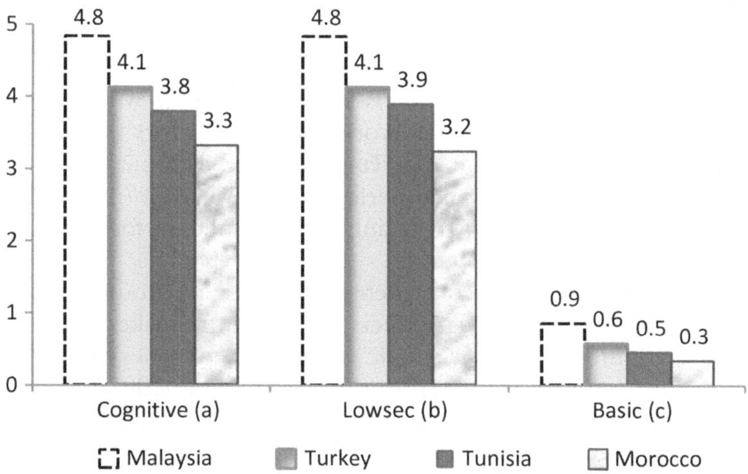


**Fig. 2.16** Average scores in cognitive skills (Source: Data from the Hanushek and Woessmann (2012). (a) Average test score in math and science, primary through end of secondary school, all years. (b) Average test score in math and science, only lower secondary, all years (scaled to PISA scale divided by 100). (c) Share of students reaching basic literacy (based on average test scores in math and science, primary through end of secondary school, all years))

### 2.4.2 *What Can Explain the Relatively Poor Quality of Education in the Tunisian Public Schools?*

In his field study, Milovanovitch (2014) reveals the increasing distrust in the Tunisian public schools' ability to fulfill their mission. The study identifies the low accountability of public schools and teachers as well as problems in the assessment of students. It also identifies the absence of accreditation and evaluation mechanisms. It urges the authorities to mobilize the concerned stakeholders (parents, students, authorities, employers, education professionals and the wider public) in order to rehabilitate public education. This participatory approach is crucial to ensure the credibility and ownership of the reforms that target a strong and fair Tunisian education system (Milovanovitch, 2014).

### 2.4.3 *Knowledge and R&D*

Knowledge is recognized as the most important factor for sustainable economic development. Most of the advanced economies are intensifying their reliance on knowledge-based economic activities, generating new wealth from innovation and creating millions of knowledge-related jobs. *What is the situation of Tunisia in the knowledge and R&D arena?*

As a developing country, Tunisia is trying to catch up with the knowledge development process. The World Bank indicators of knowledge development (Table 2.2) show that Tunisia ranked 81st out of 146 countries in 2012. This relatively bad performance (Malaysia (48th), Turkey (69th) and Morocco (101st)) is mainly due to underperformance in the pillar "economic incentives regime".

Hausmann et al. (2014) constructed a measure of productive knowledge which translates into the products that a country makes. Figure 2.17 shows the evolution of Tunisia's rank (out of 120 countries) according to the Economic Complexity Index over the periods 2000–2005, 2006–2010 and 2011–2014. It could be inferred that the country improved its productive knowledge capabilities passing from an average position of 63.5 in 2000–2005 to 46 during 2011–2014.

Therefore, the Tunisian production space is not too far from those of the Malaysian economy (31.3) and the Turkish economy (42.3). However, Tunisia's rank in the Global Innovation Index deteriorated to 77th (versus 59th position in 2012), doing worse than Malaysia (35th), Turkey (42th) and Morocco (72th). Tunisia is relatively well positioned (45th) regarding "Human capital and research" (Malaysia (34th), Turkey (43rd) and

**Table 2.2** Indicators of knowledge development in 2012

| *Country* | *Rank out of 146 countries* | *Knowledge economy index* | *Economic incentive regime* | *Knowledge index* | | |
|---|---|---|---|---|---|---|
| | | | | *Innovation* | *Education* | *ICT* |
| Malaysia | 48 | 6.1 | 5.6 | 6.9 | 5.2 | 6.6 |
| Morocco | 101 | 3.6 | 4.6 | 3.6 | 2.07 | 4.0 |
| Tunisia | 81 | 4.5 | 3.8 | 4.9 | 4.5 | 4.8 |
| Turkey | 69 | 5.1 | 6.1 | 5.8 | 4.1 | 4.5 |

Source: World Bank Knowledge for Development

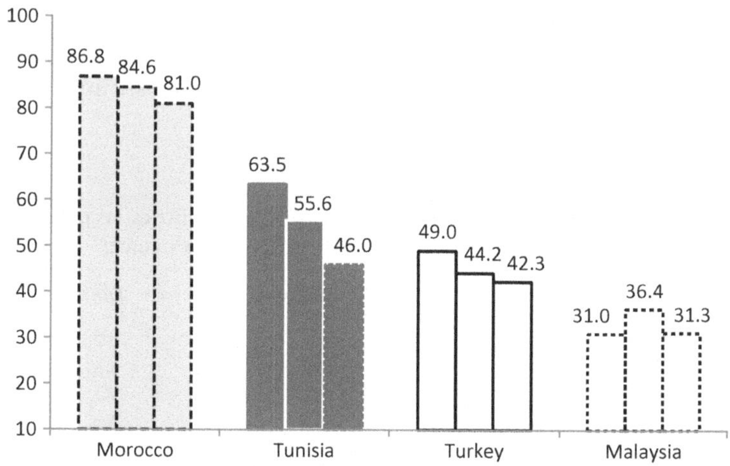


**Fig. 2.17** Average rank (out of 120) of Tunisia and other countries according to the Economic Complexity Index over the periods 2000–2005, 2006–2010 and 2011–2014 (Source: Data from Hausmann et al., 2014)

Morocco (61st)). However, the country scores very low in terms of "university/industry research collaboration" (107th), "knowledge absorption" (103rd), "market sophistication" (123rd) and "business sophistication" (107th), which are pushing it down in the ranking. The relatively good performance in scientific research (especially in pharmaceuticals, medical, biological and neuroscience) could also be inferred from the ratio of citable scientific documents per habitant over the period 1996–2015 which equals (4.97) not far from the performance of Malaysia (5.77) and Turkey (5.17) as well as by the citations per document and the h-index.

The factors explaining the inefficiency of Tunisia in innovation (namely, in terms of number of patents) are related to the lack of an adequate and modern national ecosystem to favor innovation and university/industry collaboration. (The ranks of Tunisia in the pillars "institutions", "market sophistication" and "business sophistication" are, respectively, 70th, 123rd and 107th). Despite the multiple agencies and national programs to favor innovation, the economic sectors are not knowledge-related and ties with universities and research centers are still rare. Nevertheless, success stories exist mainly in the engineering and pharmaceutical-chemical related sectors. This is not surprising given the dynamism of the mechanical, electrical, electronic and ICT sectors as well as the chemical one. Another remarkable fact revealed by Table 2.3 is the great divergence between Tunisia's rank (91st) and that of Malaysia (5th) for the subindex "state of cluster development". Tunisia clearly needs to establish an integrated national knowledge strategy.

**Table 2.3** Rank (out of 128) of Tunisia and other countries according to the Global Innovation Index and their scientific research performance

| *Index/subindex* | *Malaysia* | *Morocco* | *Tunisia* | *Turkey* |
|---|---|---|---|---|
| **Global Innovation Index** | **35** | 72 | 77 | **42** |
| Innovation efficiency ratio | 59 | 64 | 86 | 13 |
| Innovation input subindex | 32 | 75 | 82 | 59 |
| Innovation output subindex | 39 | 70 | 84 | 37 |
| University/industry research collaboration | 12 | 90 | 107 | 59 |
| Knowledge absorption | 26 | 120 | 103 | 72 |
| Knowledge and technology outputs | 35 | 72 | 89 | 45 |
| Creative outputs | 43 | 67 | 81 | 31 |
| Employment in knowledge-intensive services | 51 | 98 | 67 | 71 |
| ICT infrastructure | 46 | 45 | 55 | 63 |
| State of cluster development | 5 | 86 | 91 | 50 |
| Human capital and research | 34 | 61 | 45 | 43 |
| Citable documents per habitant | 5.77 | 1.12 | 4.97 | 5.17 |
| Citations per document | 8.07 | 4.9 | 5.83 | 6.87 |
| h-index[a] | 296 | 190 | 123 | 129 |

Source: Data retrieved from the Global Innovation Index Report, 2016, scimagojr.com and UN Population data

[a]The h-index is an indicator of both the productivity and impact of the published work of the country's scientists

## 2.5 High Youth Unemployment

I have already noted that the high level of unemployment was an important driver of the Tunisian revolution. The country is still registering a high level of youth unemployment which represents one of the major threats to its social cohesion (ILO, 2011). Figure 2.18 shows that the unemployment rate increased from 13% in 2010 to 18.9% in 2011 due to the economic recession and the return of the Tunisian Diaspora from Libya. It gradually declined but was still high in 2016 at 15.5%. The youth and particularly females are more affected by unemployment (23.2% in 2016). In 2013, 37.3% of the population between 20 and 24 years and 32.2% of the population between 25 and 29 years were jobless.

During the 2000s and even after the revolution, the state tried to tackle the unemployment problem through generous active policies.[12] Unfortunately, these policies lacked an effective impact. This is not surprising given that unemployment is related to structural deficiencies of the economy. During the last decades, the private sector had not sufficiently absorbed the university graduates who enter the job market each year.[13] Recent analysis by the World Bank (2014) reveals that the contribution of the manufacturing sector to employment growth is weak with a low productivity average. Most of the active population is employed in services (51.7%) whereas agriculture, manufacturing and non-manufacturing industries count, respectively, for 14.7%, 18.7% and 14.7%. More than half of Tunisia's highly educated workers are employed in the public sector, mainly in health and education. In 2010, only 16% of employees of the private sector had a high level of education. Therefore, it is not surprising to note the accelerated brain drain to the OECD countries.[14]

[12] Nabi and Boughzala (2009) suggested that the state shall consider the social cost of youth graduate unemployment and estimate it to be 418 TND monthly per person. This social cost is related to health, psychology and familial problems as well as to violence resulting from the frustration of being unemployed after graduation.

[13] This structural problem is not recent. In 2007, the World Bank noted that about 70% of the new entrants to the Tunisian labor market every year are not able to find a job.

[14] The percentage of male emigrants to France holding a tertiary education increased from 18% in 2007 to 20.5% in 2008 (ILO, 2011). According to the statistics published in 2018 by the OECD, Tunisia is ranked among the TOP countries in terms of brain drain with more than 20% of its university graduates working in the OECD countries. http://www.oecd.org/social/poverty/migrationandthebraindrainphenomenon.htm.

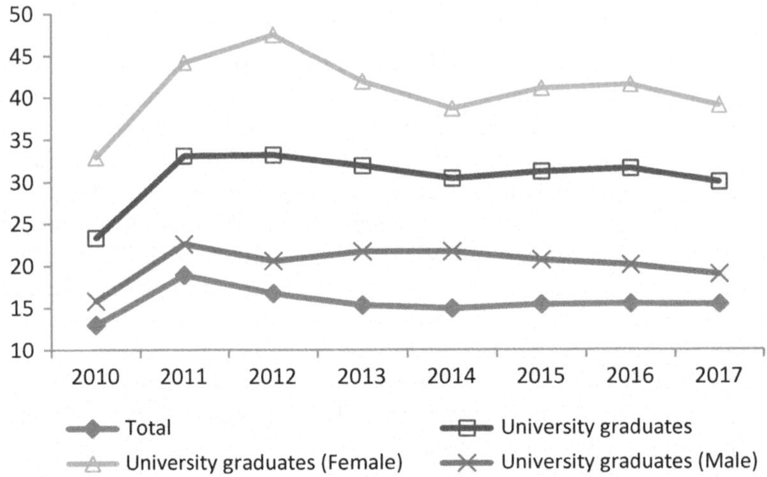


**Fig. 2.18** Unemployment rate (in %) (Source: Data from the National Institute of Statistics (INS))

Figure 2.18 shows also the high rates of unemployment among the university graduates (particularly among the females) with an average of 31.9% over 2011–2016. In 2016, 30,000 additional university graduates entered the labor market in addition to the existing 236,800 that represent around 42% of the active unemployed people. While recognizing that Tunisia is endowed with a well-educated young population, the World Bank (2016) emphasizes the priority of ensuring equal access to economic opportunities in order to unleash the energy, creativity and the immense potential of the youth. The ITCEQ (2016) report highlights the double challenge for the Tunisian economy. On one hand, it needs to create non-qualified jobs for one-third of its population over 15 years. On the other hand, qualified jobs for another one-third endowed with a university degree are also required. Figure 2.19 shows how the inner regions of the country are particularly exposed to the unemployment problem.[15] Despite some exceptions, the economic activity and private investment are still restrained to low-productivity activities, concentrated in the coastal regions and weakly intensive in jobs for the university graduates.

[15] For instance, the unemployment rate approximated 27% in the Governorate of Tataouine in 2014.

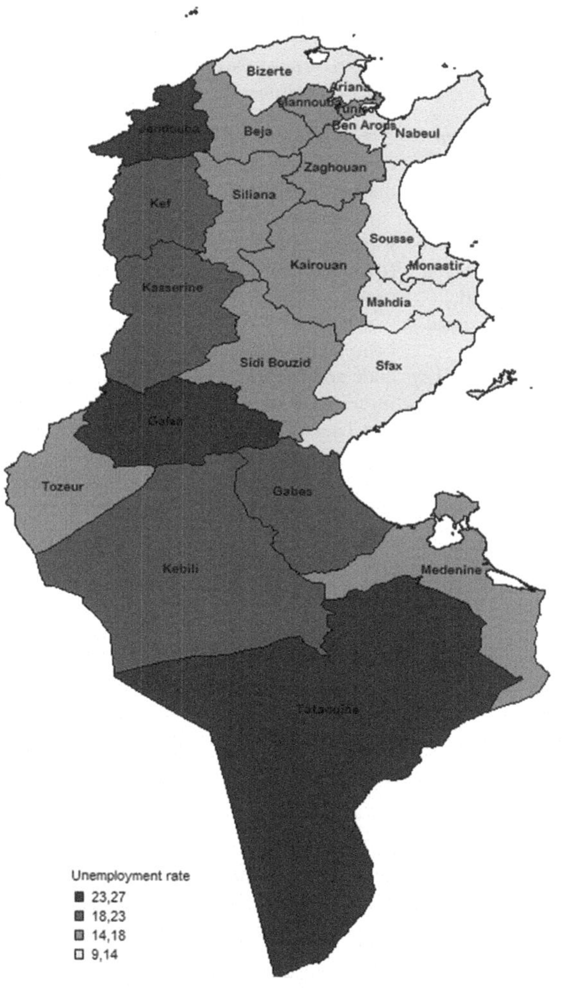


**Fig. 2.19** The unemployment rate by governorate in 2014 (Source: Data from the National Institute of Statistics (INS))

**Table 2.4** The main causes of unemployment in Tunisia

| *Demand side* | *Inefficiencies of the labor market environment* | *Supply side* |
|---|---|---|
| • Low private investment in the high productive and high-value-added sectors<br>• Lack of private initiatives owing to pessimistic prospects<br>• Weak business environment (corruption, weak infrastructure, financial constraints and fierce competition facing the SMEs)<br>• Weak impact of the active employment policies on the private sector | • Rigidities and complexity of the labor market regulations<br>• Rigidity of the wage-setting process (delinked from productivity)<br>• Rigidity and complexity of the labor code and the social insurance system<br>• Lack of follow-up and support to the beneficiaries of the active employment policies | • Skill mismatches and weak capacity of the educational system to fulfill the demand of the labor market (namely the lack of soft skills)<br>• Higher attractiveness of the public sector relatively to the private sector for the university graduates<br>• High reservation wage among the youth coupled with lack of trust in the social and economic environment<br>• Weak entrepreneurial culture |

Source: Abdelkafi and Nabi (2013) (extended and modified)

*What are the causes of the high unemployment in Tunisia*? Many reports and studies analyzed the main causes of unemployment in Tunisia. Table 2.4 summarizes the main causes of unemployment in Tunisia.

An additional binding constraint on hiring new employees by the private sector is the decline of labor productivity. Figure 2.20 shows that labor productivity increased at an annual rate of 2.5% during the period 2000–2010 and only 0.6% over 2011–2017.

There is a large agreement that improving the business environment, revisiting the incentive policies (especially with regard to investment) and modernizing the educational system are the main required reforms to reduce unemployment. Robalino et al. (2015) emphasize the need to remove the barriers to investing in higher-value-added activities.[16] They also highlight the importance to boost labor demand by lowering the tax wedge

[16] Around 52% of the active population in Tunisia is employed in services. This means that improving the competitiveness of the services sector is crucial to generate jobs.

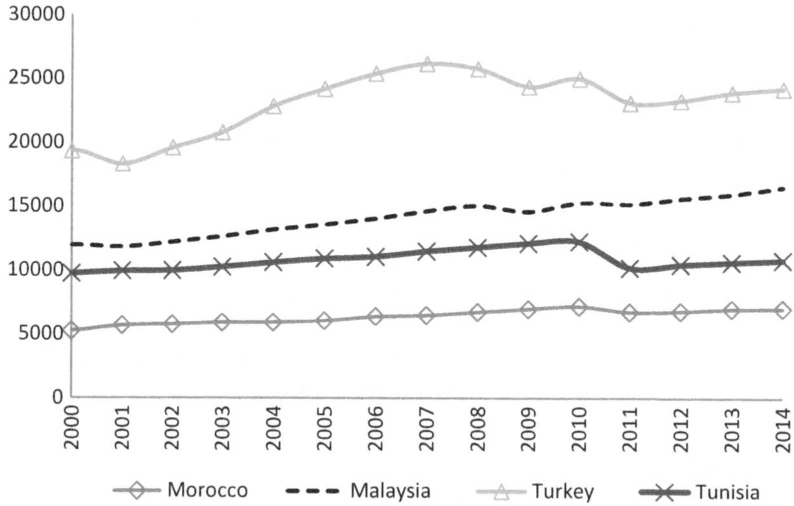


**Fig. 2.20** Labor productivity (Y/L) GDP (constant 2010 US$) (Source: Calculus of the author based on data from World Development Indicators)

on labor, reforming the pension system and changing the firing rules.[17] These reforms should be based on a flexi-security approach that strengthens the workers' protection and sets social insurance programs in case of firing. Among the recommendations included in the IsDB Group's report "*Member Country Partnership Strategy for Tunisia 2013–2015*", the need to set an active and integrated state strategy to tackle the unemployment problem shall be piloted by an inter-sectoral ministerial commission.[18]

[17] Namely by removing the dichotomy between the firing of those under open-ended and fixed-term contracts.

[18] In my quality of senior economist of the Islamic Development Bank Group, I participated in field missions and meetings with senior officials from the Tunisian government, in preparation of the "*Member Country Partnership Strategy for Tunisia 2013–2015*" (MCPS). With other economists who participated in the elaboration of the MCPS, I was aware about the importance of developing short-term policies and an integrated strategy to restore confidence and calm the social unrest, two necessary conditions to undertake the structural reforms.

## 2.6 Constrained Integration in the Global Economy

Since the late 1980s, Tunisia initiated a process of prudent integration in the global economy by gradually lowering its restrictions on international trade and financial transactions. The country signed many bilateral free trade agreements and regional (multilateral) agreements. In 1995, it signed an Association Agreement with the European Union (EU) with the objective of achieving a free trade zone for the industrialized sector in 2008. Negotiations with the EU for the liberalization of the services and agricultural sectors have been under way since 2009. Figures 2.21 and 2.22 present the changes of the KOF economic globalization de facto and de jure indexes for Tunisia and for Malaysia, Morocco and Turkey over the period 1986–2015.[19] It can be clearly noted that the de jure index of

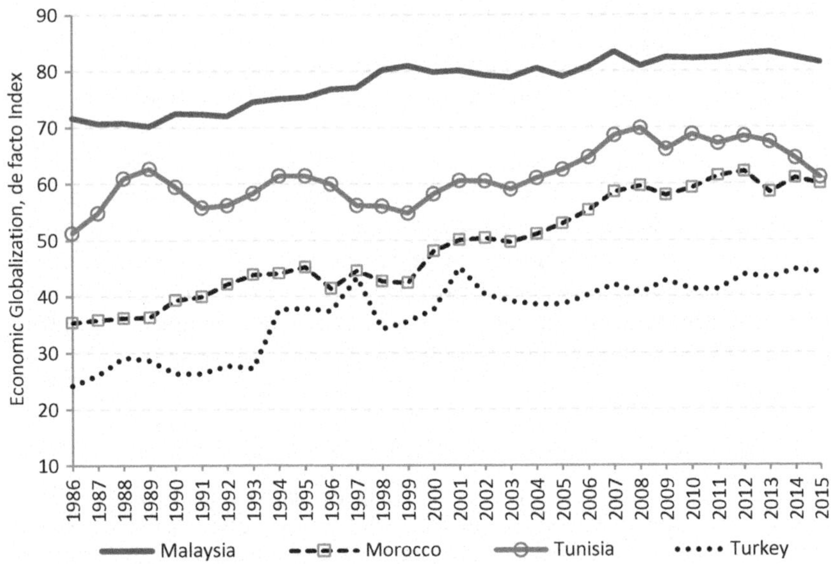


**Fig. 2.21** KOF economic globalization, de facto index (Source: Data retrieved from http://globalization.kof.ethz.ch/)

[19]The economic globalization, de facto index, quantifies trade and investment flows, whereas the economic globalization, de jure index, focuses on "hidden import barriers", "mean tariff rate", "taxes on international trade" and "capital account restrictions".

Tunisia declined in 2011, 2013 and 2015, attaining 31.3, a value lower than that of 1997 (Fig. 2.22). This evolution reflects the difficult and instable environment for trade and foreign investment transactions since 2011. Despite these constraints, the de facto globalization index for Tunisia is still higher than that of Morocco and Turkey (Fig. 2.21).

It is important to recall what was already mentioned by many reports regarding the concentration of foreign direct investment (FDI) in labor-intensive and low-value-added activities (e.g. textile, tourism, call centers) that do not require high skills. Tunisia needs more skill and technology-intensive FDI that generate more job opportunities to the unemployed university graduates. This type of FDI, which is still rare (despite the presence of many foreign firms in electronics and aerospace activities), would also generate positive externalities benefiting the entire economy through technology transfer and innovation spillovers that enhance the total factor productivity of the country.

As shown in Fig. 2.23, the exports of Tunisia are still well diversified. The share of "energy and lubricant" exports declined from 52% in 1980 to 8% in 2015. Meanwhile, the "mechanical and electrical industries"

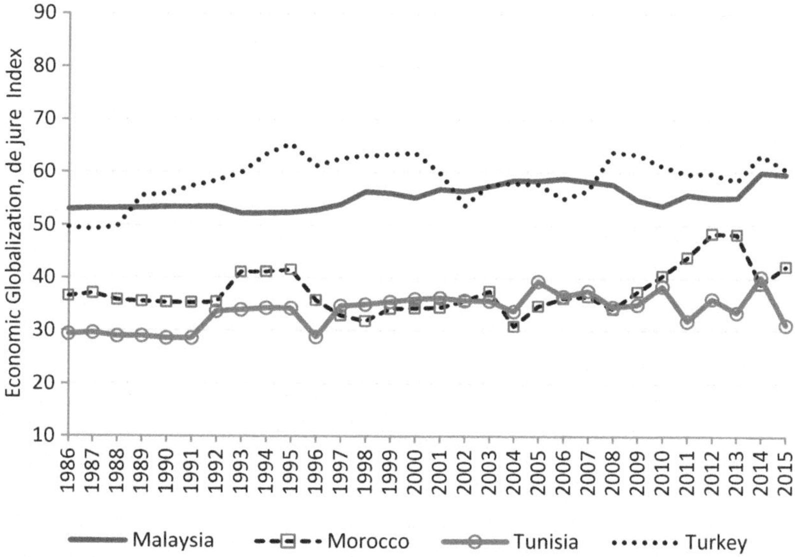


**Fig. 2.22** KOF economic globalization, de jure index (Source: Data retrieved from http://globalization.kof.ethz.ch/)

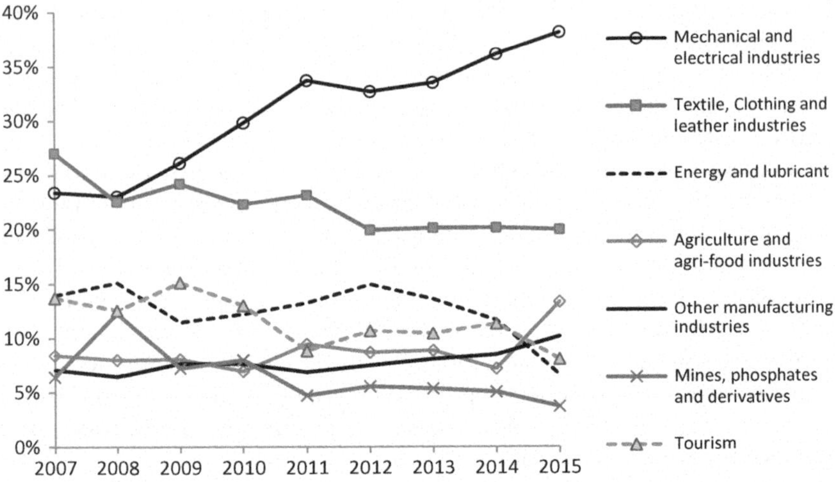


**Fig. 2.23** Exports' shares by categories of products (Source: Data retrieved from National Institute of Statistics)

became the first in contributing to exports with a share of 38% in 2015. This sector benefited from the offshore firms which are integrated into the EU automobile production networks. The "textiles and clothing" share is stabilizing around 20% since 2012. The "tourism" and "mines, phosphates and derivatives" were largely impacted by the social unrest and terrorist attacks that took place after 2011. Their respective shares declined from 13% and 8% in 2010 to 8% and 3.7% in 2015. As shown in Fig. 2.24, Europe is the main trade partner of Tunisia, but exports to Africa and imports from Asia are increasing. The concentration of the Tunisian exports in the European market intensively exposes Tunisia to the fluctuations of Europe's economic cycle and is pushing the diversification of the exports markets towards the Americas, Asia and Africa.

The Tunisian SMEs are suffering from multiple constraints, which, if not alleviated, will prevent them from integrating the global production networks. The World Bank (2013) identifies the following difficulties faced by the Tunisian SMEs: (1) identifying the target market, the product segment and the distribution channel, (2) adapting the products to markets, (3) understanding the competition, (4) launching marketing campaigns, (5) training and hiring in response to the market demand and (6) delivering the product on time and being paid. The report observes also that for some key Tunisian sectors in manufacturing and services, the logistic costs represent 20–73% of the gross markup (2010). In addition,

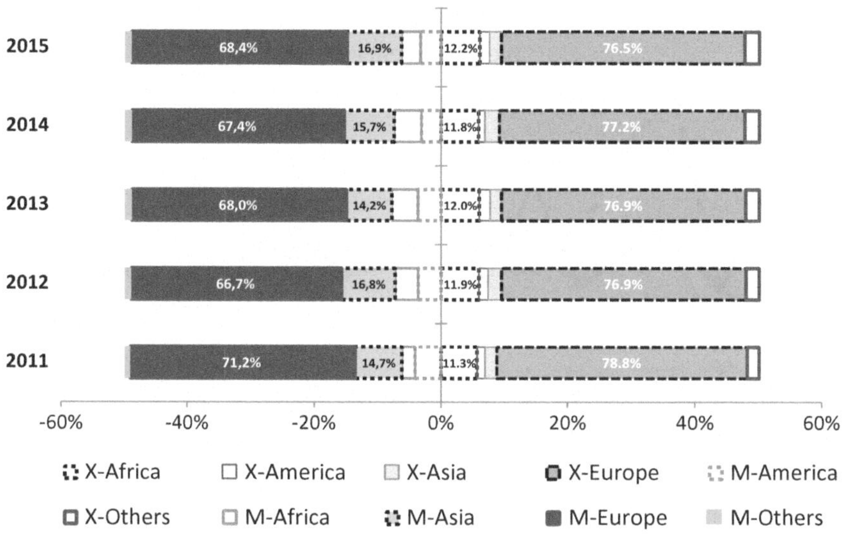


**Fig. 2.24** The composition of Tunisia's trade by destination (Source: Data retrieved from National Institute of Statistics)

in some Tunisian sectors, recent technical requirements in the export markets (like improving the traceability of the products, namely in the agri-food industry) create additional constraints in the domestic supply chain.

## 2.7 Weak Macroeconomic Fundamentals

The revolution exacerbated the economic difficulties and generated new challenges, mainly the deterioration of the macroeconomic fundamentals. In the following subsections I analyze the evolution of the macroeconomic indicators.

### *2.7.1 Economic Growth and the Economic Activity*

Tunisia realized an average annual growth of approximately 4.4% over the period 2000–2010. Following the revolution, the Tunisian economy was exposed to several economic shocks that impacted many sectors. Recurrent social upheaval and strikes reduced the activity of many companies with major impact on the phosphate sector—one of the main sources of foreign exchange receipts of Tunisia. The successive terrorist attacks reduced the number of tourists and impacted tourism—one of the most important

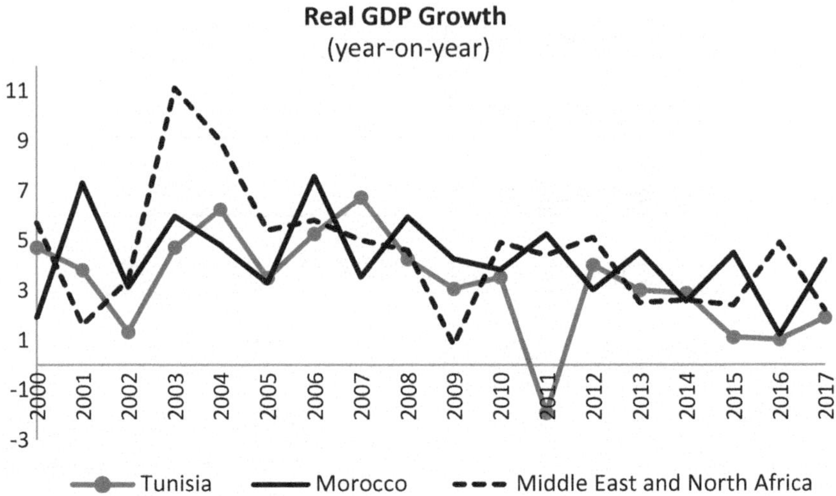


**Fig. 2.25** Evolution of Tunisia's real GDP growth in comparison with other upper-middle-income countries (Source: Data retrieved from the World Development Indicators 2018)

exporting sectors of the country. An additional negative shock was the reduction of the Tunisian workers' remittances and the FDI just after the revolution. The recession in Europe, the main destination of the Tunisian exports, exacerbated the macroeconomics difficulties. As shown in Fig. 2.25, the pace of the real GDP growth decelerated, resulting in an average of 1.7% over the period 2011–2017.

The current economic situation has multiple aspects. The socioeconomic situation and the political instability impacted the total factor productivity (TFP). The average annual growth of the TFP was around 1.8% during the period 2000–2010. The remaining contributors to the 4.4% average annual growth were capital and labor accumulation with 1.4% and 1.2%, respectively. During the period 2011–2017 the growth of the TFP was negative and equaled −0.9%. The average annual economic growth resulted from the accumulation of capital (2.2%) and labor (0.4%).[20] The latter was mainly due

[20] My calculi are based on the following Cobb-Douglas function $Y = AK^{0.4}L^{0.6}$. Data of the stock of physical capital are based on Berlemann and Wesselhöft (2014) for the period 2000–2010. Additional estimations for the years 2012–2017 were calculated using data from the Gross Fixed Capital Formation of the WDI based on the perpetual inventory method with a depreciation rate of 4%.

to massive recruitment in the public sector under the pressure of social protests. Seen from another angle, the final consumption was the main driver of the weak economic growth after 2011. As shown in Figs. 2.26 and 2.27, the current account deficit deteriorated from 4.8% of GDP in 2010 to 8.8% in 2016. This was mainly due to the trade balance deficit.

### 2.7.2 *Country Risk Assessment and External Balance*

The sovereign rating of Tunisia deteriorated since 2011 passing from the investment grade to the speculative grade (Fig. 2.28). The most recent downgrade was made by Moody's in August 2017. The rating passed from Ba3 to B1 with negative outlook. The rating agency justified this downgrading by (1) continued structural deterioration in Tunisia's fiscal strength, (2) persistent external imbalances and (3) reduced institutional strength and government effectiveness.

In order to reduce the exposure to higher risk premium when raising funds on the international financial markets, the Tunisian government asked for sovereign guarantees from the United States and Japan. In 2015, Tunisia raised 1 billion USD with 10 years maturity and 5.75% of annual yield. Looking at the composition of the net capital inflows to Tunisia

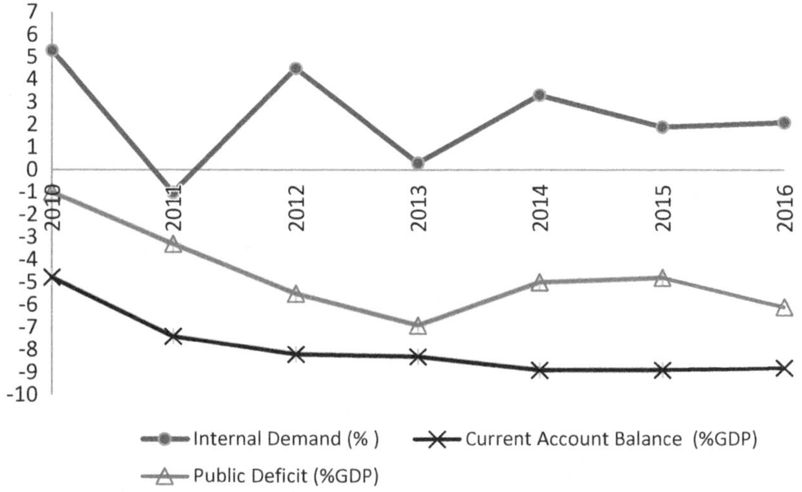


**Fig. 2.26** Evolution of the internal demand, the current account and the public deficit (Source: Data retrieved from the Tunisian National Institute of Statistics and the Tunisian Ministry of Finance)

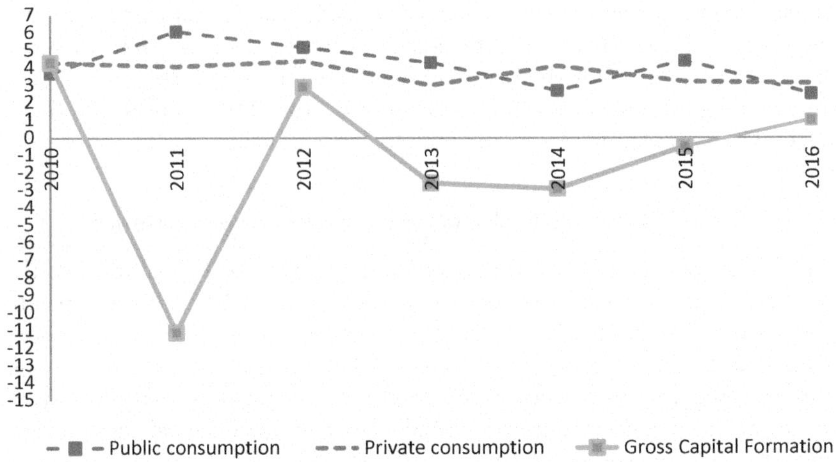


**Fig. 2.27** Evolution of the components of the internal demand (Source: Data retrieved from the Tunisian National Institute of Statistics and the Tunisian Ministry of Finance)

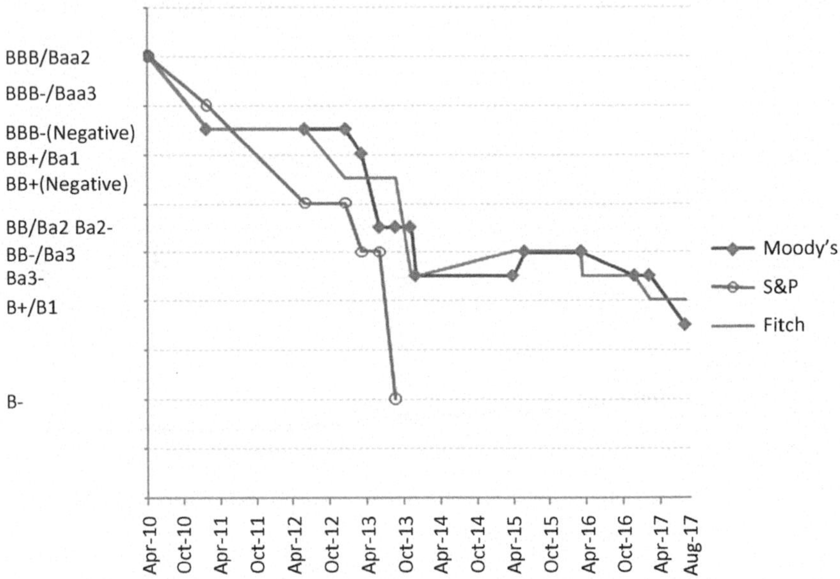


**Fig. 2.28** Evolution of Tunisia's rating by Moody's, S&P and Fitch (Source: Data retrieved from http://countryeconomy.com)

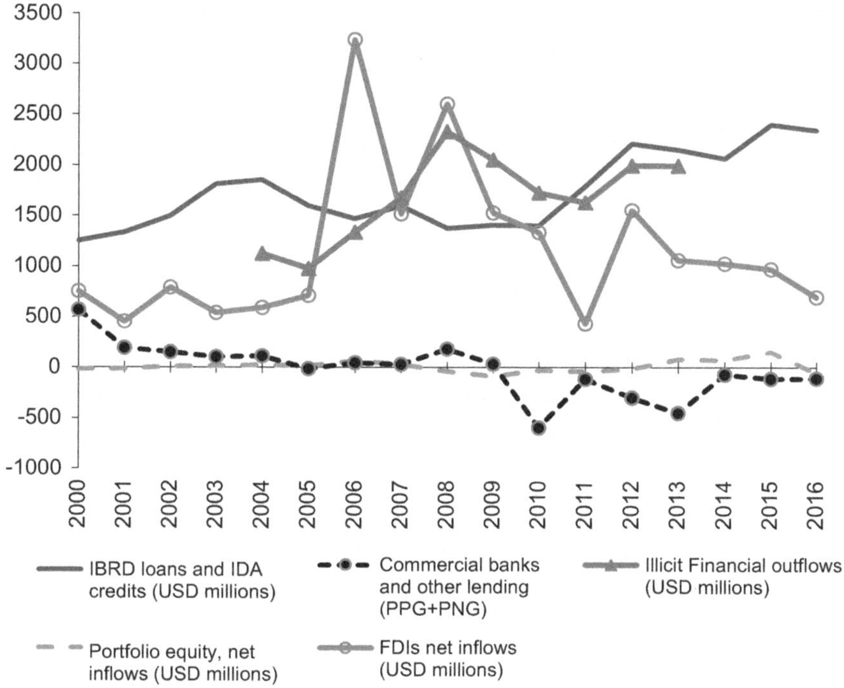


**Fig. 2.29** Evolution of the net capital inflows and the illicit capital outflows (Source: Data retrieved from the World Development Indicators and the Global Financial Integrity Report)

(Fig. 2.29) we note the decrease of FDI since 2009, a tendency which accelerated from 2012 to 2016. This deceleration is not surprising given the political instability and the deterioration of the business investment climate. Meanwhile, the financing of the economy in the form of IBRD loans and IDA credits[21] increased (2205 million USD per year on average), which is pushing the external indebtedness of the country to higher levels. It is also notable that the Tunisian stock exchange is still unable to attract

[21] IBRD (International Bank for Reconstruction and Development) and IDA (International Development Association) credits are public and publicly guaranteed debt extended by the World Bank Group.

sufficient amounts of foreign investments despite the positive tendency. This is mainly due to its small size.[22]

Figure 2.29 shows also the huge amount of illicit financial outflows from Tunisia which reached a cumulative amount of 16.8 billion USD over the period 2004–2013 (representing a yearly outflow of 19.6% of the market capitalization in 2013). In 2013, the illicit financial outflows represented 4.3% of the GDP a rate higher than that of Turkey (2.8%) and Morocco (3.7%) but much lower than that of Malaysia (14.9%).

Since the 1990s Tunisia adopted an exchange rate policy focused on maintaining a stable real exchange rate. Given its scarce resources in foreign reserves and the gradual liberalization of its capital account, a fixed exchange regime is clearly unsuitable. The country adopted instead a managed float with no predetermined path and no official fluctuation band. Currently, the value of the dinar (TND) is determined on the interbank foreign exchange market with reduced interventions of the Central Bank of Tunisia (CBT) which stabilizes the exchange rate against excessive depreciation. Figure 2.30 shows the continuous depreciation of the Tunisian currency against the American dollar and the Euro since 2011.

This trend is mainly due to the increasing current account deficit.[23] The level of foreign reserves declined from around 41% of the imports' value in December 2010 to 31% in December 2016. Meanwhile, the ratio of short-term debt to foreign reserves (one of the indicators of the pressure on the exchange rate) increased from 55% in December 2010 to 121% in December 2016. This higher ratio was driven by the increase of the external indebtedness level and its changing maturity. The percentage of short-term debt in total debt increased from 13.4% in 2010 to 19.3% in 2015. As shown in Fig. 2.31, the post-revolution is characterized by a widening of the current

[22] The ratio of market capitalization of listed domestic companies in percentage of GDP equals 19.6% in 2012. For the same year this ratio was much higher in Morocco (53.4%), Turkey (40%) and Malaysia (148.4%).

[23] In April 2017, the Tunisian currency was exposed to speculative pressure after the speech of the minister of finance regarding the slow convergence of the dinar to the parity of 3 against the European currency. This obliged the governor of the central bank and the economic adviser of the government to intervene in the media trying to restore confidence in the value of the dinar. These interventions were clearly motivated by the fear of exacerbated macroeconomic difficulties via the well-known self-fulfilling expectations mechanism. Yet, the speculative pressure obliged the central bank to inject 100 million American dollars in order to limit the acceleration of the dinar's depreciation.

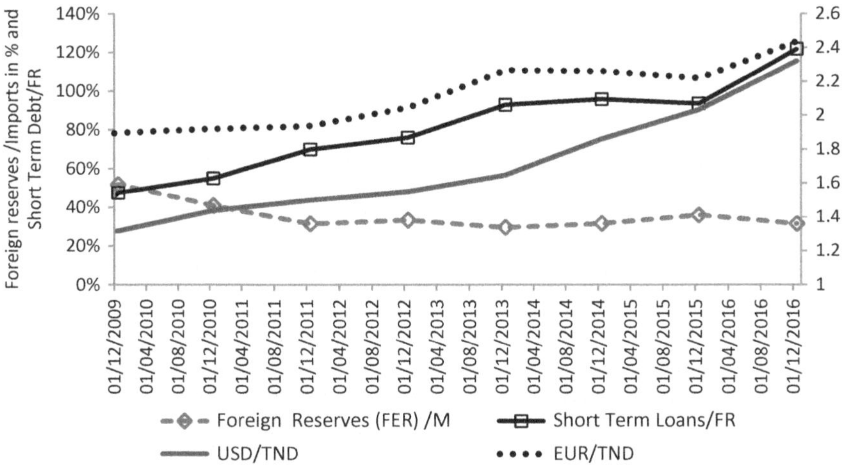


**Fig. 2.30** Foreign exchange reserves/imports and exchange rates EUR/TND and USD/TND (Source: Data retrieved from the Central Bank of Tunisia and the Tunisian National Institute of Statistics)

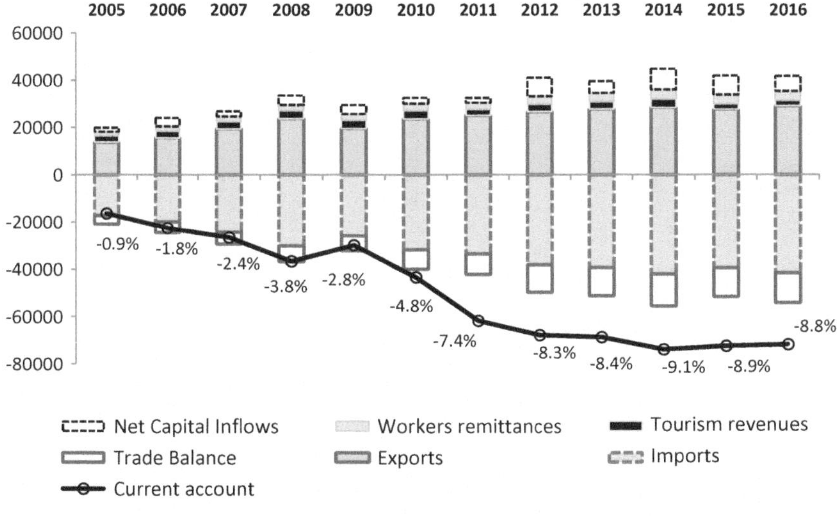


**Fig. 2.31** FDI, remittances, current account and trade volume (in TND millions) (Source: Data retrieved from the Central Bank of Tunisia)

account deficit and the decrease of the foreign exchange reserves. This trend was mainly caused by the widening of the trade deficit, the reduction of the workers' remittances and the shrinking of the FDI inflows.

### 2.7.3 *Public Deficit, Public Debt and the Tax System*

Before 2011, Tunisia pursued a prudent public financial management. In 2010, the public deficit was 1% of GDP and the public debt equaled 40.7% of GDP (16% of external debt and 24.7% of internal debt). Therefore, the Tunisian economy had sufficient fiscal and debt spaces to raise its public expenditure coping with the resurgence of huge social demand with the revolution. Figure 2.32 shows that the operating public expenses doubled from 2010 to 2017 with a share in the total budget passing from 55.9% to 62.7% over the same period. The social transfers increased (in the form of financial support to the poor, increased subsidies of food and energy after the increase of the international prices). Besides, the government was obliged to increase wages in the public sector twice while pursuing a laxest recruitment policy with approximately 20,000 new public servants each year. This has contributed to an

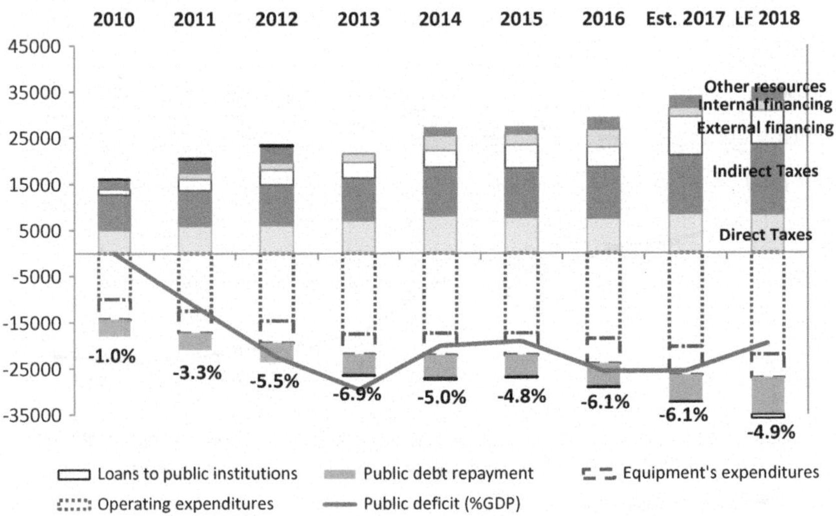


**Fig. 2.32** Structure of the state's revenues and expenditures and evolution of the public deficit (Source: Data retrieved from the Tunisian Ministry of Finance)

increase of the wages bill in the public sector from 10% of GDP to approximately 14.5% of GDP in 2016. The successive governments have also dedicated special funds for financing youth unemployment programs. Given this huge increase in the operating expenses coupled with the in-deficit situation of many state-owned companies and banks, as well as the pension system, the budget space dedicated to public investment shrunk from 24% in 2010 to 18.9% in 2017. Although the government increased public investment in infrastructure in favor of the inner and disadvantaged regions, the growth of this type of expenditure was just 42% from 2010 to 2017, much lower than the 100% increase of the operational expenses.

The slow economic growth coupled with the inefficiency of the tax system reduced the capacity of the government to finance its budget from tax revenues. The share of the latter in the total revenues decreased from 87.8% in 2010 to 68.6% in 2017. As a consequence, the fiscal deficit reached its high levels of 6.9% in 2013 and 6% in 2016.

The inefficiency of the Tunisian tax system is analyzed by Alm (2015). He qualifies it as outdated and an ad hoc system which has been accommodating the requests of specific individuals and specific sectors of the economy. Alm (2015) particularly identifies a wide range of distortions affecting the individual and firm behavior and generating significant efficiency costs. He concludes that the extensive system of incentives and the corporate tax are leading firms to base their investment decisions in tax considerations rather than on market opportunities. It is worthwhile to note that tax evasion is high, as 50% of the one-person limited liability companies are not fulfilling their duties. The recovery of unpaid taxes is inefficient and the good taxpayers are feeling injustice. The government announced a plan to modernize the tax administration including the hiring of 1600 dedicated civil servants and the development of a modern IT system. Many experts are appealing for the simplification of the taxation framework and its readjustment in cohesion with the economic development strategy of the country. Figure 2.33 shows that the ratio of public debt to GDP increased to almost 70% in 2016 (48% as external debt and 22% as internal debt).

As previously noted (Fig. 2.29), most of the external financing was in the form of IBRD loans and IDA credits (2205 million USD per year on average). It is also important to note that the repayment of the interest and principal of the public debt is an overwhelming burden. In 2017, it represented 95.3% of the investment expenses or 18% of total public

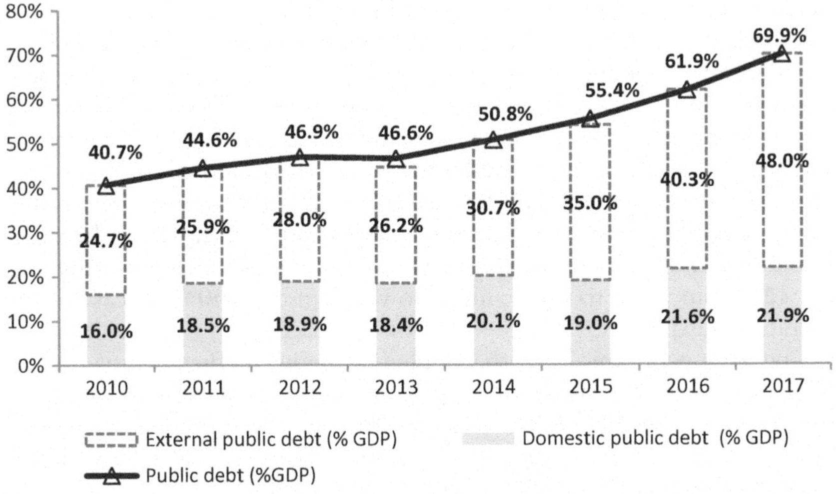


**Fig. 2.33** Evolution of the public debt in % of GDP (Source: Data retrieved from the Tunisian Ministry of Finance)

expenses. Most of the public external debt was contracted in Euros and American dollars. Therefore, the Tunisian government is exposed to the additional cost of the dinar's continuous depreciation. Given this difficult public finance situation, the government recurred to exceptional measures during the preparation of the 2017 budget. It imposed an exceptional increase of 7.5% on taxes on corporate profits. Meanwhile, it agreed with the labor unions to reschedule the wage increases planned in 2017 and pay it in the form of tax discounts. Therefore, it is clear that the country is exposed to a difficult situation in public finances. Meanwhile, the financial gap[24] increased in recent years, obliging the authorities to seek external financing mainly in the form of debt and issuance of sovereign bonds.[25] As a consequence, the public debt to GDP ratio reached 66.9% in June

[24] Difference between investment and saving.

[25] In 2014, for example, Tunisia raised 1.8 billion USD through the issuance of sovereign bonds on the international market with guarantee of the American and the Japanese governments. Meanwhile, in June 2014 the government raised 955 billion TND on the national market through a national sovereign bond issuance which is considered as the third one after 1956 and 1964.

2017.[26] The share of the external public debt to GDP reached 46.5% in June 2017, which is likely to put the Tunisian economy on the downward part of the U-inverted curve linking the external debt to the economic growth (Pattillo et al., 2002).[27]

This situation is constraining the ability of the economy to finance its transformation. The repetitive recourse to domestic commercial banks to finance the public deficit—through sovereign bonds—is reducing their incentive to finance the investment of the private sector, which is already suffering from a weak business environment and difficult access to finance. Therefore, like many developing countries, Tunisia needs urgent activation of non-traditional mechanisms for financial resources mobilization. I will suggest a variety of such mechanisms in Chap. 6.

## 2.8 Monetary Policy and the Banking Sector

The CBT is responsible for conducting the monetary policy, supervising and regulating the financial system and ensuring its stability. The new law of 2016 concretized the independence of the CBT from the executive. It mandates the CBT with the responsibility of ensuring the stability of prices while contributing to financial stability, with the ultimate objective to support the economic policies of the state in terms of economic growth and jobs creation. The CBT uses the interest rate as an instrument to conduct its monetary policy by adjusting it to inflation and growth expectations. In circumstances such as the political transition following 2011, it is comprehensible that the CBT conducts an expansionary monetary policy putting more weight on the economic activity stimulation relative to price stability. That is what exactly happened after the revolution. As shown in Fig. 2.34, the CBT accommodated its monetary policy by injecting large liquidities into the monetary market to cope with the lack of liquidity of banks. Indeed, the total volume of liquidity provided to the banking sector (banking refinancing) accelerated. Meanwhile, the CBT lowered its reserve requirement ratio from 12.5% in December 2010 to 1% in December 2013. In addition,

[26] Taking into consideration the external debt of the state-owned enterprises which are guaranteed by the government, the rate is around 80%.

[27] Along this downward part of the curve, the external debt dampens the economic growth through two channels: (1) the adverse effects on the physical capital accumulation (a contribution of 1/3 on average) and (2) the negative effects on the total factor productivity (a contribution of 2/3 on average) (Pattillo et al., 2004).

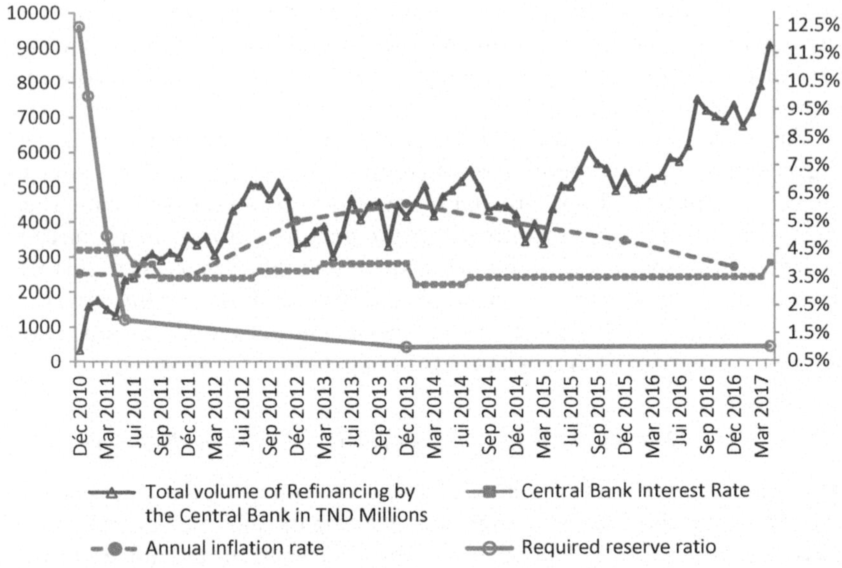


**Fig. 2.34** The main indicators of the CBT's monetary policy (Source: Data retrieved from the Central Bank of Tunisia data sets)

the CBT reduced its reference interest rate from 4.5% in December 2010 to 3.5% in July 2012. Beginning from August 2012, the CBT initiated a gradual tightening of the monetary policy in order to contain a rising inflation (5.6% on average in 2012 compared to 3.5% in 2011). However, it has again loosened it from 4% to 3.3% in January 2014 until July 2014, when it initiated a slow pace of monetary tightening, achieving 4% in April 2017.

The IMF (2015) encourages the CBT to continue its prudent monetary policy to control the inflationary pressures, preserve positive real interest rates and reduce exchange rate pressures. The Quantitative Easing (QE) policy of the CBT enabled the banking system to expand its financing of the economy (Fig. 2.35). However, it is more likely that this QE enabled the financing of the government deficit, household consumption and the working capital of well-established companies much more than new investments and financial needs of the SMEs. It has certainly contributed to the stimulation of the economic activity through the consumption channel. The negative effect is the contribution to the deterioration of the trade balance by boosting imports and reducing the value of the TND which ultimately results in higher inflation (through the exchange rate pass-through).

After 2011, the financial performance and asset quality indicators of the Tunisian banks deteriorated. However, since 2014, the aggregate performance indicators of the banking system improved. The net banking income increased at the rates of 8.03%, 8.74% and 12.95% during the periods 2015Q1/2014Q1, 2016Q1/2015Q1 and 2017Q1/2016Q1 (Table 2.5). This good performance was not accompanied by a reduction of the Non-Performing Loans (NPLs), which represented 15.8% in 2014 and 16.6% of the total gross loans in 2015, much higher than the average 4% of the higher middle-income countries to which the Tunisian economy belonged. In addition, the provisioning of the NPLs is still low, equaling 56.9% in 2015.

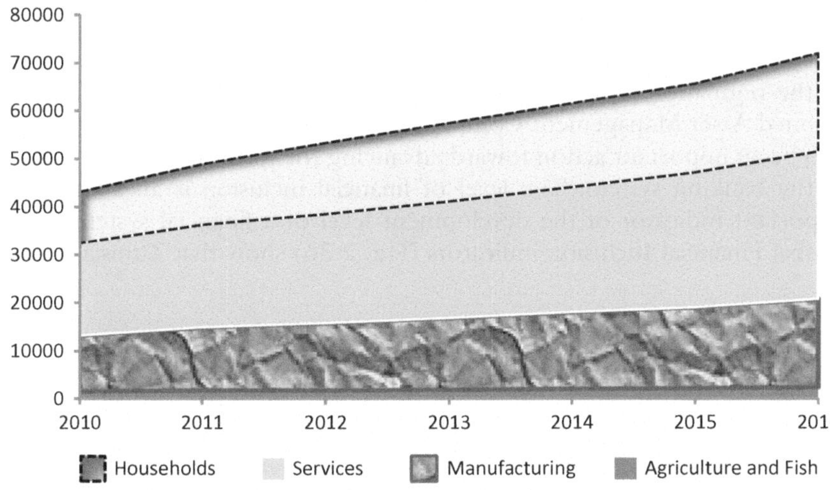


**Fig. 2.35** Sectoral distribution of banks' loans (in millions of TND) (Source: Data retrieved from the Central Bank of Tunisia data sets)

**Table 2.5** Performance indicators of the Tunisian banking system

| | *2010* | *2011* | *2012* | *2013* | *2014*[a] |
|---|---|---|---|---|---|
| ROA | 0.9 | 0.6 | 0.6 | 0.3 | 0.9 |
| ROE | 10.2 | 5.9 | 7.2 | 3 | 11.2 |
| NPLs | 13.0 | 13.3 | 14.9 | 15.2 | 15.8 |

Source: Data retrieved from the IMF and World Bank Data sets

[a]Estimations

The assets of the 36 onshore banks equaled 31,117.1 million TND in 2015. Three of the six public banks were recapitalized due to financial problems resulting from bad governance practices and crony capitalism that characterized the dictatorship period. The IMF (2015) stressed the importance to update the underlying business plans and ensure regulatory compliance of these banks throughout the restructuring period. It also emphasized the necessity to endow the Tunisian economy with a modern banking resolution and supervisory framework as well as an effective bankruptcy framework. In February 2016, Standard & Poor's classified the Tunisian banking sector of Tunisia in group "9". The main stressed negative aspects concerned weak achievement in terms of banking regulation and supervision and the regulatory. However, it is expected that the new banking law adopted in July 2016 will improve the banking supervision and governance framework. It will helpfully contribute to the convergence of the regulation with the international standards. The creation of the planned Asset Management Company for the banks' distressed assets will also be an important action toward advancing the institutional framework of the banking system. The level of financial inclusion is an additional important indicator of the development level of a financial system. The Global Financial Inclusion indicators (Fig. 2.36) show that Tunisia needs

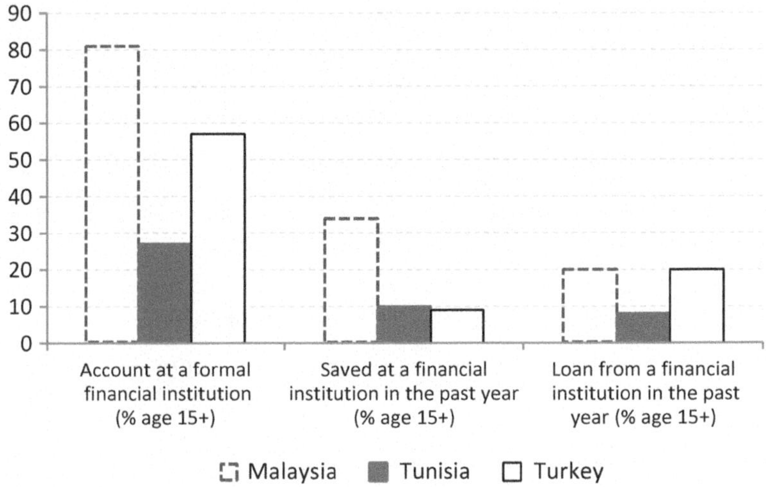


**Fig. 2.36** Financial inclusion indicators in 2014 (Source: Global Financial Inclusion Database)

to improve the "access to finance". Indeed, only 27% of the Tunisians over 15 years had an account at a formal financial institution (81% in Malaysia and 57% in Turkey). In regard to the two other indicators related to "saving" and "benefiting from a loan", Tunisia does not have better performance.

## References


Abdelkafi, R. and M. S. Nabi (2013) "A proposal for jobs creation based on Islamic microfinance and cooperatives," Sfax 2nd International Forum on Islamic Finance, 27–29 June 2013.

African Union Commission, UNECA, AfDB and UNDP (2013) "Food security in Africa: Issues, challenges and lessons," MDG Report 2013. Assessing Progress in Africa toward the Millennium Development Goals.

Alm, J. (2015) "Analyzing and reforming Tunisia's tax system," CEQ Institute, Working paper No. 34.

Ayadi, L., N. Benjamin, S. Bensassi and G. Raballand (2013) "Estimating informal trade across Tunisia's land borders," Policy Research working paper No. WPS 6731, World Bank Group, Washington, DC.

Barro, R. and J.-W. Lee (2013) "A New Data Set of Educational Attainment in the World, 1950–2010," Journal of Development Economics, Vol. 104, 184–198.

Ben Cheikh, N. (2013) "The extension of social protection to informal economy under the challenge of Tunisia's transition," Mai 2013 CRES. Centre de Recherches et d'Etudes Sociales.

Berlemann, M. and J.-E. Wesselhöft (2014) "Estimating aggregate capital stocks using the perpetual inventory method: A survey of previous implementations and new empirical evidence for 103 countries," Review of Economics, Vol. 65, No. 1, 1–34.

Boughzala, M. and M. T. Hamdi (2014) "Promoting inclusive growth in Arab countries rural and regional development and inequality in Tunisia," Global Economy & Development Working Paper N° 71.

Buehn, A. and F. Schneider (2009) "Shadow economies and corruption all over the World: Revised estimates for 120 Countries," Economics: The Open-Access. Open-Assessment E-Journal, Vol. 1, No. 2007–9, 1–53 (Version 2).

Hanushek, E. A. and L. Woessmann (2012) "Do Better Schools Lead to More Growth? Cognitive Skills, Economic Outcomes and Causation," Journal of Economic Growth, Vol. 17, No. 4, 267–321.

Hausmann, R., C. A. Hidalgo, S. Bustos, M. Coscia, A. Simoes and M. A. Yildirim (2014) "The Atlas of Economic Complexity: Mapping Paths to Prosperity," MIT Press.

ICC (2013) "Tunisia's Borders: Jihadism and contraband," Middle East/North Africa Report N° 148. International Crisis Group.
ILO (2011) "Tunisia: A new social contract for fair and equitable growth," Studies on Growth with Equity, ILO.
ILO (2015) "Background note for the panel on "Transition from the informal to the formal economy in Africa: The way forward". AFRM-13-D4-Note-informal-economy".
IMF (2015) "Tunisia 2015 article IV consultation, sixth review under the stand-by arrangement, and request for rephasing," press release; staff report; and statement by the executive director for Tunisia.
INS (2012) "Mesure de la pauvreté, des inégalités et de la polarisation en Tunisie 2000–2010," Institut National de la Statistique.
ITCEQ (2016) "Rapport sur l'économie du savoir," Février 2016. N° 6.
Kouki, M. (2017) "Efficacité des services publics," IACE.
Leaders News (2011) "Mohamed Ennaceur: Pourquoi continuer à aligner les rémunérations sur celles des moins productifs?," 11 April 2011.
Milovanovitch, M. (2014) "Trust and institutional corruption: The case of education in Tunisia," Edmond J. Safra Working Papers, No. 44, Harvard University.
Morsay, H., A. Giamouridis and R. Selim (2017) "Rethinking the role of the state in Tunisia," European Bank for Reconstruction and Development, https://www.ebrd.com/news/2017/rethinking-the-role-of-the-state-in-tunisia.html.
Nabi, M. S. (1998) "Productivité globale des facteurs et politique salariale de l'entreprise," projet de fin d'études, Ecole Polytechnique de Tunisie, juin 1998.
Nabi, M. S. and M. Boughzala (2009) "Chiffrer le coût social du chômage en Tunisie?" Etude préparée pour la 24ème Session des Journées de l'Entreprise (11–12 Décembre 2009) organisées par l'Institut Arabe des Chefs d'Entreprises.
Pattillo, C., H. Poirson and L. Ricci (2002) "External debt and growth," IMF Working Paper WP/02/69, IMF, Washington, DC.
Pattillo, C., H. Poirson and L. Ricci (2004) "What are the channels through which external debt affects growth?" IMF Working Paper WP/04/15, IMF, Washington, DC.
Robalino, D., A. Kuddo, and D. F. Angel-Urdinola (2015) "Policy recommendations" Chapter 4 in "Labor Policy to Promote Good Jobs in Tunisia: Revisiting Labor Regulation, Social Security, and Active Labor Market Programs," Edited by Diego F. Angel-Urdinola. Antonio Nucifora, and David Robalino, World Bank Group.
Whiteshield Partners (2012) "Knowledge economy assessment of Tunisia: Identifying and addressing capability and innovation gaps in the Southern and Eastern Mediterranean region (SEMED)".
World Bank (2008) "Tunisia's global integration: Second generation of reforms to boost growth and employment," World Bank Country Studies, The World Bank, Washington DC.

World Bank (2013) "Projet de développement de la compétitivité et des exportations: Document d'information du projet (Pid) phase d'évaluation," Report N° 78503.

World Bank (2014) "The unfinished revolution: Bringing opportunity. Good jobs and greater wealth to all Tunisians," Development Policy Review, May 2014, Report No. 86179-TN.

World Bank (2016) "Poverty has fallen in the Maghreb, but inequality persists," Feature Story, 17 October 2016.

## Other Sources

Government of Tunisia (2018) "Livre Blanc: Rapport de synthèse sur la réforme des entreprises publiques en Tunisie," Mars 2018, www.reformes.gov.tn.

CHAPTER 3

# The Economic Reforms' Agenda and Bottlenecks

## 3.1 The Tunisian Economy Challenges

It can be concluded from the above diagnosis that the current challenge of Tunisia is to achieve two development objectives: escape the middle-income trap and break out the post-revolution vicious circle.

The middle-income class is facing a continuous deterioration of its purchasing power. The citizens do not perceive credible and well-spread signals related to the improvement of their daily life. The freedom of expression and the emergence of a vibrant civil society are frequently stressed as the only perceivable positive outcomes of the revolution.[1] The disadvantaged regions and the economically excluded population are despairing from politicians who promised them better conditions of life (at different electoral occasions). Therefore, the challenge for Tunisia is to fulfill the expectations of the deprived population through short-term programs while gaining the confidence and the adhesion of the population to a broader development strategy.

Positive signals are emerging from time to time like the relative success of the international donors' conference Tunisia 2020 held in November 2016, the Start-up Act announced by the Minister of the ICT Digital Economy in April 2017, the e-government program, the recent laws and

[1] As noted previously, the "voice and accountability" pillar of the governance indicators has clearly improved contrarily to the other pillars of the governance indicator.



M. S. Nabi, *Making the Tunisian Resurgence*,
https://doi.org/10.1007/978-981-13-3771-0_3

actions in relation to the fight of corruption and so on. Besides, many socioeconomic actions were announced by the current government. I particularly cite the announcement in April 2017 of a national program to transfer the property rights of the state's lands to poor families (who already constructed informal homes many years ago). Another example is the recent microfinance program through which the state allocated 250 million dinars to promote the creation of micro-projects by the youth. It is clear that providing lines of financing without improving logistics, reducing bureaucracy, developing the necessary IT infrastructure, setting institutions for skills to be developed and so on is far from ensuring a sustainable positive impact on the economic dynamic. Additional measures in favor of specific sectors (like real state, tourism, franchising) or specific regions are being adopted by the authorities in response to corporatist pressure or social protests.

*But are these measures part of an integrated economic reforms' agenda targeting the resurgence of the Tunisian economy? If yes, what are these reforms and the bottlenecks it is facing?*

## 3.2 The Economic Reforms' Agenda

The successive governments since January 2011 dedicated specific social programs and mechanisms (massive hiring in the public sector, financial incentives to the private sector for hiring youth, vocational programs, encouraging entrepreneurship, financial aids to the poor families, etc.) with the objective to send positive signals in the short-term while trying to conceive and undertake (at different periods and with variable engagement) structural reforms. These reforms are related to improving the Doing Business environment (e.g. a new investment code, a new competition law, a public-private partnership code, a new central bank law ensuring its independence vis-à-vis the government, a bankruptcy law and a new banking law), reducing the size of the state, lowering the huge subsidy budget via efficient targeting of the poor, resolving the permanent deficits of the state-owned enterprises and endowing it with modern governance approaches, planning the exit of the state from non-strategic sectors, restructuring the pension system, auditing and recapitalizing the in-deficit public banks. Many of these reforms are now embedded in the national development plan 2016–2020.[2] In this context, the ongoing comprehensive macroeconomic reform program is supported by the IMF's Extended Fund Facility (US$2.9 billion, amounting to 375% of Tunisia's quota over 48 months). According to the IMF (2016) it comprises the following axes:

1. Consolidating macroeconomic stability (establishing (a) an appropriate fiscal policy, (b) a prudent monetary policy aimed at containing inflation and (c) greater exchange rate flexibility)
2. Reforming public institutions and strengthening the monitoring and performance of the state-owned enterprises
3. Establishing a high-level anti-corruption entity
4. Facilitating financial intermediation and strengthening banking sector resilience and regulations (including public bank restructuring, the development of a proper resolution framework and a risk-based supervision system)
5. Improving financial inclusion (developing new credit bureaus, revising the cap on excessive lending rates, developing financing mechanisms for small and medium enterprises and microenterprises)

In September 2016, a new investment law was approved by the parliament and became effective in April 2017. The new code which comprises 36 articles intends to facilitate investment and entrepreneurship. It aims to increase the gross capital formation to GDP to 24% at the horizon of

[2] The *Council of Economic Analysis* of the *Presidency of the Government* published in January 2016 a report about the "Major National Economic Reforms for the period 2016–2020". The report develops the main pillars of the reforms: improving the financing of the economy, reinforcement of the budgetary equilibrium, development of the human resources, renewal of the social protection system and reinforcement of the institutional and regulatory framework.

I have participated in the first stage of the production of the development plan 2016–2020 through a consultation in 2014 ordered by the UN-ESCWA for the benefit of the Tunisian Government. The report I delivered was entitled "Structural reforms for the Tunisian Economy: A smart matrix". It was the result of a detailed and methodological analysis of 12 strategic reports developed by various actors: the civil society (UTICA, UGTT and independent experts), the main political parties and the government agencies. I have constructed a smart matrix covering the priority structural reforms classified into three categories: institutional reforms, industrial reforms and economic programs with a geographic dimension. In cooperation with colleagues from ITCEQ and my students from Tunisia Polytechnic School (in the context of their End of Studies Project) we have generated multiple scenarios and simulated their economic impacts as well as their financing needs.

2020. To that end, it removed many administrative obstacles facing the foreign investors. In March 2017, the Minister of Investment and International Cooperation announced the creation of the Higher Council of Investment that will play the coordination role between the multiple stakeholders (Central Bank of Tunisia, the multiple concerned ministries and the private sector) and be in charge of developing the government investment strategy and monitoring the reforms intended to improve the business environment. In its press release of 12 June 2017, the IMF recalls that the authorities are willing to enhance the governance framework and improve the business environment. Meanwhile, it notes that the establishment of the high anti-corruption authority and the creation of the one-stop shop for investors as well as Tunisia's participation in the G20 Compact with Africa will support these objectives (IMF, 2017).

## 3.3 The Economic Reforms' Bottlenecks

During a seminar, a senior adviser from the government announced that two conditions are required for the country to join a sustainable macroeconomic path: (1) an average growth rate of 3.7% over 2017–2020 and the implementation without delay of the major reforms. I expressed my skepticism about the likelihood of fulfilling these two conditions in the absence of national cohesion and consensus around an integrated development strategy. Without achieving national cohesion and consensus, the implementation of the reforms is likely to generate even more social tensions and exacerbate the economic difficulties.

The slow progress in fighting corruption and improving public services (health, education, transport and judiciary), the declining trust in the political elite and the deterioration of the purchasing power are fueling social tension and despair among the Tunisian population. This climate is going to complicate the ability to conduct the transformation of the country. At several times, the government was not able to apply administrative and tax measures and procedures which targeted specific professional activity (doctors, lawyers, agricultural intermediaries, etc.). One of the reasons that explain the resistance to change (corporatist resistance) is the lack of trust in the ability of the state's institutions to conduct effective and fair integrated reforms. This lack of trust in the state's institutions to conduct the transformation of the country seems to result from the following factors that will be detailed respectively: (a) lack of an integrated development strategy, (b) lack of consensus and weak institutional capacities and (c) extractive political institutions.

### 3.3.1 Lack of an Integrated Development Strategy

For a successful transformation of the Tunisian economy the government (state and the public sector) shall produce a development strategy which identifies the areas of the country's (dynamic) comparative advantage (resulting in identifying entry into new technologies or new industries) as well as pinpointing the impeding barriers to an inclusive economic growth (Stiglitz, 1998).[3] Despite the adoption of the national development plan 2016–2020 by the assembly in April 2017, Tunisia lacks a broader and integrated development strategy defining the role of the state in transforming the economy. The Tunisian economy is still exposed to partial approaches of reforms emerging annually (often at the occasion of the preparation of the state budget), lacking the guarantees that it will result in a positive and shared outcome for the entire society.[4]

### 3.3.2 Lack of Consensus and Weak Administrative Capability

The slow progression of the reforms is also due to the lack of political and social consensus and the absence of a strong political leadership assuming full responsibility within its electoral mandate. Although there is a large awareness among the social partners and the elite on the necessity for the country to implement a series of structural changes, divergences are due

[3] As we will note in the next chapter, this transformation is not an easy task as it requires the conjunction of policy choices based on the following fundamentals: inclusive social contract, inclusive national identity and narrative, and inclusive social covenant. The policy choices are multidimensional in relation to the rule of the law, security, education, transitional justice, elections and political party, institutional design, political dialogue, taxation and the administration of public resources, nation-building programs and economic growth.

[4] This recalls me the introductory remarks in "*Rethinking economics after the crisis*" by Benoit Coeuré in June 2014. He noted that economists tend to progress step by step toward answering the bigger questions which interest the policy makers. At the opposite, the latter have a different temporality and need short- and medium-term actions in response to complex questions. It also recalls me the remarks of one of the political leaders of Tunisia, Ahmed-Néjib Chebbi, during the *Forum of the Future of the Tunisian Association of Economists* in February 2016. After assisting to a plenary session about the long-term challenges of Tunisia and the need for drastic structural adjustments to cope with the changing trend of the labor force, he asked the panelists about the short-term economic urgency and how to fulfill people's expectations mainly in the disadvantaged regions. Benoit Coeuré is Member of the Executive Board of the European Central Bank. His entire speech is available here https://www.ecb.europa.eu/press/key/date/2014/html/sp140624.en.html.

to the lack of a comprehensive and fair approach for implementing it during a post-revolution and socially instable environment. The risk for the Tunisian economy is to remain in the "middle-income trap" and not to be able to create sufficient jobs for the youth, to reduce regional disparities and to limit the proliferation of corruption and informality.

I have already presented the important role played by the National Dialogue Quartet[5] in resolving the conflicts between the political parties. These conflicts disrupted the political transition process and would have degenerated in civil violence. It was in recognition for that role that the Quartet received the Nobel Peace Prize in 2015. The time is now for the socioeconomic development (transformation) of Tunisia. It is worthwhile to extrapolate the consensus-building approach to deal with divergent point of views in matter of resolving the socioeconomic challenges. As argued by Stiglitz (1998), this approach constitutes a precious ingredient for the transformation process to succeed. In this regard, he notes that the process of constructing a development strategy could itself serve in building a consensus not only about a broad vision of the country, key short- and medium-term objectives, but also about the necessary conditions for achieving those goals. During this process, the consensus-building improves the political and social stability and enables the "ownership" of policies and institutions, which in turn increases the likelihood of their success (Stiglitz, 1998).

In Nabi (2011), I called for the constitution of an "economic pact" gathering the different political actors around the main economic urgencies in order to minimize the ambiguity about the future orientations of the Tunisian economy and to restore the confidence of the economic actors. Unfortunately, the country was trapped in a political turmoil for many years and the economy suffered from the absence of a clear development strategy. What I called for at that time was not the unification of the political parties' ideas and conceptions of the economic policies. After all, it is normal to have pluralistic visions about the remedies to the challenges facing the economy of the country. What I suggested at that time of extreme ambiguity, was a consensus on the economic priorities and the respect of the principles of a market economy and openness on the global economy, letting each political party the freedom to suggest its

[5] A consortium of four organizations: The Tunisian General Labor Union (UGTT), the Tunisian Confederation of Industry, Trade and Handicrafts (UTICA), the Tunisian Human Rights League (LTDH) and the Tunisian Order of Lawyers.

own remedy. Regrettably, such an "economic pact" was not considered as an urgency. The political competition and instability fueled by ideological conflicts had priority in the public debate and the media. In February 2016, the civil society exemplified in the *Association of Tunisian Economists* (ASECTU) organized the "Forum of the Future: The main economic and social choices to support the democratic process in Tunisia". The objective was similar to that of the national political dialogue, but focusing on achieving consensus on main broad economic issues.[6] The forum aimed to just enhance the awareness of the political actors and the civil society to the main challenges facing the Tunisian economy.

The report of the *Council of Economic Analysis* of the *Presidency of the Government* published in January 2016, identifies the institutional bottlenecks facing the implementation of the reforms. The emphasis is on the difficult coordination and dialogue between the multiple stakeholders of the Tunisian economy even within the executive, as well as the lack of institutional capacity within each ministry to conceive the details of the reforms. Lant Pritchett[7] qualifies this failure as the weak "administrative capability of the state". He argues that the implementation of the public policies is constrained by the real-world context. The latter creates different norms that shape the people at the implementation level (Clappison, 2011).

Pritchett distinguishes between the formulation of the policy and its implementation. The main issue is the ability of the state to ensure that the planned objectives are met. In the case of Tunisia, the execution of many planned public investment expenditures was not realized due to the limited implementation capacity of the government. In addition to these institutional deficiencies, most of the governments performed very poorly in terms of communication strategy.[8] During the last two years the

[6] The main issues were unemployment, taxation policy, social transfers, role of the state, role of the private sector, institutionalizing the social dialogue, reform of the administration and the social security system.

[7] From Harvard University on the occasion of the Economic Research Forum Annual Conference in Egypt in March 2011.

[8] On the occasion of my participation in the meeting of the *Council of Economic Advisory* of the *Presidency of the Government* (chaired by the President of the Government in June 2016), I have had the opportunity to raise the importance of developing an efficient communication strategy in order to restore the confidence of the citizens, especially during the transition period. Among the suggested ideas are developing an interactive map of the

governmental communication improved mainly through better utilization of the social media channels. "People have had enough of experts" written by Sheila Dow[9] emphasizes the "post-democratic" era in which policy decisions are made on the basis of experts' opinions rather than any democratic process.[10] In Tunisia, it seems that people have had enough of experts due to the ambiguity they are diffusing among people via the media in relation to the economic policies.[11] Hence, it is important for the government to benefit from new technologies in order to improve its communication policy.

### 3.3.3 *Extractive Political Institutions*

The governance framework comprises mechanisms, processes and institutions determining how power is exercised, how issues of public concern are considered and how citizens articulate their interests, exercise their legal rights, meet their obligations and mediate their differences (UNDP, 2010). It is clear that in most of the developing countries such a governance framework is weak and suffering from the capture of the state by the political elite. Acemoglu (2006) develops a conceptual framework where the political institutions are not inclusive and controlled by the elite. This group sets policies to increase its income and extract resources from the rest of the society. This political configuration generates an inefficient

country (encompassing the 24 governorates), enabling the user to discover the planned projects and public investments, as well as the achievements and the progress. I have also suggested improving communication about the priority subjects which interest the citizens: the fight against corruption, the governance of the state-owned enterprises, the modernization of the administration, the solution to the chronic deficit of the pension system, the tax evasion and the informal economy. I have also stressed the importance of improving the coordination between the Ministry of Finance, the Ministry of Development and International Cooperation and the Central Bank of Tunisia.

[9] In the blog of the Institute for New Economic Thinking in February 2016. See https://www.ineteconomics.org/perspectives/blog/people-have-had-enough-of-experts.

[10] The article criticizes the functioning of the policy-making institutions in developed countries mentioning how they have been captured by vested interests.

[11] In the absence of a credible national institution capable of communicating efficiently and transparently about the economic situation, the economic policies' choices and the progress toward the implementation of the reforms, the media often invited experts who criticized the economic choices from a political opposition lens. The systematic "opposition" of some experts has to some extent fueled the ambiguity in the future of the economy.

economic equilibrium through the following mechanisms: (1) revenue extraction, (2) factor price manipulation and (3) political consolidation. In this framework, the only chance for the economy to escape the inefficient policies of the dominant political group is the emergence of long-term investments combined with improvements of the marginalized groups' property rights.[12]

Therefore, it is urgent to immunize the Tunisian economy from the conflict of interests between politicians and economic actors. The deterioration of people's trust in the ruling political parties has already increased in recent years due to the prolonged socioeconomic crisis. Fortunately for the country a vibrant civil society is emerging and gaining the citizens' confidence. Nucifora et al. (2015) note that the openness of the Tunisian economy requires a new policy infrastructure which eradicates social exclusion and corruption. They argue that the previous system of laws and regulations remains largely in place, perpetuates cronyism and corruption in the business environment and limits the economic opportunities for the unconnected Tunisians. Therefore, I deem it crucial to empower the civil society so that it can play an important role in calibrating the choices in the political economy arena and reinforce the checks and balances in Tunisia. In 2011, Joseph Stiglitz noted that in order for Tunisia to prevent special interests from capturing its government, it shall restrict lobbying and ban the private financing of electoral campaigns. In addition, it shall establish transparent procedures of privatization auctions and competitive bidding for procurement in order to reduce the scope of rent-seeking behavior (Stiglitz, 2011). Another Nobel Prize laureate in economics, Edmond Phelps, talked about the development transformation of the Tunisian economy a few months after the revolution. He emphasized two prerequisites for the modernization of the economic system. The first prerequisite is to free the business sector from the control of the privileged set. The

[12] In the case of Colombia, Acemoglu and Robinson (2012) observe that the economic and political institutions have become more inclusive progressively. However, they note that major extractives dimensions such as lawlessness and insecure property rights remain due to the lack of control by the national state in many parts of the country. They explain this fact by the prevailing vicious circle: the lack of incentives for politicians to provide public services and law and order in many parts of the country. They also argue that the existing political institutions do not put enough constraints on politicians to prevent their collusion with paramilitaries and thugs (Acemoglu and Robinson, 2012).

second one is to end the bureaucratic control on entrepreneurship through licenses and other barriers (Phelps, 2011).[13]

The new constitution adopted in 2014 assigned an important role to the institutional building in order to favor an inclusive development and immunize the country against the pullback to the dictatorship regime.[14] This threat to the successful transition is generating loss of trust, especially among the Tunisian youth. They are still feeling excluded from the political system and their trust in public institutions is low, especially in the rural regions.[15] Without fairness and trust in the state's institutions, it would be difficult for Tunisia to peacefully undertake the set of necessary economic reforms.[16] The need of trust to conduct reforms is emphasized by many Tunisians with various professional backgrounds. For instance, Mohamed Meddeb—a retired General of the Tunisian Army—emphasizes the need of minimum political audacity, sincerity and pedagogical as well as communicational efforts from the government toward the citizens. These are necessary conditions for the emergence of a national will and citizens'

[13] He advocated a modernization approach à la developed countries in the nineteenth century that he baptized "capitalism 1.0" with the following components: rights against the government, property rights, rights of contract, rule of law, local banks supporting local entrepreneurs, financial firms supplying venture capital, free entry of new companies into industries and so on. In addition, respect of individual rights, tolerance toward differences and acceptance of competition are stressed as important values that shall be shared in the society for the modernization process to succeed.

[14] Yet, the building of the new institutions and the implementation of the new spirit—of designing reforms for the benefit of the entire society and not for privileged groups—is still an unachieved long process as exemplified by the tugging around the rules governing the decisions of the newly created independent *Supreme Judicial Council*.

[15] According to a study conducted in 2014 by the World Bank and the Tunisian National Youth Observatory, the trust in politics was quantified to less than 5% among the young in the rural regions and around 30% in the urban regions. The average scores of trust in police, justice, military and family were respectively around 50%, 60%, 80% and 100% (World Bank, 2014). In March 2017, the blogger Mhamed Mestiri tried to answer why many skilled young Tunisians are still leaving the country. He focused on the profile of four different individuals who tried to contribute to the development of their country but finished by leaving it. They cited the following common factors: the absence of equal economic opportunities and the unfairness in professional promotion (Mestiri, 2017).

[16] In commenting on the success of his government in undertaking the delicate reform of the social security system in his country, the prime minister of Turkey declared in 2013 that "*the people need to be able to trust those who govern them and not feel that their interests are being betrayed. Without that trust, we would not have been able to make the very difficult readjustments in our social security system*" (Erdogan, 2013).

general adhesion to the revival of the economy. He notes that citizens are just requesting equity and fairness before the law and the necessary sacrifices (Meddeb, 2016).

Porter (2015) argues that instability and unrest often result from the imbalance between economic growth and social progress. Indeed, failing in addressing basic human needs, in equipping citizens to improve their quality of life, in protecting the environment and in providing opportunities for citizens are signs of a fragile[17] and failing state. Thus, it becomes clear that there is an urgency to restore citizens' confidence in the Tunisian state institutions in order to avoid further fragility. To this end, the elite should develop and implement an inclusive growth strategy encompassing both economic and social progress dimensions.

### 3.3.4 *The Difficulty of Reforms During the Transition: A Personal Experience*

In January 2014, I joined *Tunisia Polytechnic School*[18] (TPS) in the position of Associate Professor of Economics after almost three years in the research institute of the *Islamic Development Bank Group* where I served as Senior Researcher Economist. TPS was established in 1991 to provide Tunisia with multidisciplinary engineers to lead teams, contribute to the modernization of the economy and occupy high administrative positions. It has been also assigned the national mission to contribute to the acquisition and development of technology. Despite many successful achievements, the institution has been suffering from governance problems and the inadequacy of the administrative framework it is obliged to operate in. Just after joining it, the management of TPS charged me with leading the *Governance and Quality Commission* mandated to undertake a diagnostic of the situation and to suggest recommendations to modernize the institution. In cooperation with other colleagues, we distributed questionnaires to multiple stakeholders, benchmarked with the international standards, orga-

[17] According to the definition of OECD/DAC (2007), states are fragile when there is a lack of political will and/or capacity to reduce poverty, to generate development and to guarantee the security and human rights of their populations.

[18] TPS is a public Engineering School founded in June 1991, and welcomed its first students in September 1994. The school is accessible only to the top 50 ranked students selected among more than 2000 students who pass a competitive national exam following two years of intensive university-level preparation in mathematics and physics after the Baccalaureate.

nized meetings and finally published a report entitled "Unlocking the potential of TPS: The required reform" in October 2014 on the occasion of the 20th anniversary of TPS.[19] Among the recommendations of the report was the adoption of a new legal status that guarantees the operational autonomy of the institution. The latter is required to enable sufficient flexibility in dealing with the administrative processes and improve its efficiency. In addition, the report suggested a new governance framework and made various recommendations related to the updating of the curriculum as well as the status of the faculty staff. At the time of its publication, the reform received the support of the *University of Carthage*. In February 2016, the reform gained the support of more than 60 eminent academicians and executives.[20] However, a conflict between the director of TPS and the presidency of the *University of Carthage* emerged in 2015 and undamaged the functioning of TPS. It resulted in impeding further advances in the legal reform, but fortunately the faculty staff had sufficient legitimacy to update the curriculum and obtain its official recognition.[21] From January 2014 to January 2017, the *Ministry of Higher Education and Scientific Research* was marked by the turnover of three ministers. This instability was an additional impediment to the implementation of the recommended reforms.[22] Indeed, the priority of the successive ministers was given to the reforming process of the entire national system of higher education. This broader reform is progressing very slowly after 2011, given the complexity of the tasks and the diversity of the involved stakeholders including the association of the elected presidents of the Tunisian public universities. As a consequence, the reform of TPS has not yet begun and many international cooperation opportunities have not yet been materialized.[23] The

[19] The report can be downloaded here: https://goo.gl/bNFBWo. See also the article "Révolution à l'École Polytechnique" by Tahar Abdessalem, Romain Bordier and Jonathan Nussbaumer for a presentation of the reform http://goo.gl/1UkvRS.

[20] See the article "69 universitaires, experts et dirigeants appellent à la réforme de l'Ecole Polytechnique de Tunisie", Leaders.com.tn, News 19 January 2016.

[21] The reform of the curriculum improved the chances of the TPS students to compete for internships and jobs at the international level in multiple domains (e.g. data science, financial engineering, supply chain management, IT, electronics and mechanics).

[22] Not only in TPS but also in other engineering schools, as the ministry itself published a report in October 2015—produced by an ad hoc independent committee of experts—joining several recommendations of the TPS's report published in October 2014.

[23] Including a comprehensive cooperation with an economics school ranked within the top 200–300 by the *Times* higher education world university rankings.

situation at TPS became unsupportable to the extent that obliged its director to resign in February 2017 and the Alumni of the School to intervene trying to resolve the structural administrative problems.

## References


Acemoglu, D. (2006) "A Simple model of inefficient institutions," Scandinavian Journal of Economics, Vol. 108, No. 4, 515–546.

Acemoglu, D. and J. A. Robinson (2012) "Why nations fail: The origins of power, prosperity and poverty," New York: Crown Business.

Clappison, A. (2011) "Building new democracies: Norms shape practice not policies," ERF 17th Annual Conference, https://erfblog.org/category/erf-17th-annual-conference/.

Erdogan, R. T. (2013) "The Turkish economy meets EU entry criteria," huffingtonpost.com.

IMF (2016) "Tunisia: Program note," August 2016, https://www.imf.org/external/np/country/notes/pdf/tunisia.pdf.

Meddeb, M. (2016) "Dans quelles conditions l'armée nationale peut-elle contribuer à réduire le chômage?" Leaders, 9 February 2016.

Mestiri, M. (2017) "Immersion au cœur de la fuite des cerveaux," Nawwat.org, 27 March 2017.

Nabi, M. S. (2011) "Moins d'ambiguïté, plus d'optimisme et de cohésion pour une reprise rapide de l'économie tunisienne," Leaders, 31 May 2011.

Nucifora, A., E. Churchill and B. Rijkers (2015) "Cronyism, corruption, and the Arab Spring: The case of Tunisia," Chapter 4 in 2015 Index of Economic Freedom: Promoting Economic Opportunity and Prosperity, The Heritage Foundation.

OECD/DAC (2007) "The principles for good international engagement in fragile states and situations," OECD, Paris.

Phelps, E. (2011) "For a successful Arab revolution," http://web.stanford.edu/~johntayl/PHELPS LeMonde On G8 Proposal 2011-5-20.pdf.

Porter, M. (2015) "Why social progress matters," Project Syndicate, 9 April 2015.

Stiglitz, J. E. (1998) "Towards a new paradigm for development: Strategies, policies, and processes," Prebisch Lecture at UNCTAD, Geneva, 19 October 1998.

Stiglitz, J. E. (2011) "The Tunisian catalyst," Project Syndicate, 4 February 2011.

UNDP (2010) "A Guide to UNDP democratic governance practice," http://www.undp.org.

World Bank (2014) "Tunisia: Breaking the barriers to youth inclusion," World Bank, Report No. 89233-TN.

## Other Sources

IMF (2017) https://www.imf.org/en/News/Articles/2017/06/12/pr17217-imf-executive-board-completes-first-review-under-eff-arrangement-with-tunisia.

CHAPTER 4

# Toward an Inclusive Development Strategy

## 4.1 Toward an Inclusive Development Approach

The debate on the economic growth versus economic development goes back to the early 1970s. The Tunisian economic path is another manifestation of the partial approach focusing solely on economic growth. Through the lens of the Washington consensus, Tunisia was among the best-performing countries in Africa and the Middle East and North Africa (MENA) region, and was considered a successful economy by the World Bank and the IMF.[1] This is not astonishing given that the country realized an average annual growth rate of 4.75% over the period 1990–2010 and ensured solid macroeconomic fundamentals. The problem is that little attention was given to the growth inclusiveness and the quality of the institutional environment in the Washington consensus.[2] Stiglitz (1998) notes that the problem with the development strategies based on the Washington consensus is their narrow focus on economics. He argues that development was seen by the "mainstream" economists as mainly a matter of how to improve the allocation of resources and increase capital stock.

[1] Despite their concern about the unemployment problem and the soundness of the banking system.

[2] The Washington consensus is criticized for its focus on privatization, trade liberalization, price stability and the controls of budget deficit and money supply much more than on the resilience of the financial system, the stability of output, the inclusiveness of growth and the quality of the institutional environment.



M. S. Nabi, *Making the Tunisian Resurgence*,
https://doi.org/10.1007/978-981-13-3771-0_4

He adds that the only divergence between the economists of the left and those of the right concerned the role that the government shall play in the economy and the extent to which the allocation of resources shall be improved (Stiglitz, 1998). Therefore, it is not surprising that the economic dynamic of a developing country like Tunisia was not inclusive and slowed progressively, resulting in a social economic divide and an intense duality at the regional and sectoral levels. Clearly, market distortions, rent-seeking behavior, corruption and crony capitalism have largely damaged the Tunisian economy. Therefore, these impediments to the "hypothetic" trickle-down mechanism constrained the emergence of an inclusive economic growth.

The current situation of Tunisia requires a development strategy embedding institutions, politics, economics and individuals in an interlinked framework. The task is difficult since the conception and implementation of such a strategy shall be done in a political transition period. The economics and politics being tightly interlinked, I need to back my recommendations with multidimensional frameworks that take into account this complexity. In the following sections I present the pillars of three multidimensional development approaches that I consider insightful for the Tunisian context. Then, I motivate the role of inclusive institutions in developing a successful development strategy. The need to reengineer a new social contract and reinvent leadership in the Tunisian context will also be examined.

## 4.2 A Multidimensional Approach for an Inclusive Transition

Kaplan and Freeman (2015) develop a multidimensional approach for building an inclusive regime during the transition from a fragile and fragmented state. In order for the transition to succeed it is necessary to tackle the bad practices that generated social conflicts and exclusion. These practices are deeply rooted in the economic, political, administrative, legal, security and sociocultural dimensions of the society (Kaplan and Freeman, 2015). Figure 4.1 summarizes the anatomy of an inclusive transition such as suggested by the authors. While noting the fact that groups who are advantaged from the initial situation will not favor an inclusive approach, Kaplan and Freeman (2015) recognize that achieving partial solutions is sometimes inevitable, especially in matters of how to divide power and resources equitably. The pace of achieving such solutions and conceiving

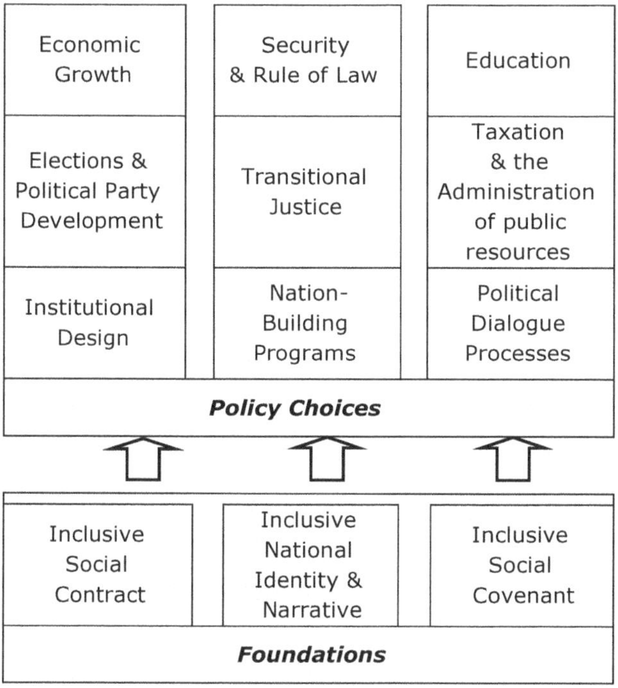


**Fig. 4.1** Anatomy of an inclusive transition

consensus about the necessary reforms is increased if successive political wins and positive economic dynamic are generated, improving the confidence in the transition process and its actors. Here, I deem interesting to recall again the analysis of Lant Pritchett when he argues that the economic reforms cannot succeed without the creation of a social movement among the dominant forces of the society (Clappison, 2011).

This task is mainly the responsibility of the political leaders who shall strengthen the belonging of various groups and key actors to a common national project. For that to happen, people shall be brought together around a common set of goals, norms, rules and larger vision that activate the positive dynamic of a constructive and peaceful collaboration (Kaplan and Freeman, 2015). Kaplan and Freeman (2015) bring also attention to a serious threat that undermines the success of the transition, which is the accentuation of corruption. In this regard, the legitimacy of the ruling elite in the eyes of the public is vulnerable to suspicion of corruption.

The authors also pinpoint an equally important ingredient for the success of the transition; it is the engineering of an inclusive change process. It should be inclusive even for those who used to benefit from the previous political regime. Avoiding losers saves the country from the resurgence of a new excluded group which might accentuate the negative forces that undermine the democratization process.

## 4.3 Lessons from Ibn Khaldun's Development Theory

### *4.3.1 The Multidimensional Framework of Ibn Khaldun*

The second multidimensional framework that I deem relevant to the Tunisian context remounts to Ibn Khaldun (1332–1406). In al-Muqaddimah[3] he develops a model explaining the rise and fall of a dynasty or civilization. Chapra (2008) notes that Ibn Khaldun did not explain development and decline through the lens of the economic variables alone. He rather analyzed how the interrelationships between social, moral, economic, political, historical and demographic factors lead to the rise and fall of societies. This multidisciplinary and dynamic approach enabled Ibn Khaldun to explain why some countries develop faster than others, what are the drivers of sustainable development and what are the ingredients of the true well-being.

Chapra (2008) represents the civilizational dynamic of Ibn Khaldun through a circular causation chain including bidirectional interaction of a set of socioeconomic and political factors: political authority (G), beliefs and rules of behavior (S), people (N), wealth or stock of resources (W), development (D) and justice (J) (Fig. 4.2). Although it might be triggered by a single factor, the development (D) of a country could not materialize and be sustainable if the causal relationships involving moral, social, political and demographic factors are not engaged in a virtuous interdependent dynamic. He argues that human well-being could not be attained merely through the rising of literacy and income. It also depends on the quality of

[3] Which means "introduction" and constitutes the first volume of a seven-volume book entitled *The Book of Lessons and Record of Cause and Effect in the History of Arabs, Persians and Berbers and their Powerful Contemporaries.*

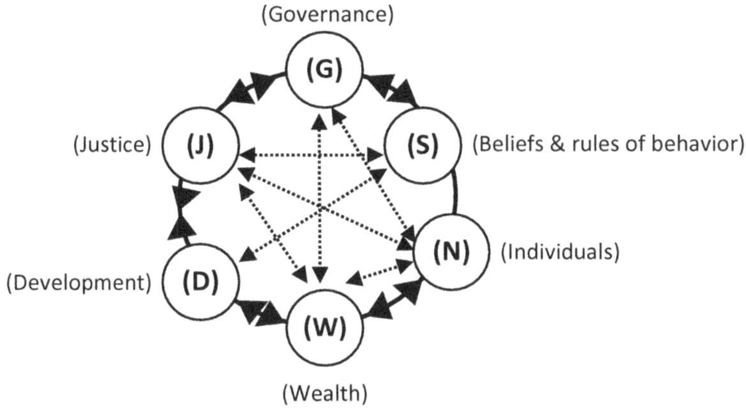


**Fig. 4.2** The causal relationships in Ibn Khaldun's development theory

education and the socioeconomic uplift. Another ingredient is the moral caliber which is the source of honesty, integrity and conscientiousness. These moral qualities which favor developments are generally ignored in the neoclassical economics (Chapra, 2008).

### *4.3.2 Role of Islam and Importance of Governance in Ibn Khaldun's Theory*

In the sixth century, Islam (S) was the triggering mechanism that activated the development dynamic of a Bedouin society and led to the moral and material uplift of its individuals (N).[4] Chapra (2008) notes that Islam changed the character of the society through three main channels: (1) providing development-friendly institutions (S); (2) creating a framework of good governance (G) by ensuring justice, dignity, equality and

[4] It is particularly important to note that women benefited from equal rights as men and were accorded property rights since that time. As a result, 41% of the charitable endowments (*awqaf*) in the Othman Aleppo were founded by women (Roded, 1994). The inheritance-sharing rules commonly reduced to a "2:1 ratio" in favor of men are a misleading interpretation which undermines the financial obligation under the shelves of the latter and ignores many cases where the inheritance ratio is equal or is in favor of women.

self-respect and (3) guaranteeing that the benefits of development are shared by all, particularly the poor and the downtrodden (J).[5]

Chapra (2008) argues that Muslim countries shall benefit from the moral values of Islam (socioeconomic justice, accountability of the political authority, rule of law) and its emphasis on education and dialogue, in order to achieve justice and undertake socioeconomic and political reforms (Chapra, 2008). Unfortunately, in the majority of Muslim countries, the deficient governance framework constitutes a major constraint to the triggering of a virtuous civilizational dynamic à la Ibn Khaldun. Chapra (2008) particularly criticizes the absence of political legitimacy, freedom of expression, honesty, efficient judiciary and the absence of accountability of the political elite. He concludes that Islam's principles are not sufficient because the current decline of Muslim countries is the result of combined internal factors (moral degeneration, loss of dynamism in Islam after the rise of dogmatism and rigidity, decline of intellectual and scientific activity, internal revolts and disunity) and external invasions and warfare (having weakened investment and economic growth).

After 2011, it was expected that Tunisia will begin a new civilizational cycle triggered by an improvement in the political system and governance framework (factor "G"). This would have progressively led to less corruption and better allocation of public resources for education, health, judiciary and building development-friendly institutions. Unfortunately, after the revolution, corruption expanded and the institutional reforms are slowly progressing. It will be inferred from the next sections that such new civilizational cycle will not likely emerge if Tunisia will not accelerate the building of inclusive economic and political institutions.

[5] Chapra (2008) also notes that the institutional ingredients for development emphasized by North (1990) and North and Thomas (1973) were available and contributed to the rise and supremacy of the Muslim civilization from the eighth to the middle of the twelfth century. He adds that the analysis of Ibn Khaldun reveals that the political illegitimacy triggered the reverse declining dynamic. It started with the hereditary succession initiated by the fifth Caliph (*Muawiyah*) who appointed his son *Yazid* to the Caliphate in 679. This event had progressively led to the deterioration of the political system and governance framework (deterioration of "G"). Authoritarian and arbitrary governments progressively emerged, resulting in shrinking the scope of accountability of the rulers and the political elite, as well as impeding the freedom of expression. Chapra (2008) notes that many religious scholars (*ulama*) were persecuted, which led to their progressive separation from the political sphere (deterioration of "S"). The vicious dynamic accelerated leading to gradual deterioration in the quality of life ("J" & "D") as a consequence of misuse of the state resources for the royal court's luxury, increase in taxes, disincentives to working, production and innovation.

## 4.4 Stiglitz's Paradigm for an Inclusive Development

Invited by the *Cercle of the Tunisian Economists* in June 2012 to animate a conference on "*Rethinking Macroeconomics: Policy Recommendations for Developing Countries*", Joseph Stiglitz emphasized the possibility for an economy to couple higher growth with greater economic efficiency, lower wealth inequality and more equality of opportunity. As chief economist of the World Bank, he has advocated since 1998 a dynamic approach of development. The "*transformation of society*"—as he qualified—requires the adoption of "*scientific*" ways of thinking in order to identify the constraints (based on available data) and conceive new relations, new methods of production and administration. This dynamic shall be triggered by individuals and societies through a participatory approach for setting forth the transformation vision (the society in 10 or 20 years, for example) and embracing the targets (quantitative goals) to be reached. He notes that the new development strategy shall not only raise GDP per capita, but also improve living standards in relation to health and literacy, reduce poverty and improve the quality of the environment. For these targets to be achieved the underlying policies shall be durable, which requires a real societal transformation (Stiglitz, 1998).

He does not ignore the role of institutions in development. Instead of being static, it shall evolve endogenously as part of the transformation process: traditional institutions might weaken and be replaced by new institutions enriched by new social capital and new capacities. At the opposite, the development strategies derived from the Washington consensus focused on privatization with insufficient attention to the building of the institutional infrastructure that is necessary for the market economy to function (Stiglitz, 1998). In this development paradigm, one can find again the multidimensional interrelationship that characterized the development theory of Ibn Khaldun. Indeed, Stiglitz's paradigm focuses on the interrelationships[6] between five components (levels) of the development strategy: the individual, the family, the community, the private sector and the state (the public sector) (Fig. 4.3). Hence, conceiving efficient mechanisms of coordination between the public agencies and ministries, the

[6] For example, education occupies the center of the "individuals'" development, but is also important for the "private sector" strategy and the women ("family") empowerment.

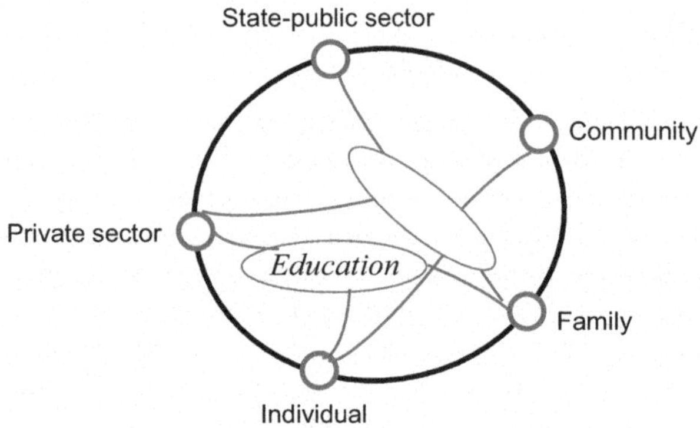


**Fig. 4.3** The interrelationships in Stiglitz's development paradigm

private sector and the civil society is crucial for the smooth implementation of the transformation strategy.

Stiglitz's paradigm emphasizes the role of "social/organizational capital" in shaping the pace of the change and the speed of transformation. It includes institutions and relations that mediate transactions and resolve disputes. The development approach framework suggested by Stiglitz is based on the abovementioned five levels (components) and the pillars presented in Table 4.1.

The acceptability of the transformation process requires the protection of the poor while moving to market outcomes. Pittman (2009) emphasizes the necessity of this component for the success of the economic reforms in developing countries. He notes that for the reforms to be both initially accepted and irreversible they should carefully address employment, access and income distribution (Pittman, 2009). Therefore, it is important to endow Tunisian development strategy with a pillar dedicated to its rural regions which are suffering from high levels of poverty and unemployment, weak infrastructure and low investment and so on.

In addition to the abovementioned pillars, the development strategy shall set priorities and sequencing. In particular, it is crucial to determine the ordering of the tasks to be undertaken. For example, privatization of state-owned firms should take place after establishing a competition and a regulatory framework. Similarly, the internal and external financial liberalization shall be subsequent to the establishment of a financial regulatory framework (Stiglitz, 1998).

**Table 4.1** The pillars of Stiglitz's development strategy

| *Pillars of the development strategy* | *What a development strategy shall outline?* |
|---|---|
| Social and organizational capital | • Develop social and organization relations and institutions which are essential for the pace and success of the development transformation. |
| Economic management | • Identify the most important distortions in the economy, and policies to address them while taking full account of their social costs and distributional impacts. |
| Resources | • Plans for developing physical capital and human capital, preserving natural resources.<br>• Plans for encouraging saving and investment and for filling the gap between the two.<br>• Plans for schools and for financing them.<br>• Plans for using and renewing natural resources. |
| Knowledge management | • Plans for reducing the knowledge gap by creating capacities to absorb, adapt, create and disseminate knowledge (through investments in human capital, technologies and research institutions). |
| Sector and subnational strategies | • Narrowing focus to a sector/industry.<br>• Setting integrated solutions region/city (an urban strategy)/rural areas. |

## 4.5 Building Inclusive Institutions

### *4.5.1 Why Inclusive Institutions Are Important for Development?*

There is a global awareness that the degree of inclusiveness of growth and its ability to improve the living standards depend on various structural and institutional economic policies beyond education and redistribution (Schwab, 2015). Galal and Selim (2012) argue that the underdevelopment of the Arab countries is rooted in the lack of inclusive economic and political institutions. According to Stiglitz (2014), the socioeconomic problems of developed economies are related to the functioning of the political system rather than to how markets should or do work. Instead of ensuring that markets are competitive, the political elite designed rules that generated markets' distortions, leading to the control of the economy by corporations and the rich (Stiglitz, 2014). Guerrero et al. (2009) argue that when a country's institutions are weak, the market functioning is inefficient and the policy design is distorted to serve the benefit of few powerful groups at the expense of the broader society and future generations (Guerrero et al., 2009).

The institutions that can be influenced by the powerful groups are diverse. They comprise the regulatory bodies, the judicial system, the legislature, the public agencies that administer rules and incentives, the political parties and the executive. Guerrero et al. (2009) argue that policy makers can be forced by the powerful to undertake suboptimal policies instead of the first-best ones. These policy distortions serve the powerful interests. In *Why Nations Fail*, Acemoglu and Robinson (2012) analyze the vicious circle of interaction between extractive political institutions and extractive economic institutions. They argue that extractive political institutions generate extractive economic institutions which benefit the few at the expense of the majority. In order to remain in power, the few defend the system through several channels like building their (private) armies and mercenaries, buying their judges and arranging their elections (Acemoglu and Robinson, 2012). Boughzala and Ben Romdhane (2015) analyze the factors underlying the Tunisian uprising and the prospects for consolidating the transition to democracy. They recall the analysis of Acemoglu and Robinson (2012) and recall that the development of inclusive economic institutions is the outcome of inclusive political institutions. They note that inclusive economic institutions and widely distributed prosperity cannot be sustainable in the long run if the political institutions are not inclusive. This finding is not surprising given that political institutions modulate how competition for power among the various actors of the society evolves. I have already noted that Kaplan and Freeman (2015) recognize this fact when they argue that a transition period is opportune for the reengineering of the political institutions. The resulting benefits would be more effectiveness and more equity with regard to the distribution of power and resources.

### *4.5.2 Reengineering the Political Institutions*

Reengineering political institutions is a long and difficult process that shall tackle many dimensions: the electoral system, the judicial system, the decentralization, the independence of public institutions like the central bank. It also requires a great sense of openness and inclusiveness from the side of the political leaders. In this regard, Kaplan and Freeman (2015) argue that advances in reshaping institutions to increase their independence and inclusiveness shall take into consideration the balance of power in the transition. Otherwise, the interests of the powerful groups that are threatened by too fast or deep reforms will oppose it by catalyzing extremism, elite domination, one-party rule, ethnic conflict, secessionism, corruption or gridlock (Kaplan and Freeman, 2015).

Aoki (2014) criticizes the example provided by Acemoglu and Robinson (2012) to illustrate the prerequisite of an inclusive political institution in order to achieve inclusive economic development. His critic is based on the historical evolutions of the Republic of Korea and the Democratic People's Republic of Korea. Aoki (2014) recalls that the inclusive political regime of the Republic of Korea emerged after it had already achieved a middle-income status and was not the catalyst of its economic development. This observation leads him to question if the polity necessarily precedes the economy. He notes that Acemoglu and Robinson (2013) recognize the possible mutual dependency of the political and economic institutions. More precisely, the political equilibrium could be dependent on the market failure and rest upon it.

Aoki (2014) shows that the development processes of China and Japan favor a theory of permanent interactions between the political and the economic institutions (Fig. 4.4). To illustrate this permanent interaction, he constructs a game model with three types of agents (the rulers, the peasants and other intermediate organizations) and illustrates how the two types of institutions are emerging, sustaining and changing interactively through the strategic behavior of agents. He concludes that multiple types of dynamic relationships linking the political and economic institutions can exist. It could be strategic complementarity, substitutability or rivalry relations that link the individual actors as well as the political and economic domains and determine their co-evolution.

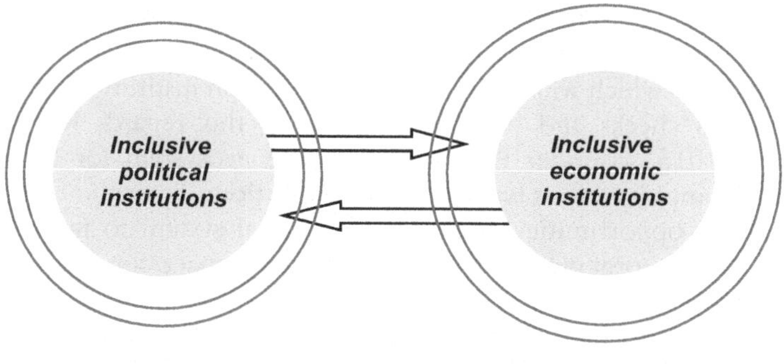


**Fig. 4.4** The relationship between economic and political institutions

## 4.6 Importance of Leadership

### *4.6.1 Leadership and Change*

Leadership generates a set of actions that create the change space and mobilize people, ideas, meaning and resources to achieve the change objectives. Meanwhile, the essence of leadership is to enhance the acceptance of change through the encouragement of change-oriented beliefs and commitment. It involves complex iterative steps and feedback loops (Andrews et al., 2010). Andrews et al. (2010) represent the change space as the intersection of three expanding spheres: the acceptance for the change, the accountability of the change and the necessary abilities to achieve the change. Their key message is that leadership actions should intend to expand the space change with the objective of institutionalizing the change process at the timely (context-dependent) stage.

### *4.6.2 Institutional Leadership*

I believe like many Tunisians that the leadership of Habib Bourguiba played an important role in founding the pillars of a modern state. However, for the current situation I believe that Tunisia needs an institutional leadership. Kaplan and Freeman (2015) note that beyond charisma, the effectiveness of leaders depends on their capacity to be pragmatic, to respond to changing needs and to build the durable institutions that exploit their vision. I am convinced that Tunisia cannot escape the current politico-economic trap without an institutional leadership. This is mainly due to the multidimensional aspects of the required change space. For each dimension (social cohesion, political system, economic system), Tunisians have no choice but to build an ecosystem for the crowd (people/civil society) to participate in the emergence of an inclusive change process which will result in building modern institutions governed by perpetual checks and balances process. In this regard, Kaplan and Freeman (2015) consider that a constructive ecosystem for leadership should encompass various types of social institutions, favor the emergence of education opportunities, modernize the legal system to facilitate the creation of new organizations and create ample space for dialogue and development.

I am convinced that Tunisia needs to facilitate the emergence of not only organizations which stimulate dialogue and contribute to more social cohesion and political and economic inclusiveness, but also those which develop creativity and entrepreneurship. As noted by Shiller (2014), people need to collaborate within organizations that facilitate synergy, creativity and which are led by people of integrity. Instead of being dominated by central leaders as is the case with corporatist institutions, the new type of economic institutions should be collectively governed through the fluid actions of modern crowds that promote concerted creative actions. Shiller (2014) defends the need of this new type of economic institutions to favor creativity in order to generate a continued economic growth. I believe that this suggestion is equally valid for the other dimensions of the space change. Without the emergence of such type of institutions, it will be difficult for Tunisia to succeed in converging to a full-scale democratization. I affirm this while recalling the framework developed by Acemoglu and Robinson (2000) ("*Inequality, Growth and Development: Democratization or Repression*") where the interests of the rich elite (initially controlling the political system) are to choose either a repression (dictatorship) regime or to initiate the transition to a full democracy. The reason behind this dualistic choice is that modest concessions in the form of low level of wealth/power redistribution to the other groups of the society is not sustainable and might lead to radicalization and further unrest.[7]

## References

Acemoglu, D. and J. A. Robinson (2000) "Inequality, Growth and Development: Democratization or repression?" European Economic Review, Vol. 44, 683–693.

Acemoglu, D. and J. A. Robinson (2012) "Why nations fail: The origins of power, prosperity and poverty," New York: Crown Business.

Acemoglu, D. and J. A. Robinson (2013) "Economics versus politics: Pitfalls of policy advice," Journal of Economic Perspectives, Vol. 27, No. 2, 173–192.

Andrews, M., J. McConnell and A. Wescott (2010) "Development as leadership-led change – A report for the global leadership initiative and the World Bank Institute (WBI)," Harvard Kennedy School, Faculty Research Working Paper Series, RWP10-009.

[7] The interaction between "sustaining democracy" and developing an "inclusive economic system" is not particular to developing countries like Tunisia. Reich (2015) emphasizes the need for an upsurge in the public in order to rescue the democracy and to take back the economy in the US, Europe and Japan. Noam Chomsky argues that financial institutions expanded enormously and a vicious cycle between finance and politics accelerated. This is because wealth was concentrated in the financial sector and politicians were facing the rising cost of campaigns (Polychroniou, 2016).

Aoki, M. (2014) "Economic and political transitions from Pre-modern to modern states in the Meiji restoration and Xinhai revolution: A Strategic approach," ADBI Working Paper Series No. 486.

Boughzala, M. and S. Ben Romdhane (2015) "Transition from autocracy to democracy in Tunisia: Factors underlying the Tunisian uprising and the prospects for consolidating the transition to democracy," American University of Beirut Institute of Financial Economics, Lecture and Working Paper Series No. 3.

Chapra, M. U. (2008) "Ibn Khaldun's theory of development: Does it help explain the low performance of the present-day Muslim world?" The Journal of Socioeconomics, Vol. 37, No. 2, 836–886.

Clappison, A. (2011) "Building new democracies: Norms shape practice not policies," ERF 17th Annual Conference, https://erfblog.org/category/erf-17th-annual-conference/.

Galal, A. and H. Selim (2012) "The elusive quest for Arab economic development," ERF Working Paper No. 722, November 2012.

Guerrero, I., L. Felipe, L. Calva and M. Walton (2009) "The Inequality Trap and Its Links to Low Growth in Mexico," in "No Growth Without Equity? Inequality, Interests, and Competition in Mexico," Edited by Santiago Levy and Michael Walton, A co-publication of The World Bank and Palgrave Macmillan.

Kaplan, S. and M. Freeman (2015) "Inclusive transitions framework," Institute for Integrated Transitions, July 2015.

North, D. C. (1990) "Institutions, Institutional change and Economic Performance," Cambridge: Cambridge University Press.

North, D. C. and R. P. Thomas (1973) "The Rise of the Western World: A New Economic History," Cambridge: Cambridge University Press.

Pittman, R. (2009) "Restructuring in times of crisis," Network Industries Quarterly, Vol. 11, No. 4.

Polychroniou, C. J. (2016) "Socialism for the rich, capitalism for the poor: An interview with Noam Chomsky," Truthout, 11 December 2016.

Reich, R. (2015) "What happened to the moral center of American capitalism?" robertreich.org/post/128336881225FRIDAY, 4 September 2015.

Roded, R. (1994) "Women in Islamic bibliographical collections from Ibn Sa'ad to who's who," Lynne Rienner Publishers, Boulder and London.

Schwab, K. (2015) "How can we achieve growth for the many, not just the few?" World Economic Forum.

Shiller, Robert J. (2014) "Creativity, corporatism, and crowds," Project Syndicate, 18 November 2014.

Stiglitz, J. E. (1998) "Towards a new paradigm for development: Strategies, policies, and processes," Prebisch Lecture at UNCTAD, Geneva, 19 October 1998.

Stiglitz, J. E. (2014) "Capitalism needs new rules to restore the growth and stability of postwar era," The Guardian, 2 September 2014, https://www.theguardian.com/business/2014/sep/02/joseph-stiglitz-capitalism-new-rules-growth-stability.

CHAPTER 5

# Unlocking Tunisia's Economic Potential

## 5.1 Modernizing the Tunisian State

Subsequently to the 2008 financial crisis, the collapse of the tax receipts coupled with the contraction of the economy exposed the governments in advanced countries to a difficult dilemma: raise taxes or crowd out spending on new priorities and new policies (Pisani-Ferry, 2015). The Tunisian government is facing a similar challenge: *how to finance public investment and economic reforms in a situation of low growth, continuous public deficit and increased indebtedness?*

Pisani-Ferry (2015) recommends the setting of priorities, the systematic evaluation of the efficiency of public money and enabling the rapid termination of ineffective policies once revealed via independent evaluation. He argues that structured spending reviews are necessary to bridge the gap between ends and means and favor informed democratic decision-making (Pisani-Ferry, 2015). Since 2011, the consecutive Tunisian governments have been aware that accelerating the economic development requires the modernization of the state. The current government is progressing in developing a new governance framework for the state-owned enterprises based on a contractual program with the state.[1] Beyond this new framework, it is important to benefit from new technologies by disrupting the public sector in order to improve the quality of the public

[1] This framework will set key performance indicators and tracking procedures to improve the performance of the state-owned enterprises and public agencies.



M. S. Nabi, *Making the Tunisian Resurgence*,
https://doi.org/10.1007/978-981-13-3771-0_5

services. Otherwise, the deterioration of the public services' quality might lead to the erosion of the government legitimacy and the willingness of citizens to pay taxes (Pisani-Ferry, 2015). The author recommends the following further actions:

1. Reengineering the government programs by investing in new technology, retraining employees and buying stakeholders' consent
2. Promoting the public sector innovation by setting up proper mechanisms to select and disseminate innovations initiated by public entities
3. Empowering the citizens by enabling them to access governmental data with efficiency and effectiveness

## 5.2 Developing a New Social Contract

### 5.2.1 *What Is a Social Contract?*

Remounting to Jean-Jacques Rousseau (1712–1778), we find that the social contract expresses the solution to the following fundamental problem: what is the form of consented people's grouping ("city", sovereign, state) that ensures their mutual preservation while guaranteeing their individual freedom? Indeed, the general will of all the people is stated through the creation of the laws of the state (Rousseau, 1962). The recent definitions of "social contract" are more reflective of the modern complexity. According to OECD/DAC (2008), it is the dynamic agreement between the state and the society on their mutual roles and responsibilities. This dynamic agreement emerges from the interaction between multiple factors: (1) the society's expectations about the state's role; (2) the state capacity to provide public services and to secure revenue from its population and territory and (3) the elite will to channel the state's resources and capacity to fulfill social expectations. In addition to these factors, the report emphasizes the degree of institutionalization of the bargain between state and society and the legitimacy of the involved actors, as determinants of the expectations and the facility of the bargaining process.[2]

[2] It is common to find justification of an active role of the state within a market economy in the textbooks of advanced microeconomics. For example, that role is well known in the

### 5.2.2 *What Was the Social Contract Before the Revolution?*

Before the revolution, social assistance programs and "solidarity" actions tailored by the government were conceived to reduce poverty and ensure a minimum level of social cohesion. They served as part of an implicit social contract between the state and the citizens. However, they were inefficient and had mainly served in maintaining the government political legitimacy (ILO, 2011). Gherib (2012) notes that, after independence, the relationship between the UGTT and the state evolved toward a "contentious cooperation". Meanwhile, he argues that the state played a central role in the emergence of the Tunisian capitalism. However, crony capitalism had gradually developed in the Tunisian economy to the extent that favoritism and proximity to the political sphere were determinants in Doing Business. Gherib (2012) also argues that during the economic liberalization phase (initiated in the late 1980s in the context of weak institutional environment), the state tried to control the labor union's members through its elite. This control contributed to an asymmetric social contract and a non-inclusive economic growth dynamic. As a consequence, the authoritarian legitimacy progressively vanished and the signs of social division multiplied. This in turn weakened the relationship between the state and the two social partners and germinated the Tunisian revolution.

### 5.2.3 *The Need of a Social Contract Ensuring Social Progress and Inclusiveness*

It is important that the social contract includes social progress (address human needs, build social capital and create opportunities for all citizens) as an integral part of an inclusive development strategy (Porter, 2015).[3]

theory of international trade of Hecksher-Ohlin Samuelson where workers and capitalists might be exposed to opposite effects of the trade openness. Economists know that market imperfections (accentuated in a developing country like Tunisia where inclusive institutions are still in an infant stage) prevent reaching a Pareto optimal equilibrium. They also know that the latter is not unique, and there is a need to balance the interests of the various categories of the society when conceiving economic policies that achieve social justice and favor social cohesion.

[3] Porter (2015) emphasizes the importance of monitoring social progress through social performance indicators (SPIs). He cites the example of Paraguay where SPIs are being used at the national, regional and municipal levels to measure social progress and achieve the targets of its inclusive national development plan for 2030.

Inclusiveness is a multidimensional concept which goes beyond poverty and income distribution to encompass equal access to opportunities to all citizens and sharing the benefits of economic growth among all the social classes. That was the spirit emphasized by the economist and philosopher Amartya Sen[4] who opened the field of economic analysis to the individual freedom and the ability to act to the field of capabilities. As noted by Chapra (2008), this spirit of human well-being is the center of Ibn Khaldun's civilizational dynamic that culminates when material advances are coupled with moral uplift, justice and social harmony. It is clear that social harmony is not possible in economies where economic opportunities are not accessible to all but restricted to the rich and politically connected people (Levine, 2011).

Systemizing the role of the state within a new social contract is very important for Tunisia to converge the frequent opponent positions of the social partners, namely, the UGTT and the UTICA. Such a role cannot take place without an inclusive social contract that determines fair rules of the economic system. As noted by Stiglitz (1998), laws, regulations and institutions determine the functioning of markets, economic growth and how prosperity is shared. When rules are rightly established, broad sharing of prosperity and strong economic performance are mutually reinforced (Stiglitz, 1998).

### 5.2.4 *Institutionalizing the Social Dialogue*

The UGTT and UTICA played an important role in the political transition. This role culminated in January 2014 when the political tension was extreme.[5] However, the political transition process and the difficult

[4] Amartya Sen, winner of the Nobel Prize in Economics in 1998, stresses the inequality of capabilities which is not limited to wealth and income inequality. The Nobel Prize laureate Amartya Sen opens the economic development to individual freedom and dignity, and the access to social opportunities to realize one's aspirations. In this regard, he is a pioneer in repositioning the economics discipline within the arena of the social sciences. On several occasions (e.g. a lecture given in 2013 at the research institute of the *Islamic Development Bank Group* and at the opening speech of the *Just Economy Conference* in Paris in 2014), I emphasized the important contribution of Sen to the field of economic development. The video is available here: www.goo.gl/ZiehAH.

[5] The two social partners with the Tunisian Human Rights League (LTDH) and the Tunisian Order of Lawyers formed the Quartet to conceive a solution to the political confidence crisis that exposed the country to the risk of a civil war.

economic situation made the Tunisian social dialogue between these two social partners difficult and time-consuming. Robalino et al. (2015) observe that the social contract signed in January 2013[6] between the Tunisian government, the unions and the employers' organization is a first good step toward building a national social dialogue. The authors note the good quality of the Social Pact which outlines the broad approach as well as the perimeter of the reforms. They also stress the importance of the suggested flexi-security comprehensive approach to reform the labor market rules and institutions, targeting a better protection of workers while giving firms the necessary flexibility to remain competitive (Robalino et al., 2015). It is unfortunate that, since 2013, there is no clear advancement in developing a new social contract ensuring social progress and inclusiveness. The inception of a new social contract shall help the government in going forward in setting a broader and integrated development strategy.

It is becoming clearer that there is a need for institutionalizing the social dialogue with credible and permanent mechanisms and instruments. This was one of the recommendations made by the Emeritus Professor Mongi Boughzala during the Forum of the future[7] where he suggested to mandate the *Instance Nationale du Dialogue Social* (proposed since 2013) of the social intermediation role. In November 2015, the wage negotiations between the two social partners (UTICA and UGTT) were interrupted due to the impossibility to reach an agreement. I myself called in Nabi (2015) for institutionalizing the social dialogue within the mandate of a Tunisian Development Institute.[8] The institutionalization of the social dialogue is likely to minimize the vulnerability of the negotiations to the political instability. As noted by Stiglitz (1998), the limited ability of some countries to resolve conflicts is one of the obstacles to successful development. ILO (2011) cites the successful example of the social dialogue in the Republic of Korea. It was inexistent during the military regime and

[6] Following a ten-month dialogue process supported by the International Labour Organization (ILO).

[7] The Forum was organized by the Tunisian Economists Association (ASECTU) in February 2016.

[8] In Nabi (2015), I also suggest to index the wage increase on the sectoral productivity instead of fixing a unified rate for all sectors. Such a flexible mechanism would have avoided the conflict that opposed the Textile National Federation (FENATEX) with UTICA. The main reason of that conflict was the fact that the wage increase of 6% in 2017 had not taken into consideration the difficult situation of the Tunisian textile sector.

emerged in 1993 with the transition to a democratic regime. In 1998, after the financial crisis, the Korean government created the *Korea Tripartite Commission* (KTP) in order to involve the social partners in the economic restructuring progress and updating of the labor law. This commission played an important role in building a national consensus and facilitating the economic recovery.

## 5.3 Toward an Open, Fair and More Productive Economy

Unlocking the potential of the Tunisian economy requires a broad strategy with an active role of the state and the civil society. Such a strategy shall lead to a more open and fair economy. Alkebsi and Malouche (2015) emphasize the importance of freeing the economy from the dominance of the government patronage and the regime-connected crony capitalism. As noted earlier, this will not be an easy task as the political system might be a captive of private interests. Without a deep reform of the system of law and regulations, the Tunisian economy will likely continue to be trapped in the middle-income range and could not benefit from its potentialities. It is important for the Tunisian economy to improve the productive efficiency of the public and private sectors. The new laws and regulations aiming to improve the business environment are not sufficient.

For the private sector, other types of incentives (tax, financial, PPP) shall be conceived in order for the private companies to develop and gradually implement their digital transformation. The creation of a national digital transformation agency was one of the recommendations of the IACE (2016) study. The suggested agency is intended to favor the digital transformation. For the public sector, the laws and regulations shall be completed by modern management and governance approaches of the administration, the state-owned enterprises and the public institutions (such as universities, research centers, etc.) in order to improve the quality of their services, make them attractive for high potentials and unleash their creativity and innovation potential. Initiatives by the civil servants and synergies within the different components of the public sector shall be encouraged. Employees shall be professionally promoted according to their performance in achieving predetermined key performance indicators. Such a deep reform would improve the total factor productivity through increased productive efficiency in a first stage and more innovation and technological progress in a second stage.

## 5.4 Immunizing the Tunisian Economy Against the Political Instability

During recurrent social protests, Tunisian citizens showed their maturity asking for credible development plans for their regions and not necessarily short-term programs. Unfortunately, as the years pass and governments change with slow achievements, the trust in the state's ability to fulfill its promises is declining and the credibility of the political elite is diminishing. The political transition that many thought ended by the completion of the new constitution in 2014 is likely to be revived. First, some emerging political parties revived the ideological debate on the occasion of the municipal elections (initially planned in 2017 but now expected for May 2018). Second, the presidential initiative about the economic reconciliation launched in parallel to the transitional justice process is dividing the society. In Nabi (2011), I emphasize the interrelationship between a quick economic recovery and the success of the political transition. It is well known that the behavior of the economic agents is related to their expectations about the new rules governing the triangle: economy, politics and civil society. After 2011, the private sector was in its majority stuck to the "wait-and-see" behavior concerning the political stability and improved business environment. The political ambiguity impacted the economic activity and reduced the private investment as well as the national saving. This behavior accentuated the negative economic shocks (social unrest and strikes, recession in Europe, war in Libya, terrorist attacks, etc.) and triggered the switch to a bad economic equilibrium (low economic growth, high public deficit, high current account deficit, depreciation of the dinar, higher indebtedness, spread of corruption and informality) driven by negative self-fulfilling expectations.

In Nabi (2011), I also highlight the importance of reducing the ambiguity about the country's future economic choices and of restoring the Tunisian's confidence. Unfortunately, the political instability that characterized the political transition process was very damaging. In 2017, the country had its ninth government since 14 January 2011. The political parties are not yet well structured and weakly anchored in the society. The confidence of the people in the political elite is shrinking mainly among the youth. In order to limit the interference between the political sphere and the economics management affairs, I called in Nabi (2016a) for the creation of a Tunisian Development Institute (TDI).

## 5.5 Creating a Tunisian Development Institute

As previously analyzed, there are many institutional bottlenecks that are impeding the progress of the economic reforms. *How can Tunisia alleviate these institutional bottlenecks?*

The quality of management of a nation's affairs depends on the efficiency of the mechanisms, processes, relationships and institutions that aggregate the interests of the citizens and groups, concretize their rights and obligations and mediate their differences (UNDP, 2015). In Nabi (2016a), I suggested the creation of *Tunisia Development Institute (TDI)*,[9] an independent public agency mandated by the parliament to conceive, coordinate and monitor the economic development strategy of Tunisia. Such an institution would be able to build a national consensus on a developing strategy based on a forward-looking vision for an inclusive growth. As noted by Spence (2016), building a consensus is a critical first step. This new institution shall be the place where ideally "first-best" and more realistically "second-best" economic policies could be rapidly and consensually conceived, and where the implementation and evaluation processes activated. TDI shall be inclusive and open to the multiple actors of the Tunisian economy (public agencies and private sector) as well as to the civil society and the political parties. Indeed, it is important that such a new institution benefits from the trust of the multiple actors in order for the various and opponent positions to be mediated. It shall enable the economic transformation of Tunisia by ensuring a long-term commitment of the society to a development strategy whatever the ruling political party. Endowed with high-level recognized expertise in economic development policies, it would play the role of leader through catalyzing the economic debate, prioritizing the studies and dispatching them among the multiple research centers and public administration/institutes

[9] I shared this idea with my colleague Professor Tahar Abdessalem on several occasions when debating about the economic reforms and the difficulty to achieve consensus during the political transition. The first time I thought about the TDI was at the occasion of an international symposium where I met K.C., a Senior Economist from *Korea Development Institute* (KDI). I remember that he informed me about the important role played by the KDI in South Korea's development path and how the government capitalized on the expertise of the country's best economists.

that are active in the economic advisory.[10] The idea is to immunize the debate about the economic policies, in terms of conception and evaluation, from the political interference. This debate is taking place since the revolution through fragmented channels mainly via the media. In 2014, the technocratic government launched a tentative of an "*economic dialogue*" with the objective of building a consensus among the political parties and the social partners on the main strategic economic orientations of the country. I expressed my skepticism about the success of that dialogue when commenting on a concept note draft that a colleague sent me.[11] Currently,[12] it is expected that the Assembly will revive the *Social and Economic Council*. Although it is expected that this institution will help in conducting the national dialogue among the multiple actors of the economy, its consultancy role prevents it from playing the role I assign to the TDI. The *Commission for Sustainable Development and the Rights of Future* Generations is another consultancy instance that was embedded in the new constitution. It would play a complementary role to the *Social and Economic Council*, since it shall be consulted on draft laws related to the economic, social and environmental issues, as well as to the development plans.

[10] That role was to a certain extent played from 1959 to the date of suspension of the 1959 constitution in 2011 by the *Social and Economic Council*: a constitutional organization having an advisory role to the prime minister. In 2012, the *Council of Economic Analysis* (CEA) was created as a consultancy structure to the president of the government. However, by constitution the CEA is linked to the executive and cannot play the role that I assign to the TDI.

[11] I noted: "In my opinion, since the current phase is a transitional one, the best expected outcome from the national dialogue would be the creation of a permanent institution … a sort of a national think tank—let's call it *Tunisia Development Institute* (TDI)—that can attract the best economists and establish development strategies with different political orientations. This will at least canalize the interactions of the competing parties, guarantying the sustainability of the efforts, avoiding the negative influence of the political sphere on the economic sphere. … Therefore, I suggest the Creation of a 'Tunisian Development Institute (TDI)' which absorbs all the existing Institutes and Commissions/Councils which currently operate under the Presidency of the Republic, the multiple Ministries, etc. … The TDI shall be politically neutral and independent and try to conceive many reforms options taking in account the different political orientations. This is in my opinion a more efficient way to synergize efforts and to guarantee long-term economic consistency. … We can learn from the role played by the Korean Development Institute (under an authoritarian regime) and design our TDI in a manner that takes in account the different political regime that we are setting."

[12] October 2017.

## 5.6 Daring a Pluralistic Approach of Economic Development

The failure of the capitalistic economic system in generating inclusive growth motivated many researchers to rethink capitalism. There are suggestions that advocate the inclusion of ethical dimensions and defend a more active social role of the state within the free market economy. Some other thinkers are exploring new mechanisms and institutional changes to bring inclusiveness, social justice and sustainability to the economic system.[13] Again, let me invite Coeuré (2014) who notes the importance of developing several paradigms and approaches in parallel. Criticizing the conventional economic thinking and its role in the recent economic crisis, he advocates a pluralistic approach which is likely to endow the policy institutions with alternative conceptual tools if the standard ones are not efficient. It is important for the policy-making institutions in Tunisia to be inclusive and unorthodox in some way. This shall be translated into a political commitment to a mix of development approaches: a market economy which is also open to the development of cooperatives, microfinance and other solidarity actions. The government would find in the civil society an excellent ally in developing the drivers of the social economy.[14] Beyond that, it shall not be taboo to reengineer specific economic policies for the current period; a targeted monetary policy, for example (that will

[13] For example, the social market economy, which was initially developed in West Germany by the Christian Democratic Union in 1949, combines free market capitalism alongside public social policies (Mau, 2003). Another example comes from the Islamic economists who emphasize on interest-free and participatory banking, as well as the importance of cooperation and coordination in the economy through dedicated social institutions and mechanisms. Umar Chapra considers that among the goals of the moral philosophy of Islam are the socio-economic justice and equitable distribution of income and wealth (Chapra, 1983). Zubair Hassan argues that the pursuit of self-interest is not antagonistic with caring of the interest of others and avoiding hurting them. In order to promote the interest of each other, mutual respect and cooperation shall replace rivalry and conflict (Hassan, 2011). John Fullerton from the Capital Institute is suggesting an alternative approach: the regenerative economics based on a "holistic" approach taking into account the dynamic relationships between social, economic and ecological health (Fullerton, 2015). John Fullerton qualifies "holism" as a paradigm shift which encompasses the perspectives of both capitalism and socialism.

[14] In July 2017, a workshop was organized under the patronage of the president of the government to launch a study (financed by the UNDP and the Swiss Development Agency) to make the social and solidarity economy (estimated currently to be 1% of GDP) one of the drivers of the Tunisian economy.

be detailed in the next chapter). Enabling the emergence of new financial intermediaries and benefiting from the global digital finance disruption to improve financial access shall be encouraged.[15]

Unfortunately, the economic policy-making tends to stick to the "business as usual" instinct. This is the result of inadequate incentives and rigid bureaucracy rather than the absence of creative and imaginative potentialities within the public administration. Moving toward a creative and efficient state shall unleash the creative potential of the civil servants and enable the creation of synergies with academicians and the private sector. In November 2016, during the discussions about the state budget of 2017 and the constraint it was exposed to (related to the ceiling of 14% on the public wage bill relatively to GDP), I suggested in Nabi (2016b) a payment mechanism based on the emission of sovereign zero-coupon bonds. I discussed it with a senior economic adviser who liked the idea. After a while, he suggested an adjustment to make it a gracious distribution without the need to issue bonds. I understood that my initial proposal was difficult to implement in the short run. The adopted solution had only considered the use of tax exoneration as a tool for materializing the wage increase for the civil servants. The component related to the use of the zero-coupon bonds was not considered. This was unfortunate, since it would have enabled the use of targeted monetary policy to alleviate the burden on the public wage bill in the state budget of 2019.

## 5.7 Modernizing the Judicial and the Property Rights Systems

### *5.7.1 Modernizing the Judicial System and Improving the Enforceability of Contracts*

Almost one year before the revolution of 17 December 2010–14 January 2011, I have contributed to the literature on persistent inequality by publishing Nabi (2009), a paper motivated by the "inferred" stylized facts that characterized the business environment in Tunisia (inefficient judicial system and crony capitalism). In Nabi (2009), I extend a modified version of Aghion and Bolton's (1997) model by including costly contract enforcement (judicial inefficiency) and relaxing the hypothesis of fixed-size investment opportunities. The rationale behind these two extensions relative to the basic model is the following: to enable wealthy entrepreneurs to

[15] It is a paradox that, given the absence of a specific regulation, some young Tunisian entrepreneurs are creating their Fintech start-up in France to serve SMEs in Tunisia.

enlarge their investment projects through bank loans as it is often the case in situations where less wealthy entrepreneurs lack the required collaterals. The World Bank (2014a) report confirms the relevance of these two extensions. It reveals that firms owned by the regime's clan were significantly larger than their competitors. In addition, they realized much higher levels of output, profits and growth and were financed by the Tunisian banks up to 5% of the total bank financing. Further, about 30% of the loans were granted with laxist conditions and no guarantees of repayment, contrarily to the non-connected firms that faced substantial difficulties in accessing credit from banks (World Bank, 2014a).

The costly enforcement of financial contracts and the unrestricted investment opportunity enabled me to obtain different results in comparison to Aghion and Bolton (1997). The latter show that income inequality widens in the beginning of the capital accumulation process but decreases at a later stage. In contrast, Nabi (2009) shows that inequality increases in the first stage but remains constant or increases in the second stage (depending on the deposit interest rate ceiling). Nabi and Rajhi (2013) analyze the effect of costly enforcement of the financial contracts on the dynamic of capital accumulation in an endogenous growth model. We show that higher cost of enforcement decelerates the economic dynamic through the credit-rationing channel, which in turn deprives the economy from reaching its growth potential. The importance of the judicial system efficiency was also analyzed in Nabi and Suliman (2009). We show in that paper that an improvement in the enforcement of the credit contracts intensifies the bidirectional causality relationship between banking development and economic growth mainly due to the reduction of the non-performing loans and to better quality of the institutional environment.

### 5.7.2 *Developing the Property Rights System*

Hernando de Soto tried to answer why capitalism succeeded in generating the economic development of the Western countries and failed elsewhere. By referring, among others, to Adam Smith's view about the role of capital in the production cycle as described in the *Wealth of Nations*, de Soto defines capital as an economic potential which requires to be mobilized in a form that can contribute to the creation of wealth. This mobilization is a complex process having at its core a formal property system. The formal property system unlocks the economic potential of the assets so that they can be used to produce, secure or guarantee values.[16] According to De Soto (2000) the main problem of developing countries is not the lack of entrepreneurship but rather the absence of such a formal property rights system. In order for them to benefit from the accumulated trillions of dollars of real estate, he recommends enabling the process of preserving the assets information in a recording and embodying it in titles (De Soto, 2000).

In 2012, the UTICA and the Institute of Liberty and Democracy (ILD) headed by Hernando de Soto conducted a study on the Tunisian Economy (De Soto, 2013a). In a commentary written in the *Wall Street Journal* in February 2013, De Soto presented the main findings of this study. He notes that 85% of the Tunisian enterprises are extralegal with an estimated value of 115 billion USD (among which 93 billion USD as extralegal assets). This value equals 11 times the total stock-market capitalization in 2010 and four times the amount of FDI since 1976 (De Soto, 2013b). The main message of de Soto in that commentary was about the necessity to understand the main cause of the revolution in Tunisia and the continuous instability in the MENA region in general. He noted that in the case of Tunisia, Bouazizi's ability to run his business depended on the goodwill of the local authorities rather than on an enforceable right. Even if the value of his confiscated asset was estimated to be just 225 USD, he was exposed to greater damage, which is the inability to recover from that ad hoc bankruptcy given the impossibility of resorting to a legal property right (De Soto, 2013b).

## 5.8 Disrupting the Financial System to Improve Financial Inclusiveness

The interest in the analysis of the relationship between finance and economic growth is not new. Since the fourteenth century, Abderrahmane Ibn Khaldun (1332–1406) identified in his Muqaddimah (1377) the following virtuous circle: higher wealth > more saving > greater investment > more development > higher wealth. In order to enable this

[16] According to de Soto the formal property systems of the West produce the following six effects that allow the generation of capital by the citizens: (1) fixing the economic potential of assets, (2) integrating dispersed information into one system, (3) making people accountable, (4) making assets fungible, (5) networking people and (6) protecting transactions.

virtuous circle, Ibn Khaldun emphasized the role of the state in setting the right conditions: low rate of taxation, security of life and property, healthy physical environment, and (impressively) division of labor and specialization.[17] Bagehot (1873) explained the higher productivity of capital in the UK relative to other countries by the ability of its better-developed (in terms of organization and size) financial market to screen and finance the more productive projects. More recently, Hicks (1969) affirmed that the industrial revolution was the outcome of the financial systems' expansion, which enabled the utilization of the inventions and technological progress. In general, economists assign five main functions to the financial system in economic development: (1) facilitating the exchange of goods and services, (2) mobilizing saving, (3) facilitating the allocation of resources, (4) facilitating diversification, managing and hedging risks and (5) monitoring borrowers (Levine, 1997). In practice, the efficient accomplishment of these functions varies among countries. In general, it is restrained by market imperfections (in the form of information asymmetry, market incompleteness, costly enforcement of contracts) as well as weak institutional environment (underdeveloped legal framework, inefficient judicial system, corruption, informality). For many economists (e.g. Stiglitz, 1998; Boyd and Smith, 1996) those imperfections constitute one of the causes of the non-convergence of the countries in terms of revenue and economic growth.

The emergence of new digital channels of financial services is positively disrupting the financial system at least in terms of improving the access to finance. Traditionally underserved segments are increasingly benefiting from these new channels not only for payment services but also for insurance and credit products. CGAP (2015) argues that these innovative financial channels could benefit the financial lives of the poor by driving down transaction costs, expanding customer choice, increasing customer engagement and helping financial service providers better understand the risk profile of potential customers. The same study expects that the current growth of the Smartphone penetration and the maturing of the mobile

[17] Oláh (2017) recognizes that Ibn Khaldun identified the division of labor as the basis for any civilized society and the source of surplus value on the factory, social and international levels. I have had the pleasure to recall the contribution of Ibn Khaldun in a presentation I gave during the *Global Sustainable Finance Conference 2013*, Karlsruhe/Germany, 4–5 July 2013.

money infrastructure will favor the access to finance of the poor in developing economies in the near term. For that to happen, it recommends increased commitment from the stakeholders, establishing new partnership models, increasing the understanding of the customers, improving the regulatory environment to support money platforms and new technologies (CGAP, 2015).

The World Bank (2014b)'s report for the G20 recognizes the opportunities offered by the digital payments, noting that it can increase financial inclusion through the provision of speed, security, transparency and cost efficiency of the financial transactions (World Bank, 2014). Meanwhile, it recommends that governments encourage regulators to enable digital financial services through: (1) easy entrance for the providers of new vectors of financial services and innovative business models, (2) ensuring the respect of consumer protection and risk-based prudential norms and (3) addressing the issues of anti-money laundering and the financing of terrorism. In this regard, it recommends inspiring from the guidelines prepared by the Financial Action Task Force (FATF)[18] and the successful mobile payment regulations in Brazil where nonbanks are allowed to offer payments and savings and to access the central bank's clearing and settlement system. It also acknowledges the Mexican approach in enabling the private sector to participate in the distribution of government payments and the development of new product design. The report addresses a list of additional recommendations to the governments:

1. Digitize payments and receipts, including social transfers.
2. Convene public and private sectors to create a basic payment infrastructure to enable competing product development.
3. Create an environment that fosters private sector innovation.
4. Guide digital financial service providers to educate consumers and small businesses about their options to increase confidence, competence and adoption.
5. Recognize that remittance providers offer a digital entry point to formal financial services for senders and receivers.
6. Look to multilateral development banks and comparable agencies as sources of comparative expertise in digital finance.

[18] http://www.fatf-gafi.org.

## References


Aghion, P. and P. Bolton (1997) "A Theory of trickle-down growth and development," Review of Economic Studies, Vol. 59, 151–172.

Alkebsi, A. and M. Malouche (2015) "It's time for Tunisians to take the next big step," Foreign Policy, 11 April 2015, http://foreignpolicy.com/2015/04/11/tunisians-next-big-step-arab-spring/.

Bagehot, W. (1873) "Lombard Street: A description of the money market," Homewood, IL: Richard D. Irwin, 1962 Edition. Boyd et Smith, 1997.

Boyd, J. H. and B. D. Smith (1996) "The co-evolution of the real and financial sectors in the growth process," World Bank Economic Review, Vol. 10, No. 371–396.

CGAP (2015) "Global landscape of innovations in digital finance," https://fr.slideshare.net/CGAP/the-global-landscape-of-digital-finance-innovations.

Chapra, M. U. (1983) "Monetary policy in an Islamic economy," in "Money and Banking in Islam," Edited by Ziauddin Ahmed, et al., International Centre for Research in Islamic Economics, Jeddah, KSA, 1983.

Chapra, M. U. (2008) "Ibn Khaldun's theory of development: Does it help explain the low performance of the present-day Muslim world?" The Journal of Socioeconomics, Vol. 37, No. 2, 836–886.

Coeuré, B. (2014) "Rethinking economics after the crisis," https://www.ecb.europa.eu/press/key/date/2014/html/sp140624.en.html.

De Soto, H. (2000) "The mystery of capital: Why capitalism triumphs in the West and fails everywhere else," Basic Books, New York.

De Soto, H. (2013a) "L'économie informelle. Comment y remédier. Une opportunité pour la Tunisie," Tunis, Cérès Editions.

De Soto, H. (2013b) "The Secret to reviving the Arab Spring's promise: Property rights," The Wall Street Journal, 26 February 2013.

Fullerton, J. (2015) "Regenerative capitalism: How universal principles and patterns will shape our new economy," Capital Institute.

Gherib, B. (2012) "The political economy of the Tunisian revolution: Social groups versus crony capitalism," Revue Tiers Monde, No. 212, 2012/4.

Hassan, Z. (2011) "Scarcity, self-interest and maximization from Islamic angle," MPRA Paper 29414, University Library of Munich, Germany.

Hicks, J. (1969) "A theory of economic history," Oxford: Clarendon Press.

IACE (2016) "La Tunisie en Transformation: L'impératif digital," www.iace.tn.

Ibn Khaldun, A. (1377) "The Muqaddimah" translated by Franz Rosentha, http://asadullahali.files.wordpress.com/2012/10/ibn_khaldun-al_muqaddimah.pdf.

ILO (2011) "Tunisia: A new social contract for fair and equitable growth," Studies on Growth with Equity, ILO.

Levine, R. (1997) "Financial development and economic growth: Views and agenda," Journal of Economic Literature, Vol. XXXV, 688–726.

Levine, R. (2011) "Finance, regulation and inclusive growth," paper presented at the OECD and World Bank Conference on "Challenges and policies for inclusive growth," Paris, 24–25 March.

Mau, S. (2003) Moral Economy of Welfare States. Routledge, 74, ISBN: 978-1-134-37055-9.

Nabi, M. S. (2009) "Financial imperfections, inequality and capital accumulation," Economics Bulletin, Vol. 29, No. 3, 2400–2415.

Nabi, M. S. (2011) "Moins d'ambiguïté, plus d'optimisme et de cohésion pour une reprise rapide de l'économie tunisienne," Leaders, 31 May 2011.

Nabi, M. S. (2015) "Une piste pour débloquer les négociations sociales et une proposition d'un "Tunisian Development Institute,"" Espace Manager, 16 November 2015.

Nabi, M. S. (2016a) "L'exigence d'un leadership institutionnel pour la réussite de la transition économique," Leaders, 22 February 2016.

Nabi, M. S. (2016b) "La titrisation au secours du budget de l'Etat tunisien? Quelques propositions!" 3 November 2016, https://www.espacemanager.com/la-titrisation-au-secours-du-budget-de-letat-tunisien-quelques-propositions.html.

Nabi, M. S. and T. Rajhi (2013) "Banking emergence, contract enforcement and endogenous growth," International Review of Economics, Vol. 60, No. 1, 83–100.

Nabi, M. S. and O. Suliman (2009) "Institutions, banking development, and economic growth," The Developing Economies, Vol. 47, No. 4.

OECD/DAC (2008) "Concepts and dilemmas of state building in fragile situations: From fragility to resilience," Discussion Paper, OECD, Paris.

Oláh, D. (2017) "The amazing Arab scholar who beat Adam Smith by half a millennium," http://evonomics.com/amazing-north-african-scholar-beat-adam-smith-half-millennium/.

Pisani-Ferry, J. (2015) "Reengineering government," Project Syndicate, 30 April 2015.

Porter, M. (2015) "Why social progress matters," Project Syndicate, 9 April 2015.

Robalino, D., A. Kuddo, and D. F. Angel-Urdinola (2015) "Policy recommendations" Chapter 4 in "Labor Policy to Promote Good Jobs in Tunisia: Revisiting Labor Regulation, Social Security, and Active Labor Market Programs," Edited by Diego F. Angel-Urdinola. Antonio Nucifora, and David Robalino, World Bank Group.

Rousseau, J.-J. (1962) "Du contrat social, ou principes du droit politique" in Collection complète des oeuvres, Genève, 1780–1789, Vol. 1, in-4° édition en ligne www.rousseauonline.ch version du 7 octobre 2012, http://www.rousseauonline.ch/Text/du-contrat-social-ou-principes-du-droit-politique.php.

Spence, M. (2016) "Economic decline is leading to political instability. What's the solution?," World Economic Forum and Project Syndicate, 24 March 2016.

Stiglitz, J. E. (1998) "Towards a new paradigm for development: Strategies, policies, and processes," Prebisch Lecture at UNCTAD, Geneva, 19 October 1998.

UNDP (2015) "UNDP and governance: Experiences and lessons learned," UNDP.

World Bank (2014a) "The unfinished revolution: Bringing opportunity. Good jobs and greater wealth to all Tunisians," Development Policy Review, May 2014, Report No. 86179-TN.

World Bank (2014b) "The opportunities of digitizing payments," A report by L. Klapper and D. Singer, World Bank Development Research Group of the World Bank, 28 August 2014.

World Bank, the Better Than Cash Alliance, and the Bill & Melinda Gates Foundation (2014) "The opportunities of digitizing payments," http://www.gpfi.org/publications/opportunities-digitizing-payments.

CHAPTER 6

# Daring New Financial Channels for Development and Social Inclusion

## 6.1 Securitization as a Channel of Mobilizing Funds for the State Budget

Securitization is an innovative way to mobilize funds which is not activated in Tunisia. Ketkar and Ratha (2009a) provide a clear description of a typical structure of securitization. They note that it involves the borrowing entity (originator) selling its future receivables to a special purpose vehicle (SPV). Then the SPV issues the debt instrument to the investors. The originator's debtors (obligors) are directed to pay directly a collection account managed by a trustee. The collected receivables are transferred to the SPV and are used to make principal and interest payments to the investors.

### *6.1.1 Issuing Zero-Coupon Bonds to Finance Wage Bills*

The end of the year 2016 was characterized by rich discussions of the draft of the Tunisian state budget of 2017. The government was exposed to many constraints among which was its engagement with the labor unions to increase the wage bill in the public sector for an amount of 1030 million TND (approximately 7.5% of the total wage bill). That period was characterized by intense tension between the government and the labor unions, fueled by official declarations about the impossibility to fulfill that commitment. Among the official justifications, the slow economic growth resulting in weak public receipts and the already extremely high level of



M. S. Nabi, *Making the Tunisian Resurgence*,
https://doi.org/10.1007/978-981-13-3771-0_6

**Table 6.1** Structure of the state budget of 2016

| *Expenditures (million TND)* | *Resources (million TND)* |
|---|---|
| Wage bill | Direct taxes |
| 13,700 | 9441 |
| Other operational expenditures | Indirect taxes |
| 6540 | 12,259 |
| Investment | Non-fiscal resources |
| 6210 | 2195 |
| Loans | Domestic borrowing |
| 125 | 2460 |
| Debt service | External borrowing |
| 5825 | 6045 |
| **Total** | **Total** |
| **32,400** | **32,400** |

the public wage bill (around 14% of GDP making it one among the highest in the world). At the other end, the labor unions accused the laxity of the government in collecting taxes and fighting corruption and the informal economy. In that context, I suggested in Nabi (2016b) an intuitive financial solution based on the issuance of sovereign zero-coupon (ZC) bonds. The value of the ZC bonds shall finance the wage increase and have to be subscribed by the civil servants. Table 6.1 presents the structure of the state budget which was circulated by the end of 2016, without including the wage bill increase of 1030 million TND.

The mechanism I suggested could be illustrated by the following additional line in Table 6.2.

The suggested maturity of the ZC bonds is two years, providing the government with a two-year space to generate stable financial resources for the additional wage bill. Meanwhile, the civil servants would benefit from the investment opportunity offered by the ZC bonds. If the issuance of the ZC bonds took place in January 2017 with a value of 875.5 million TND, the civil servants would have expected to benefit in January 2019 from a net additional purchasing power of 970 million TND (on the basis of an annual interest rate of 5.25%). This purchasing power is to be channeled through tax reduction. The mechanism I suggested has the advantage of avoiding a long renegotiation process and being flexible. In financial terms, it means that the government will finance 875.5 million TND of internal borrowing by the securitization of a future tax reduction of 970 million TND. In addition, despite the automatic subscription of

**Table 6.2** Impact of the suggested mechanism on the state budget of 2016

| Additional wage bill | Additional tax on revenues |
|---|---|
| **1030** | **154.5** (15% × 1030) |
| | Issuance of ZC bonds (2 years) |
| | **875.5** |

the civil servants, I suggested that the ZC bonds might be sold on secondary markets via the financial intermediaries. Although this mechanism has not been adopted (judged too complex to be implemented), its tax credit's leg was considered in the adopted solution.[1]

### 6.1.2 *Securitization to Reduce Public Subsidization of the Social Security Institutions*

In Nabi (2016b), I have also suggested another variant of the securitization in order to alleviate the burden of the subsidies allocated to the social security institutions while increasing the wage bill. Indeed, a large part of the operational expenses consists of public subsidies, in particular those channeled to the in-deficit social security institutions (SSIs) amounting to 500 million TND. The suggested mechanism consists in avoiding the direct subsidy of the SSIs and letting them issue investment certificates on the monetary market. These certificates could be sold to institutional investors or subscribed by the civil servants. The reimbursement is suggested to take place in one year (or two years) in the form of reduction of social security contributions. The new structure of the state budget is shown in Table 6.3.

Instead of an additional wage bill of 1030 million TND totally financed by the government, the latter would have financed just 530 million TND while the remaining part (500 million TND) would be channeled through the investment certificates. This financial mechanism would expose the social security institution to the market discipline and limit its systematic recourse to public subsidy.

[1] See http://www.leaders.com.tn/article/21222-qui-a-souffle-a-youssef-chahed-l-idee-du-credit-d-impot-pour-debloquer-l-accord-avec-l-ugtt.

**Table 6.3** The new suggested structure of the state budget of 2016

| *Expenditures (million TND)* | | | *Resources (million TND)* | | |
|---|---|---|---|---|---|
| Wage bill | 13,700 | **+530** | Direct taxes | 9441 | **+79.5** |
| Other operational expenditures | 6540 | **−500** | Indirect taxes | 12,259 | |
| Investment | 6210 | | Non-fiscal resources | 2195 | |
| Loans | 125 | | Domestic borrowing | 2460 | **−49.5** |
| Debt service | 5825 | | External borrowing | 6045 | |
| **Total** | **32,400** | **+30** | **Total** | **32,400** | **+30** |

### *6.1.3 Securitization to Finance Infrastructure Development*

Another variant of that financial mechanism could be applied to alleviate the burden on the state budget resulting from the public investment on infrastructure development. Hence, instead of a direct public financing for the construction of a highway, the concerned public enterprise could recourse to securitization of the future revenues that will be generated out of this new infrastructure. This suggested mechanism could also take place through the channel of sukuk.

### *6.1.4 Role of Sukuk in Raising Financial Resources*

Sukuk are investment certificates that grant their holder a share of the profit generated by the financed asset or pool of assets, proportionally to their ownership share in that underlying asset.[2] Therefore, they are hybrid

[2] Most of the sukuk are "asset-based" and not "asset-backed". The latter type of sukuk grants to the holders the legal ownership of the underlying assets so that they can sell them in case of default of the issuer. On the contrary, the "asset-based" sukuk grants investors only the ownership of the cash flows and not the assets themselves. In July 2013, I have had the

financial securities different in structure from conventional bonds and stocks. Abdullah (2011) notes that the great potential of sukuk is in transforming an asset's future cash flow into present cash flow. Wilson (2004) critiques the current offering of sukuk, noting that they are mirroring their conventional peers. He proposes an innovative way of pricing and risk sharing in order to make sukuk clearly distinctive from conventional sukuk. Nevertheless, the sukuk market has grown rapidly during the last decade. The value of global sukuk issuance was 1.2 billion USD in 2001 whereas the amount of outstanding sukuk reached 362.8 billion USD by the Q3 of 2016. According to the survey done by Thomson Reuters (2017) the sukuk issuance reached 39.8 billion USD in 2016 up to Q3, distributed as follows in term of issuers: sovereign (15.4), quasi-sovereign (12.5) and corporate (11.9).[3] In 2016, the following sectors have mostly benefited from the financial resources raised through sukuk: financial services (14.2), transport (2.7) and power and utilities (2.1).[4]

This financial instrument has served the economies of many countries globally. Malaysia is the biggest issuer with 23 billion USD issued by Q3 2016, representing 58% of the market share of total sukuk issued globally. The London Stock Exchange listed its first sukuk in 2006. In Australia, two sovereign sukuk were successfully issued in 2014 and 2015 and the state budget of 2017 emphasized the timely opportunity to issue a third sukuk (Tsang, 2016). As for Turkey, a first sovereign sukuk was issued in 2012 at the domestic and international markets. It enabled the government to raise 8 billion USD through seven domestic two-year sukuk and three international seven-year sukuk. Cobanoglu (2016) notes that the sukuk issuance enabled Turkey to reduce the overall cost of funding relative to the conventional channel through the Eurobonds. Since the end of 2012, Tunisia announced its willingness to issue its first sovereign sukuk

opportunity to animate a session on Islamic finance in the European Commission in Brussels. I remember that the participants were very interested by the project sukuk as a channel to mobilize funds and enable the PPPs for the development of costly infrastructure projects.

[3] The distribution of the type of sukuk issued in 2016 was the following: Wakala (12.1), Murabaha (11.2), Ijarah (7.3), Musharakah (2.7) and Mudarabah (2.5).

[4] The report reveals that the most preferred emerging sukuk market for investors is the US and for the issuers it is Hong Kong. But the most preferred country to issue and invest in sukuk remains the UAE.

to raise 1000 million TND. However, in 2016 the issuance was canceled.[5] It is unfortunate that the Tunisian economy has not yet benefited from such a financial mechanism.[6] The infrastructure (musharaka) sukuk enabled the raising of 73.1 billion USD between 2002 and 2012 for ten countries (among which were Malaysia (61%), UAE (7%) and Saudi Arabia (30%)). This gives us an average annual potential of raising 560 million USD through infrastructure sukuk per country. Assuming that Tunisia has the potential to raise 25% of that potential, it is not unfeasible to issue infrastructure sukuk for an amount of 140 million USD as a channel of public-private partnership (PPP) for costly infrastructure development.

### *6.1.5 Issuing GDP-indexed Bonds*

In October 2005 and April 2006, the Financing for Development Office of the United Nations Department of Economic and Social Affairs (UN DESA) and the Office of Development Studies of the United Nations Development Programme (UNDP) organized two seminars entitled "GDP-Indexed Bonds: Making It Happen" and "GDP-Indexed Bonds: An Idea Whose Time Has Come". On the occasion of the second seminar,

[5] The reason for that cancellation is not only related to a technical constraint (impossibility to transfer the ownership of the stadium of Rades—which was chosen to back the operation—to a special investment vehicle) but also due to the negative perception by the public opinion. Many Tunisians considered the operation as a mortgage of a public infrastructure in return of foreign borrowing. This led to fierce opposition fuelled by the fear to see its ownership transferred to foreign investors in case of default. I understand this opposition and think that the Tunisian authorities should not have opted for that particular type of sukuk (called ijara sukuk) (although the documentation of the issuance was not available in order to judge the terms related to the ownership transfer in case of insolvency).

[6] In Tunisia, the juridical foundation of sukuk took place in July 2013 by the law n° 2013-30. However, as mentioned by Moncef Cheikhrouhou, Tunisia has already used such a financial mechanism for the infrastructural arrangement of the region Lac of Tunis in the 1980s. Contrarily to the enthusiasm of Moncef Cheikhrouhou in relation to the opportunity offered by sukuk to the Tunisian economy, the economist Radhi Meddeb was skeptical about their usefulness. Indeed, Meddeb (2013) argues that sukuk will cost the state the payment of higher interests relative to the conventional financial markets. He adds that these products are developed in the same manner as conventional bonds but are just adapted to the Islamic financial markets, namely, investors from GCC.

The reader might consult "Tunisie: Moncef Cheikhrouhou pour l'adoption des Sukuk", http://www.investir-en-tunisie.net/fr/index.php/2013/07/19/tunisie-moncef-cheikhrouhou-pour-ladoption-des-sukuk/.

Stephany Griffith-Jones noted that the main benefits of the GDP-indexed bonds are (a) stabilizing the debt-to-GDP ratio and limiting procyclicality; (b) reducing the likelihood of defaults and debt crises and (c) offering a new investment instrument that helps investors diversify their investments (UNDP, 2006).

For the current situation of Tunisia such an instrument would be beneficial if the variability of the coupon and the GDP insurance premium are well tailored. This financial mechanism has the potential to stabilize public expenditures and limit the procyclicality of fiscal pressures. Indeed, the growth-indexed bonds require low-interest payments at times of slower growth and vice versa. They can therefore limit the recourse to cutting social spending during recessions (Griffith-Jones and Sharma, 2009). In the case of the Greek crisis, Stiglitz (2015) recommended the use of such a financial instrument observing that the country would benefit from converting its current bonds into GDP-linked bonds.

### *6.1.6 Issuing Diaspora Investment Bonds*

Diaspora bonds constitute a source of long-term foreign financing channeled to investment. As noted by Ketkar and Ratha (2009b), they have similarity with Islamic bonds (sukuk) but are different in terms of remuneration (since interest payments are forbidden for the latter). They also argue that Diaspora purchases of bonds are generally motivated by a sense of patriotism and desire to contribute to the development of their country. The authors give examples of the bonds issued by Israel in 1951 which have totaled more than 25 billion USD from the Jewish Diaspora. They also cite the example of the State Bank of India, which raised over 11 billion USD. Bradlow (2008) notes that the Reconciliation and Development (R&D) bonds were originally conceived to involve the South African Diaspora in the national reconciliation process. They evolved to become a channel for raising financing from residents and expatriates for small-scale revenue projects that generates jobs, services and opportunities in the disadvantaged regions. Bradlow (2008) emphasizes the important role played by the Diaspora bonds in channeling domestic and international funding for development projects and in promoting reconciliation in post-conflict societies. A similar initiative called the Diaspora Investment in Agriculture (DIA) was launched by the United States Department of State and the International Fund for Agricultural Development (IFAD) in 2006. According to IFAD (2006), the partnership aims to leverage the contributions of migrant workers and to favor their contribution to the sustainable economic development by financing agricultural projects particularly in rural areas. Among the objectives of the DIA initiative are improving the lives of the poor rural people by financing sustainable agricultural projects and building the capacity they need to undertake investment and gain access to markets.

The infrastructure projects that Tunisia needs are very costly and require a huge amount of capital, exceeding the financial resources of the state. In June 2016, I suggested during my participation in the meeting of the *Council of Economic Analysis* that the Tunisian government issues Diaspora Investment Bonds to channel resources toward structured projects in targeted inner regions of Tunisia.[7] The funds raised through the Diaspora bonds could be managed by the *Caisse des Dépôts et des Consignations*[8] and channeled to the pre-identified projects. Meanwhile, the remittance flows constitute an important financial resource for Tunisia. It amounted to 1794 million USD in 2016, representing 4.6% of the GDP. Let us assume that the government will issue Diaspora Investment Bonds to finance identified and preannounced infrastructure projects in different regions of the country. It is not unrealistic to estimate that it will be possible to attract 5% additional resources from the Tunisian Diaspora or equivalently almost 90 million USD.

### 6.1.7 Activating the PPP

The cooperation with the private sector shall also be considered in financing the infrastructure projects in Tunisia. It could be done through the issuance of dedicated financial securities (Diaspora bonds, sukuk, bonds, etc.) and based on PPP under multiple models, one among which is the

[7] A similar idea was announced by Mohamed Bichiou of Tunis Exchange Market in 2013. In September 2016, Habib Karaouli launched quite a similar idea through the magazine leaders. He suggested the issuance of bonds in foreign exchanges (but reimbursable in domestic currency) for the Tunisian Diaspora to participate in the financing of MSMEs.

[8] In 2011, Tunisia created the Caisse des Dépôts et des Consignations (CDC), a public financial institution under the control of the ministry of finance. The CDC is in charge of investing a part of the national saving (coming from the postal banking) in long-term financial investment accompanying the sectoral policies of the state, namely in social housing, energy projects, investment in rural regions and investment in environmental projects.

Build, Operate and Transfer (BOT) model.[9] The ADB report (2015) recalls that the financing landscape changed and that sustainable development could no more be financed by governments solely. While recognizing that strategic initiatives need to be backed by public funds, it notes that a diverse range of sources (public, private and joint financing, south-south cooperation) shall be mobilized to meet the development funding needs. Despite the adoption of the law No 2015-49 in November 2015 setting the legal framework for the PPP in Tunisia, there is still a widespread skepticism among Tunisians about this cooperation channel between the public and private sectors. This skeptical reaction is related to the fear of weakening the state and its ability to guarantee affordable public services. Nevertheless, Tunisia has practiced PPP since the 1980s on the occasion of the layout of the Lac de Tunis (from 1985 to 1988).[10]

## 6.2 Developing Equity Finance and Crowdfunding to Improve Access to Finance

Policy makers have to ensure better access to financial services and particularly to banking services. The access to finance has been acknowledged by the World Economic Forum (WEF) as one of the criteria to assess the development level of a financial system. Indeed, the WEF (2012b) defines financial development as the combination of factors, policies and institutions that leads to effective financial intermediation, efficient markets and deep and broad access to finance. Improving the access to finance is particularly important for SMEs.[11] In Tunisia, SMEs contribute to approximately two-thirds of the economic activity and 65% of the employment.[12]

[9] Let us note here that some recent critics are globally emerging regarding the social optimality of the PPP (see Leigland, 2018).

[10] http://www.leaders.com.tn/article/13630-vivement-la-loi-sur-les-ppp.

[11] The International Finance Corporation considers SMEs to be key engines of job creation and economic growth in developing countries noting that they represent 90% of businesses and more than 50% of employment globally. The World Bank considers that four out of five new formal jobs in emerging markets are created by SMEs. http://www.worldbank.org/en/topic/financialsector/brief/smes-finance.

[12] In April 2010, I conducted a study in cooperation with CJD Sousse on "SMEs and Export". Among the results, I found that 60% of the enterprises are using less than 60% of their production capacity. Among the questioned enterprises, there were 50% which were not exporting due to problems and constraints related to transport, bureaucracy, finance and insurance and fierce competition.

According to the IFC Enterprise Finance Gap Database, there are 400 million MSMEs in developing countries with only 15% having access to credit and 25% among them considering access to finance as a major constraint. According to the same database, the total unmet demand for formal SME financing is estimated by the IFC for 2011 to be 1.5 trillion USD (two-thirds in emerging markets and developing countries). The European Central Bank considers the SMEs as a pillar of the euro area economy which depends on bank loans and are exposed to higher cost and higher rejection rate relative to larger firms (Cœuré, 2012). The WEF (2012a) notes that many emerging economies shall develop their financial systems in order to generate economic growth and prosperity for their people. It emphasizes in particular three areas: consumer financial services, SMEs financing and corporate bond markets.

In order for Tunisia to escape the middle-income trap, it shall move toward a knowledge-based economy based on human capital accumulation rather than physical capital accumulation. Such a transition will be difficult with the existing financial system, as the knowledge-based models are exposed to more severe credit constraints from the banking system. Indeed, the innovative enterprises and particularly the start-ups do not have the physical collateral that enables them to access the traditional bank financing.[13] Therefore, it is important to develop the equity-finance component of the financial system. Such a component is more willing to finance R&D activities and technological start-ups. This can be done by developing the stock markets' role in financing the private sector and promoting entrepreneurship. It can also be done by favoring the emergence of new channels for raising funds like crowdfunding.

### *6.2.1 Governmental Intervention to Improve Access to Finance*

Clarke et al. (2003) note that even if policy makers are aware of the urgent need to enhance access to finance, they might be unarmed with the right and effective financial instruments. However, Cressy (2002) identifies a successful active governmental role in improving access to finance to the small, young and often high-tech firms. This intervention is taking place in many developed countries (the US, Japan, Western Europe) as well as

[13] As recalled by Pofeldt (2012), it is opportune for the economies which are becoming technology-based to take into account the value of the intangible assets of such enterprises.

in developing countries of Eastern Europe. It is realized through the development of financial schemes such as loan and equity guarantee schemes, venture capital trusts, soft loan schemes, government grants and government equity investment. Cressy (2002) presents arguments from the literature that justify this state intervention. It is related to the existence of R&D spillovers and positive externalities to innovation. In Germany, for example, there are specific state support measures for the high-growth innovative enterprises (HGIEs). Among the most frequent financial support identified by Lilischkis et al. (2013) are those targeting investment (i.e. production factor capital), employees (i.e. production factor labor) and support to research (i.e. production factor knowledge).

In Nabi (2016b), I suggest an original equity contract and compare it to the traditional debt in regard to access to finance and economic inefficiency.[14] The suggested equity contract embeds a dynamic incentive that links the entrepreneur's share in the project's payoff to his own invested funds.[15] Based on the proven results, I recommend governmental intervention to improve access to finance through equity and by reducing the deadweight cost of debt finance.

### 6.2.2 *Unlocking the Crowdfunding*

Crowdfunding is an Internet-enabled channel to raise funds for artisans, Non-governmental organizations (NGO), entrepreneurs and early-stage enterprises. It emerged during the financial crisis of 2008 in reaction to the credit crunch. The large-scale adoption of ICT and the development of social networks enabled the online collection of funds in the form of donations or investment by many people. In 2014, it is estimated that 16.2 billion USD was raised globally (InfoDev, 2013). In 2015, it increased to 34 billion USD constituting P2P Lending (25 billion USD), Reward and

[14] This is done in a model with moral hazard in the form of hidden effort by a risk-neutral agent (entrepreneur) financed by a risk-neutral principal (financier).

[15] I showed that equity and debt are feasible for a determined range of projects' sizes and entrepreneurs' wealth. However, debt is less financially constraining than equity for large projects. In contrast, equity is more accessible to small projects. Another interesting result is the fact that extending the financial contracting to two periods enhances the access to debt under the necessary incentivizing termination threat (financing nonrenewal). As for the suggested equity contract, access to finance improves over a larger horizon only for small projects undertaken by sufficiently foresighted entrepreneurs.

Donation Crowdfunding (5.5 billion USD) and Equity Crowdfunding (2.5 billion USD).[16] In France, the collected funds increased from 152 million EUR in 2014 to 296.8 million EUR and 628.8 million EUR respectively in 2015 and 2016 (KPMG, 2017). In 2016, there were 1,019,488 subscribers to the Crowdfunding platforms in France who contributed to the financing of 21,375 projects in different sectors (19% in culture, 25% in social activities, 47% in the economic sector, 9% in other activities). Those subscriptions took the form of donations (6035), loans (720,703) and investment (448,779). One would have expected that such a financial channel would have developed rapidly in the developing countries. The urgent need for alternative sources of finance to the unbaked or credit-rationed organizations and artisans in those countries do not need argumentations. However, most of the Crowdfunding platforms are located in developed countries.[17] This might be the result of the institutional rigidity and/or the lobbying of traditional financial intermediaries. The World Bank report InfoDev (2013) notes that Crowdfunding helps developing countries in alleviating the constraints on the entrepreneurial finance by facilitating access to capital for SMEs, cultivating high-growth entrepreneurs, supporting access to export markets and catalyzing flows of capital within and between communities.

Despite the advocacy done in 2015 and before by many organizations in Tunisia for enabling such a channel, there are always no clear signals of progress in that direction from the concerned authorities.

## 6.3 Daring Targeted Quantitative Easing

### 6.3.1 *The Monetary Policy Framework of the Central Bank of Tunisia*

The law n°2016-35 of 25 April 2016 mandates the Central Bank of Tunisia (CBT) with the principal objective of price stability. Its seventh article equally mentions that the CBT strives for a perfect coordination of

[16] http://crowdexpert.com/crowdfunding-industry-statistics/.

[17] InfoDev (2013) reports the following distributions of crowdfunding in selected countries: the US (344), France (53), the UK (87), Canada (34), the Netherlands (34), Spain (27), Germany (26), Brazil (17), Italy (15), Australia (12), India (10), South Africa (4), Russian Federation (4), Belgium (1), Hong Kong SAR, China (1), China (1), UAE (1) and Estonia (1).

its monetary policy with the state's economic policies. This coordination shall take place while respecting the independence of the CBT vis-à-vis the government. This independence has been emphasized in many articles of the new law.[18] In the economic literature, the conduct of the monetary policy is often modeled as the minimization of a loss function $L = f(y - y*, \pi - \pi*)$ having two arguments: the output gap (difference between the effective output ($y$) and the potential output ($y^*$)) and the difference between the effective inflation ($\pi$) and the inflation target ($\pi^*$). The weights assigned to each argument in the loss function depend on the relative importance assigned by the central bank to the price stabilization relative to the economic activity. In developed economies having reached an advanced stage of institutional development, the most important weight is assigned to price stabilization. Meanwhile, the conduct of the monetary policy is endowed with the necessary flexibility to adjust with the fluctuations of the economic cycle.

### *6.3.2 Weak Efficiency of the Quantitative Easing*

In Tunisia, the main transmission channel of the monetary policy is the "credit channel".[19] As noted in Chap. 2, the CBT increased the capacity of Tunisian banks to create money after 2011. This has been done through an expansionist monetary policy based on lowering its interest rate, decreasing the obligatory reserve rate and pursuing an extensive quantitative easing (QE) policy. As we have seen, this policy has much more resulted in increasing the credits for consumption rather than financing the private investment. This policy has certainly avoided a deeper contraction of the economic activity in Tunisia, by stimulating the private consumption and avoiding a credit crunch.

However, the efficiency of QE relative to other policies in reviving the economy is questionable even in developed countries. In their article entitled "*What's Holding Back the World Economy?*" Stiglitz and Rashid (2016) analyze why fiscal retrenchment and QE have timidly stimulated household

[18] In terms of monetary policy, article 10 clearly prohibits the use of seigniorage for financing the public deficit.

[19] As the majority of the central banks in the world, the CBT has the monopoly of issuing the monetary base but delegates to the commercial banks the creation of the scriptural money (which constitutes the main component of the money in circulation).

consumption, investment and growth.[20] The authors regret that the phenomenal decrease of the interest rate around zero for approximately seven years has not been exploited by governments to borrow and invest in infrastructure, education and social sectors. Such a policy would have stimulated the economic activity through the channel of the aggregate demand. They draw a negative assessment of the QE as practiced in developed countries, noting that it generated sharp increases in leverage, market capitalization and financial-sector profitability with timid positive impact on the real economy. Meanwhile, they suggest corrective measures in order for the QE to result in positive effects on the real economy: (1) restoring impaired lending channels, especially those concerning SMEs; (2) setting specific lending targets for banks and (3) penalizing the holding of excess reserves by banks.

### 6.3.3 *Introducing a Targeted Quantitative Easing*

In Nabi (2016a), I suggest a TQE tailored for the Tunisian context.[21] The idea is to enable the monetary creation for financing public investment in infrastructure, providing credit lines to microfinance institutions and financing public pension system and the state-owned enterprises. The originality of the suggested mechanism is to back the money creation by future financial flows resulting from productive investments. In the suggested mechanism, the CBT would act as an institutional investor that delegates to the financial intermediaries the role to grant loans (on its behalf while benefiting from predetermined commission fees) for specific targets with agreed-on rules of reimbursing. The created and injected money will be reversibly punctured over a horizon of five to ten years. I suggested four channels: TQE bank-based, TQE Infrastructure, TQE public assets and TQE pension system. The four channels have in common the following features: (1) they serve specific targets, (2) they are limited in time and (3) they respect the legal framework of the CBT. Table 6.4 presents more details of each channel.

[20] The authors note that "in 17 of the 20 largest developed economies, investment growth remained lower during the post-2008 period than in the years prior to the crisis; five experienced a decline in investment during 2010–2015".

[21] I published it on my LinkedIn profile in June 2016 and later in November 2016 on the web magazine investir-en-Tunisie.

**Table 6.4** The proposed channels of the targeted quantitative easing

| *Channel* | *Details* |
|---|---|
| TQE bank-based | The CBT shall fix a ceiling (bank-specific depending on its liquidity position and total loans/deposits, for example) for conventional refinancing. Beyond that ceiling, the refinancing shall be conditioned by the financing of investment, exports or working capital of MSMEs. |
| TQE infrastructure | The idea is that the CBT creates money to finance (it could be within public-private partnership) public infrastructure mainly in the inner and isolated regions of Tunisia. The beneficiary in that case shall be a company (such as Tunisie Autoroute [TA]) specialized in building and operating the public infrastructure or public service.<br>The CBT provides financing to the company (TA) through a credit line operated by a public bank. The beneficiary company reimburses the principal and a fixed share of the revenues generated by the new infrastructure (e.g. highway) over a determined period of time.<br>Another way to finance the infrastructure could be through the issuance of investment certificates by TA indicating the final use of the raised funds. The CBT could refinance at lower cost the commercial banks that will purchase these investment certificates. It could also acquire a direct portion of the issued assets. |
| TQE public assets | The idea is to create an independent public assets management company (PAMC, a kind of special investment vehicle) to which the state delegates the management of its shares in the state-owned companies for a determined period (let's say ten years). The PAMC could issue investment certificates of ten years maturity with an annual remuneration indexed on the future generated cash flows and the risk profile of each state-owned enterprise.<br>As in the previous case, the investment certificates could be purchased by commercial banks. In that case, the CBT could refinance at lower cost the commercial banks which purchase these investment certificates. It could also acquire a direct portion of the issued assets.<br>This operation enables the state to raise important revenues while disciplining it since it is not a classic seigniorage operation, but rather a securitization of future revenues (it could be seen as an inter-temporal trade-off where the government accepts a certain amount of money at a discount relative to the future cash flows.<br>This trade-off is important given the economic context characterized by large public deficit, slow economic growth and higher public indebtedness and costly recourse to external financing). This mechanism has also the advantage of avoiding the privatization of the beneficial state-owned enterprises (largely contested by Labor Unions).<br>The successful experience of Singapore shall inspire the Tunisian authorities. Indeed, in 1974, Singapore created Temasek, a state-holding company, to hold government assets and introduce modern governance practices to the state-owned enterprises (Cheng-Han et al., 2015). |

(*continued*)

**Table 6.4** (continued)

| *Channel* | *Details* |
|---|---|
| TQE pension system | The Tunisian pension system is in deficit and the government is preparing its restructuring. In order to reduce the burden on the public finance, the social insurance institutions shall be able to issue investment certificates on the financial market backed by their future revenues. As in the two previous cases, the investment certificates could be purchased by commercial banks and the CBT. |

This targeted money creation will increase the financing space for public investment and reduce the burden of the external public indebtedness. It is limited in time and reversible since it is backed by the securitization of the future public revenues. Taking into account that the refinancing of the commercial banks by the CBT increased by 1000 million dinars between March and April 2017, it is not unrealistic to target an annual amount of 500 million dinars for the TQE. The negative effect of such a mechanism in terms of inflation could be offset by the positive impact in the form of a lower recourse to external financing (with its negative effect on the value of the TND and the stock of the external debt). Besides, the financing of targeted public investment would improve the attractiveness in the beneficiary regions. Given that Tunisia has not fully liberalized its capital account, this type of monetary policy is possible since it does not expose it fully to the incompatibility trilemma of Mundell-Fleming.

## 6.4 Participatory Banking, Cooperatives and Microfinance

### *6.4.1 The Debate on Wealth and Income Inequality*

The *Capital in the Twenty-First Century*, a book by Thomas Piketty, revived the debate on wealth and income inequality and engaged a planetary debate on this issue. Basically, with a high return on private wealth relative to the economy's growth (high r–g), wealth inequality might reach or surpass the nineteenth-century levels. In order to prevent this scenario, Piketty suggests the implementation of progressive wealth tax at the global scale. In an interview published on the Blog of the Institute of New Economic Thinking, Stiglitz (2015) identifies two types of measures that might contribute to the reduction of wealth and income inequality.

The Nobel Prize laureate suggests that "the before-tax and transfers income" measures in relation to improving the institutional environment (stronger unions, higher minimum wages, stronger enforcement of antitrust laws and corporate governance laws, better education). He also stresses the importance of redistributive policies and addressing preferential treatment benefiting mainly rich people.

I believe that the role of the financial system in reducing income and wealth inequalities is another important dimension. Hence, the debate on the institutional reforms to set, in order to reduce the income and wealth inequality, shall not ignore the dimension of a positive "disruption" of the financial system. This positive disruption is to be catalyzed by introducing new types of institutions and innovative financing mechanisms that fulfill the access to the finance gap. I have already justified in Chap. 5 the importance of the new digital channels in positively disrupting the financial system. In the next section, I motivate another vector of disrupting the banking system by introducing a new type of business model.

### 6.4.2 *Can Participatory Banking Reduce Wealth Inequality?*

Observing the recent widening of income inequality in most of the countries, one might conclude that the impact of policy makers on "finance" through taxation and monetary policy is ineffective. Noting this, I explored in Nabi (2015) the impact of a new type of banking on the dynamic of wealth and income inequality. The exercise I conducted could be considered as a contribution to the opening of the debate about income inequality on a new perspective: *what if we disrupt the banking system by introducing a new type of business model?*

The exercise I conducted is also related to the debate on the "optimal" structure of the banking system.[22] In Nabi (2015), I consider an equity-based banking (participatory banking), financing the economy through

[22] De Grauwe (2009) argues that the reforms implemented since the 1930s in order to enhance the stability of the banking system and to prevent large-scale banking crises (central bank's lender of last resort role, deposit insurance mechanism and banks' capital regulation) have shown their limits. He argues that the solution is narrow banking where banks act as money market funds that use the sight deposits they collect to buy riskless financial securities. Meanwhile, the traditional role of transforming deposits to loans should be assigned to financial firms (investment banks) involved in financial markets with close matching of the average maturities of their assets and liabilities.

equity contracts instead of conventional debt contracts (as is the case in conventional banking). I wanted to analyze if this substitution changes the dynamic of wealth and income inequality.[23] The suggested participatory financial intermediaries are atypical on the assets and liabilities sides. On the assets side, they finance investment projects on the basis of equity contracts and therefore behave as investment companies. On the liability side, they remunerate the collected deposits contingently on their aggregate return (which is certain under the assumption of complete risk sharing).[24] In Nabi (2015), I consider overlapping generations of populations comprising individuals having identical entrepreneurial abilities. They initially belong to one of two classes: the poor or the wealthy. Despite the presence of credit market imperfections (costly enforcement of financial contracts and moral hazard), I prove that the poor class has the possibility of catching up with the wealthy class. This catching-up process ends with the decrease of income inequality and is triggered once the poor class reaches a sufficient level of wealth accumulation. This result diverges with the one I obtained in my previous related article (Nabi, 2009) presented in Chap. 5. This divergence is due to the particularity of participatory banking relative to conventional banking. The new financial contracting relationship (based on equity contracts) between banks and agents has two distinctive features: (1) it loosens the importance of the collateral constraints and (2) it discourages excessive borrowing of the wealthy classes beyond a particular threshold of wealth accumulation (thus reducing the concentration of wealth). In particular, borrowing from the financial intermediaries

[23] The full substitution of conventional banking by participatory banking in this modeling exercise is motivated by the simplification of the mathematical framework.

[24] In practice, the features of the financial intermediation I consider are typical of an ideal business model of the participatory (Islamic) bank. Indeed, under Islamic banking, assets and liabilities are (ideally) expected to be integrated such that borrowers share their profits and losses with the bank, which in turn shares profits and losses with depositors. One advocate of the participatory business model of the financial intermediaries is Chapra (1985), who argues that the entrepreneur and the financier should share equitably any gains and losses. Khan (1987) argues that the business model of participatory banks can successfully fill the failure of conventional banks in maintaining stability. Indeed, it requires the separation of investment deposits (funds) from demand deposits (on which 100% reserve is constituted). While demand deposits are perfectly guaranteed and yield no return, investment deposits should be similar to mutual fund shares and not guaranteed a fixed return. It is clear that the "theoretical" or ideal business model of a participatory bank has some commonalities with narrow banking.

under the equity contract exposes wealthy agents to higher sharing ratios, which increases the cost of borrowing. Consequently, the incentive to borrow to enlarge the investment projects gradually vanishes and wealthy agents tend to self-finance their projects or become depositors. Consequently, the financial constraints on the poor classes are relaxed and its agents can finance their entrepreneurial aspirations.

### 6.4.3 Participatory Banks for Rural Development

*Can participatory banks improve access to finance and boost the economic activities in the rural regions of Tunisia?*

The development of participatory (Islamic) banks in Indonesia and their success in increasing financial access to micro, small and medium enterprises (MSMEs) is worthwhile to mention. Sitorus (2013) notes that Indonesia counts more than 50 million MSMEs, which represent around 97% of all the enterprises. In 2012, half of the total Islamic bank financing went to MSMEs. The latter declared more accessibility and reactivity to their financing needs from the participatory banks in comparison to their conventional peers. The positive contribution of participatory banks is also needed in improving the access to finance in rural regions.[25] As discussed in the previous section, the business model of a participatory bank requires less collateral on the side of the borrowers. Creating participatory banks at the regional levels while inspiring from the German saving and cooperative banks[26] shall be considered as a way to improve access to finance and boost the economic activities in the rural regions of Tunisia. In Germany, saving banks are the market leaders in mobilizing local depos-

[25] Besley (1994) identifies the various forms of governmental intervention in rural credit markets in developing countries. They range from government ownership of banks (e.g. India, Mexico) to the obligation imposed on commercial banks to open branches in rural areas (Nigeria). The subsidization of credit to farmers is another form of intervention. Besley (1994) notes that what makes rural credit markets in developing countries different from other credit markets is the intensity of the following imperfections: scarce collateral, underdevelopment in complementary institutions (insurance, credit bureaus) and covariant risks.

[26] In 2014, the group of saving banks in Germany comprised more than 500 institutions that employed 341,000 staff members. The German banking system comprises also a cooperative banking group with around 1050 institutions (including around 1000 local cooperatives) employing 200,000 staff members (Behr and Schmidt, 2015).

its and transforming them into loans to SMEs and private households (Behr and Schmidt, 2015).

### 6.4.4 *Coupling Microfinance with Cooperatives*

*What role can microfinance and cooperatives play in rural development and jobs creation?*

Hu and Khan (1997) delve into the sources of China's high growth post 1978 (with an average of more than 9% a year). It appears that sustained increase in productivity was the main driver in addition to capital and labor accumulation, which played a secondary role. Indeed, the contribution of productivity growth to output growth exceeded 50% by the early 1990s while that of capital formation was below 33%. The reason behind the high and sustained growth of labor productivity is linked to the economic reforms that were undertaken since 1978. The main factor explaining the rapid growth of productivity is the introduction of profit incentives to rural collective enterprises (owned by local governments and guided by market principles), family farms, small private businesses and foreign investors and traders. These incentives encouraged the factory owners and small producers to increase their profits and to reinvest more in order to improve the performance of their business (Hu and Khan, 1997). It is therefore clear that introducing profit incentives in the rural collective enterprises played an important role in the economic growth of China. *Can this successful experience be tailored to the Tunisian context?*

The success of the Association de Défense des Oasis de Jemna in recent years in doubling the benefits of the agricultural farm by operating as a local cooperative reveals that it is possible for Tunisia to benefit from the cooperative system at the regional level. According to the FAO's (2013) report, there are only 151 cooperatives active in the Tunisian agricultural sector. They were managed by the public authorities for a long time, have no more credibility from the financial institutions and lack the confidence of farmers. Abdelkafi and Nabi (2017) note that throughout the world "*cooperatives play a major role in the development of rural areas where private investors are reluctant to invest and basic public services are generally absent. … They help generate employment opportunities, health, education, clean water, improve sanitation, roads, market access, and enable rural citizens to be better organized and to be listened by public authorities. The International Labor Organization issued in 2002 recommendations on the Promotion of Cooperatives (No. 193) encouraging governments to put in place the institutional and legal frameworks for the development of cooperatives*" (Abdelkafi and Nabi, 2017, 10). In 2012, I suggested with my colleague Rami Abdelkafi an innovative program to stimulate the creation of short-term job opportunities for university graduates.[27] The idea is to exploit the huge potential of microfinance and cooperatives.[28] The IBM Belgium (2010) study financed by the European Union in 2010 estimated a potential of 1 million new clients of micro-credit in Tunisia. Meanwhile, the potential of job opportunities created through cooperatives is still timidly exploited in Tunisia. For that reason, we suggested a national program articulated on the cooperative structure in rural areas of Tunisia, based on PPP for the training and promotion of the entrepreneurship abilities of young graduates and coupled with an incentive financial contracting through the microfinance institutions.

**Box 6.1 Steps of the Proposed Program to Support Young Graduates**
The first step consists in selecting (according to credible and transparent criteria) regions and young graduates who will benefit from the program. In parallel, training structures should be selected (based on a set of specifications) by the Ministry of Employment to provide training (theoretical and practical) related to the creation and the management of projects. Meanwhile, private companies existing in the beneficiary regions should be encouraged to participate in training the beneficiaries of the programs.

Successful trainees will benefit from the government financial support to create their own cooperative. The financial support has two components: (1) X% (<50%) of shares of the cooperative will be distributed to the trainees for free and (2) the remaining 100%–X%

[27]We conceived this program on the occasion of our participation to a workshop organized by the IMF Institute and the World Bank Institute on "*Employment Policies in the MENA Region*". Then, I have had the opportunity to present it at a national conference in 2013 before publishing it in Abdelkafi and Nabi (2017).

[28]The microfinance sector received particular attention by the successive governments since 2011. In January 2013, a new legal framework for the microfinance sector was promulgated enabling (1) the emergence of companies specialized in microfinance and the change of the legal status of existing associations, (2) the expansion of the range of microfinance services to include micro-insurance and (3) the establishment of a monitoring and regulatory framework.

of shares will be the state participation in the cooperative through the microfinance institution.

At the end of each fiscal year, each graduate (cooperator to the institution) pays an amount enabling him to buy a fraction of the state's shares in the cooperative. This funding scheme as decreasing partnership (Musharaka Moutanakisa) has the advantage of encouraging all the graduates (now cooperators) to provide the necessary effort for the success of their cooperative and to acquire the state's shares in the capital. The management of the cooperative will be undertaken by the graduates themselves even if we can conceive an initial stage where monitoring is realized by the microfinance institution via the services of a specialized expert.

Note that our proposed program will reduce the moral hazard problems that characterized the program "Amal", since the grant of the premium (free distribution of the cooperative' shares) will take place at the end of the training cycle. Moreover, the largest proportion of the premium is granted in the form of state participation in the capital of the cooperative created for the beneficiaries who succeeded their training.

Source: Abdelkafi and Nabi (2017)

In 2013, the *Ministry of Employment and Vocational Training* identified 3500 profitable micro-projects. Those micro-projects lacked self-financing and were likely to benefit from the E4E Initiative for Arab Youth which aimed to address the labor demand and the skills mismatch. At that time, the Ministry also stressed the importance of supporting the Vocational Education and Training for Employment Project, which targeted 7000 students, 208 trainers and 51 supervisors in three disadvantaged regions. Among the recommendations included in the MCPS report,[29] I cite the following recommendations:

[29] In my quality of senior economist of the *Islamic Development Bank Group*, I participated in field missions and meetings with senior officials from the Tunisian government, in preparation of the "Member Country Partnership Strategy for Tunisia 2013–2015" (MCPS).

1. Financing micro-enterprises in the disadvantaged regions with the pooling of the unemployed youth in clusters after succeeding their vocational program
2. Accelerating the emergence of the Islamic microfinance sector in order to tackle the self-exclusion from the conventional financing
3. Enhancing the public local agencies' role in accompanying new entrepreneurs
4. Providing financial incentives to the private sector investment in the disadvantaged regions through hiring trainees and encouraging business angels
5. Enhancing the solidarity actions between the various regions, encouraging the civil society to participate in poverty's alleviation efforts and incentivizing the hiring of the youth by the private sector especially in the rural and inner regions (IsDB, 2013)[30]

## 6.5 Social Impact Bonds for Modern and Efficient Philanthropy

### 6.5.1 *Philanthropy: Zaqat and Waqf*

*How can Tunisia benefit from its philanthropic potential to reduce extreme poverty and generate social solidarity?*

Bensoussan et al. (2013) encourage governments to raise voluntary contributions from citizens and private corporations through dedicated matching programs. By developing such large programs they can leverage on their credibility to resolve social issues on a large scale. Tunisia launched the *Fond National de Solidarité* (National Solidarity Fund) (called 26-26) in 1992. However, this fund lacked credibility in the absence of transparency and accountability rules. Another national initiative was launched in 1992 when the Tunisian Union of Social Solidarity NGO (*Union Tunisienne de Solidarité Sociale* "UTSS") created regional funds to collect

[30] Similar recommendations were suggested by the *International Labor Organization* in its report ILO (2015). For instance, the report suggests the following: (1) rethinking the institutional support to the micro-projects, (2) revalorizing the vocational specialties and encouraging the private initiative, (3) supporting the social and solidarity economy by setting specific mechanisms in cooperation with the vibrant civil society.

and distribute Zaqat.[31] The Zakat (meaning purification) is viewed as a "compulsory charity" equaling 2.5%[32] of an individual's wealth and assets.[33] The annual payment of Zaqat is considered as an accomplishment of the third pillar of Islam for those whose annual wealth exceeds a minimum threshold.[34] In the Quran it is specified that "*Zakat is for the poor, and the needy and those who are employed to administer and collect it, and the new converts, and for those who are in bondage, and in debt and service of the cause of Allah, and for the wayfarers, a duty ordained by Allah, and Allah is the All-Knowing, the Wise*" (al-Tauba, 9:60). Beyond the direct individual channels and in order to increase the social impact of Zaqat, the *International Shari'ah Board on Zakat* (ISBOZ) recommended its utilization in financing development projects, educational services and healthcare services as long as the beneficiaries of such projects are the targeted recipients of Zakat. Mohieldin et al. (2012) find supporting evidence that a proper Zakat collection and management can alleviate the poorest class living with an income under 1.25 USD per day out of the poverty line in 20 out of 39 OIC[35] countries.

After 2011, there was a renewal call for the creation of a national Zaqat institution to collect, manage and distribute Zaqat funds at the national level. The idea was subject to political conflicts and seen as a tool of political propaganda by the Islamic party. During my participation in the meeting of the *Council of Economic Analysis* in June 2016, I suggested to the chief of the government to renew the mandate of the *Tunisian Union of Social* Solidarity in collecting, managing and distributing Zaqat funds by activating the regional funds that were initially conceived[36] and coordinating the exercise of reducing extreme poverty with the Ministries of Social and Religious Affairs. It is urgent to activate this channel in order to improve the social impact of the Zaqat funds and avoid its interaction with

[31] See objective 4 on the website www.utss.org.tn.

[32] There are other rates for agricultural products, mining produce and animals.

[33] Cash, gold and silver, commercial items and assets, excluding long-term business capital and housing owned not for resale.

[34] This threshold is called Nissab, which equals 3 ounces of gold (87.48 g) or its cash equivalent.

[35] The *Organization of Islamic Cooperation.*

[36] In 1992, my father (www.salahnabi.net) was designated the President of the Regional Fund at the Governorate of Monastir. I found documents mentioning meetings during the inception phase of the regional Zaqat funds.

the political arena. Modern management practices are to be identified at the international level. In Bangladesh, for example, Zaqat funds can be collected by the microfinance institutions that channel it to the extreme poor in the context of an economic empowering strategy (including basic financial literacy, training in undertaking simple micro-projects, etc.).

Waqf (endowment, pl. Awqaf) is a second Islamic philanthropy channel which is subject to ideological opposition in Tunisia. It was abolished by President Habib Bourguiba just after the independence. It was considered as latent physical capital losing its economic value progressively without a sufficiently positive contribution to the economic dynamic of the country. It is worthwhile to note here that the majority of Awqaf were in general allocated to groups of individuals belonging to the same families. It is clear that this type of Awqaf is not the most beneficial to the society. At the opposite, Awqaf for public purposes are providing a wide range of services, especially in education and community services, in both Muslim and non-Muslim countries where they are called endowments (Mohieldin et al., 2012). Syed Ali et al. (2013) note that "Awqaf are distinct from Zakat in two fundamental ways. First, they are voluntary philanthropy, not obligatory like Zakat. Second, the beneficiaries of Waqf can be assigned by the people who created the Waqf. Thus, Awqaf can be used not only to provide charity for the poor but also to provide public and social goods to a specific group or to the population at large. ... This is in addition and parallel to the normal public sector controlled by the government" (Syed Ali et al., 2013, 78).

In Kuwait, Qatar and Singapore, Awqaf are being managed according to modern governance rules. Their proceeds are contributing to wide benefits to the society through building hospitals, universities and commercial and office complexes. In Morocco, the revenues of Awqaf are financing the building of townships (Tong, 2007). Recognizing this positive contribution to the social welfare of Singaporeans,[37] Tong (2007) noted that the trust laws and the new regulatory framework will help Singapore to become a center for the development of Waqf, which requires the same ecosystem as the conventional charitable trusts. Syed Ali et al. (2013) argue that Awqaf can be used to build social and public institutions which enable the private sector development. "*For example, institutions for better*

[37] He added that proceeds of Waqf helped needy Singaporeans regardless of race and religion by providing them with medicine.

*governance, development of accounting standards, providing education and training, creation of system of property and collateral registration, and institutions to settle minor trade disputes all are possible through awqaf*" (Syed Ali et al., 2013, 78). Abdelhady (2013) proposes the establishment of a multilateral food security Waqf to improve food security of the Middle East. The suggested Waqf would serve as a financial channel for investment and financing of research and development, capacity building and income generation in the agricultural sector. It would also facilitate the access to finance for small farmers, SMEs and other parties across the food supply chain (Abdelhady, 2013). She observes that there are examples of successful utilization of the Waqf structure by Muslims and non-Muslims for the promotion of public interest and the facilitation of investment in culturally and geographically diverse countries. From that perspective, she argues that this tool should neither be overlooked nor underestimated.

Given the flexibility and the wide range of public services that can be financed through Awqaf, it is important to utilize their huge potential within the state's strategy to generate an inclusive economic development. In the following section, I suggest the utilization of Zaqat and Awqaf funds through Social Impact Bonds to serve the state's social programs.

### 6.5.2 Social Impact Bonds

Social Impact Bond (SIB) ("social innovation financing" or "pay for success projects") is a PPP which has recently emerged to improve the impact of public social expenditure. Helbitz et al. (2016) define SIB as a PPP which drive resources toward effective social programs that measurably improve lives. It enable public authorities to partner with performing service providers by using private investment to develop, coordinate and expand effective programs. The repayment of the original investment takes place only if the program achieves the expected results. The evaluation of the program is made by an independent agency using predetermined outcomes and performance metrics (Pettus, 2013).

This performance-based contract functions as follows. In the first step, the government decides the social problem to address (criminality, homelessness, child welfare, early childhood education, youth development, etc.). Then, it signs a contractual agreement with an intermediary (Social Impact Bond Issuer). The latter raises capital from investors (institutions or individuals) and donators (foundations or individuals). The intermediary is also responsible for contracting with a nonprofit service provider. In the case the initially stated objectives are achieved (through the appraisal done by a neutral evaluator who is hired to measure the outcomes and resolve possible disputes), then the government repays the investors (Pettus, 2013). According to Helbitz et al. (2016), there have been 60 SIBs launched in 15 countries until June 2016. The first emission was done by the Social Finance UK in 2010 with the target of reducing reoffending. The following countries issued their first SIB in the year indicated between brackets: the US, Australia, Germany, Netherlands (2013); Belgium, Canada (2014) and Portugal, India, Switzerland, Austria, Israel, Finland (2015). In 2016, the UK had more than 30 active programs based on SIBs over ten years. For the same year, the US had more than ten active SIBs channeling over 100 million USD of private capital to solve social challenges (Helbitz et al., 2016).

Therefore, the SIB enables efficient and measurable cooperation between the government, the social sector, philanthropists and the investment community. The SIB could be therefore seen as a mechanism which transfers the risk of social programs from the public sector to investors and donators. The state pays investors only in case of success with clear and measurable deliverables. This mechanism enables the saving of public money and the timely achievement of social targets. Shirazi and Bin Amin (2009) estimate, for a sample of OIC countries, Zaqat proceeds to GDP. They found that it varies between 1% and 7.5%. Assuming that the amount of Zaqat paid by Tunisians individually equals 1% of GDP, it is not unrealistic to assume that issuing SIBs in Tunisia could attract half of this amount or equivalently 0.5% of GDP (approximately 500 million dinars).

### 6.5.3 *Creating a National Solidarity Institution*

I suggest the transformation of the *National Solidarity Fund*, created by the law No 92-122, to an independent public institution (e.g. National Solidarity Institution (NSI)) which is accountable in the same way as the Financial Market Council (Conseil du Marché Financier). This is in line with the announcement made by the chief of the government in July 2017 about the creation of an independent and public structure in charge of the development of the social and solidarity economy. The NSI shall be responsible for developing a national strategy in coordination with the *Ministry of Social Affairs* and the civil society. The NSI shall also play an active role in implementing national programs and initiatives for alleviating the social problems. It could play the role of intermediary in the Social Impact Bonds' governance framework, by enabling the channeling of diverse types of funds (including those channeled through Zaqat and Awqaf) to dedicated social programs.

The NSI shall also play an active role in transposing to the Tunisian context the best practices at the international level in matters of utilization of philanthropic funds. Venture philanthropy, for example, is a new concept which uses tools of venture funding for the promotion of start-ups and risky social ventures.[38]

## References

Abdelhady, H. (2013) "Islamic finance as a mechanism for bolstering food security in the Middle East: Food security WAQF," Sustainable Development Law & Policy, Vol. 13, No. 1, 29–35.

Abdelkafi, R. and M. S. Nabi (2017) "Integrating microfinance and cooperatives for jobs creation in Tunisia," IRTI Policy Paper Series No. PP/2017/02, Jeddah: Islamic Research and Training Institute.

Abdullah, A. K. (2011) "Overcoming the weaknesses in sukūk: Toward risk-sharing instruments in Islamic finance," Islam and Civilisational Renewal, Vol. 2, No. 4.

ADB (2015) "Beyond the MDGs: Technology, finance and statistics to unlock sustainable development in Asia Pacific," News Release, 28 May 2015.

Behr, P. and R. H. Schmidt (2015) "The German banking system: Characteristics and Challenges," White Paper No. 32.

Bensoussan, E., R. Ruparell and L. Taliento (2013) "Innovative development financing," McKinsey.

Besley, T. (1994) "How do market failures justify interventions in rural credit markets?" The World Bank Research Observer, Vol. 9, No. 1, 27–47.

Bradlow, D. (2008) "An experiment in creative financing to promote South African reconciliation and development," in "Africa's finances: The contribution of remittances," Edited by R. Bardouille, M. Ndulo, and M. Grieco, Cambridge Scholars Publishing, 2008.

Chapra, M. U. (1985) "Towards a just monetary system," The Islamic Foundation, Leicester, UK.

Cheng-Han, T., D. W. Puchniak and U. Varottil (2015) "State-owned enterprises in Singapore: Historical insights into a potential model for reform," LAW, National University of Singapore, Working Paper 2015/003.

[38] http://www.socialinnovator.info/ways-supporting-social-innovation/third-sector/mission-related-investment/venture-philanthropy.

Clarke, G., L. C. Xu and H.-F. Zou (2003) "Finance and income inequality: Test of alternative theories," Policy Research Working Paper Series 2984, The World Bank.

Cobanoglu, M. (2016) "Sukuk as an alternative instrument for public finance: The experience of Turkey," https://medium.com/@CASEresearch/sukuk-as-an-alternative-instrument-for-public-finance-the-experience-of-turkey-1878c6247694.

Cœuré, B. (2012) "SME financing – A euro area perspective," speech at the Conference on Small Business Financing, Frankfurt, 13 December 2012.

Cressy, R. (2002) "Funding gaps: A symposium," The Economic Journal, Vol. 112, F1–F16.

De Grauwe, P. (2009) "Lessons from the banking crisis: A return to narrow banking," CESifo DICE Report 2/2009.

FAO (2013) "Tunisie: Financement du secteur agricole," Centre d'investissement de la FAO, Zoom sur les Pays.

Griffith-Jones, S. and K. Sharma (2009) "GDP-Indexed Bonds: Making It Happen," in "Innovative Financing for Development," Edited by S. Ketkar and D. Ratha, The World Bank, ISBN: 978-0-8213-7685-0, 79–98.

Helbitz, A., R. R. Lotan, J. Newman, G. C. Sims, A. Zaroulis (2016) "Social impact bonds: The early years," Social Finance.

Hu, Z. and M. Khan (1997) "Why is China Growing so Fast?" International Monetary Fund, Economic Issues No. 8.

IBM Belgium (2010) "Etude sur le marché de la microfinance en Tunisie: Contexte réglementaire, offre, demande et conditions de développement".

IFAD (2006) "Diaspora Investment in Agriculture (DIA) initiative," Financing Facility for Remittances, www.ifad.org/remittances/pub/dia.pdf.

ILO (2015) "Background note for the panel on "Transition from the informal to the formal economy in Africa: The way forward". AFRM-13-D4-Note-informal-economy".

InfoDev (2013) "Crowdfunding's potential for the developing world," Finance and Private Sector Development Department, World Bank, Washington, DC.

IsDB (2013) "Member country partnership strategy for Tunisia," Country programs Department, Islamic Development Bank Group, June 2013.

Ketkar, S. and D. Ratha (2009a) "Future-flow securitization for development finance," in "Innovative Financing for Development," Edited by S. Ketkar and D. Ratha, The World Bank, ISBN: 978-0-8213-7685-0, 79–98.

Ketkar, S. and D. Ratha (2009b) "Development finance via Diaspora Bonds," in "Innovative Financing for Development," Edited by S. Ketkar and D. Ratha, The World Bank, ISBN: 978-0-8213-7685-0, 79–98.

Khan, M. (1987) "Islamic interest-free banking: A theoretical analysis," in "Theoretical studies in Islamic banking and finance," Edited by Mohsin Khan and Abbas Mirakhor, The Institute of Islamic Studies, 15–36.

KPMG (2017) "Baromètre du Crowdfunding, 2016" Financement Participatif France.

Leigland, J. (2018) "Public-Private Partnerships in developing countries: The emerging evidence-based critique," World Bank Research Observer, Vol. 33, No. 1, February 2018, 103–134.

Lilischkis, S., M. Janssen and F. Barjak (2013) "Policies in support of high-growth innovative enterprises," Revised Draft Final Policy Brief 2, Version 1.6, November 2013.

Meddeb, R. (2013) "Les Sukuks au secours de l'économie tunisienne: mythe ou réalité?" Leaders, opinions, 19 July 2013, http://www.leaders.com.tn/article/11874-les-sukuks-au-secours-de-l-economie-tunisienne-mythe-ou-realite.

Mohieldin et al. (2012) "The role of Islamic finance in enhancing financial inclusion in Organization of Islamic Cooperation (OIC) Countries," Islamic Economic Studies, Vol. 20, No. 2.

Nabi, M. S. (2009) "Financial imperfections, inequality and capital accumulation," Economics Bulletin, Vol. 29, No. 3, 2400–2415.

Nabi, M. S. (2015) "Equity-financing, income inequality and capital accumulation," Economic Modelling, Vol. 46, April 2015, 322–333.

Nabi, M. S. (2016a) "Politique monétaire En Tunisie, Osons un Targeted Quantitative Easing !" 10 November 2016, http://www.investir-en-tunisie.net/fr/index.php/2016/11/10/politique-monetaire-en-tunisie-osons-un-targeted-quantitative-easing/.

Nabi, M. S. (2016b) "Revisiting equity and debt: Access to finance and economic inefficiency," International Review of Economics, December 2016, Vol. 63, No. 4, 393–429.

Pettus, S. (2013) "Social impact bonds," Harvard Magazine, 11–12, July–August 2013.

Pofeldt, E. (2012) "An untapped source of entrepreneurial financing," https://www.forbes.com/sites/elainepofeldt/2012/08/30/an-untapped-source-of-financing-for-job-creation/#36252d4b435e.

Shirazi, N. S. and M. F. Bin Amin (2009) "Providing for the resource shortfall for poverty elimination through potential zakat collection in OIC-member countries: Reappraised," The Pakistan Development Review, Vol. 48, No. 4, 739–754.

Sitorus, D. (2013) "Smart policy: Why Islamic banks matter in Indonesia," CGAP Blog, http://www.cgap.org/blog/smart-policy-why-islamic-banks-matter-indonesia.

Stiglitz, J. E. (2015) "A Greek morality tale," Project Syndicate, 3 February 2015, https://www.project-syndicate.org/commentary/greece-eurozone-austerity-reform-by-joseph-e%2D%2Dstiglitz-2015-02.

Stiglitz, J. E. and H. Rashid (2016) "What's holding back the World economy?" Project Syndicate, 8 February 2016, https://www.project-syndicate.org/commentary/whats-holding-back-the-global-economy-by-joseph-e%2D%2Dstiglitz-and-hamid-rashid-2016-02?barrier=accessreg.

Syed Ali, S., N. S. Shirazi and M. S. Nabi (2013) "Role of Islamic finance for the development of IDB-member countries: A case study of Kyrgyz Republic and Tajikistan," IRTI Occasional Paper No. 14.

Thomson Reuters (2017) "Sukuk perceptions & forecast Study 2017".

Tong, G. C. (2007) "Opening Speech, Singapore International WAQF Conference 2007," Integration of AWQAF (Islamic Endowment) in the Islamic Financial Sector, 6 March 2007.

Tsang, J. C. (2016) "The 2016–17 Budget," Speech on Wednesday 24 February 2016.

UNDP (2006) "Report on the meeting on "GDP-indexed bonds: An idea whose time has come," Washington, DC, 21 April 2006.

Wilson, R. (2004) "Innovation in the structuring of Islamic sukuk securities," Humanomics, Vol. 24, No. 3, 170–181.

World Economic Forum (2012a) "Redefining the emerging market opportunity: Driving growth through financial services innovation".

World Economic Forum (2012b) "The financial development report 2012," http://www.weforum.org/reports/financial-development- report-2012.

CHAPTER 7

# Tunisia's Integration in the Global Economy

## 7.1 Integrating the Global Economy with Method

### *7.1.1 The "Flying Geese" Catching-Up Process and the Industrial Policy*

*What Strategy Shall Tunisia Pursue in Integrating the Global Economy?*
In "Globalization and its discontents," Joseph Stiglitz observes that the most successful developing countries are the Asian ones which opened their economies slowly and gradually. They benefited from globalization to increase their exports, while accompanying the emerging of new economic activities. Hence, trade liberalization shall be conceived and implemented strategically to enable the Tunisian economy to increase its exports markets while enabling the development of high-value-added economic activities.

Tunisia shall inspire from the East Asian "flying geese" model of economic development.[1] In the 1990s, Japan played the role of leader in that model, followed by the New Industrialized countries NIES (Korea, Taiwan, Hong Kong, Singapore) and the ASEAN-4 (Philippines, Thailand,

[1] The flying geese model describes the shifting of industries from more advanced countries to those catching up from behind (Kwan, 2002).



M. S. Nabi, *Making the Tunisian Resurgence*,
https://doi.org/10.1007/978-981-13-3771-0_7

Malaysia, Indonesia) and China. The regional economic dynamism was based on the specialization of each country in exporting according to its comparative advantage. The specialization of a country was not antagonist with upgrading its industrial structure by accumulating capital and technology. The technology transfer was enabled by the progressive relocation of industries, through FDI, from the most advanced economies to the catching-up ones.

Kwan (2002) observes that the catch-up process of China disrupted this sequential specialization in the production of knowledge-intensive goods. He observes that China increased its competitiveness not only in labor-intensive products, but equally in IT and other technology-intensive products. Therefore, it is important for Tunisia to conceive an industrial policy in relation with its current and targeted comparative advantage while cooperating with its international economic partners, which are leaders in the targeted sectors. Partnership with the European Union, and the regional integration and cooperation with Algeria, Morocco, Mauritania and Libya within the Maghreb Regional Integration shall be developed on the basis of selected industrial cooperation.[2] In order to catalyze such regional cooperation, the central banks of these countries shall conceive specific payment mechanisms. Nabi et al. (2015) develop an intra-OIC trade financial support mechanism based on the issuance of Trade-based Special Drawing Rights (T-SDRs) inspired from the SDRs of the IMF. Such a mechanism could be implemented within the Maghreb Union.

Tunisia shall conceive its industrial policy to catalyze a dynamic of exports diversification coupled with accumulation of knowledge and upgrading to higher value-added activities.[3] Fanelli (2014) observes that the rationale for an industrial policy has changed. During the 1970s–1990s, it was commonly acknowledged within the Washington consensus that there is no need for an active industrial policy since government failures were judged worse than market failures. With the beginning of the 2000s the focus has moved to the design of an institutional setting by enabling the coordination between the government and the private sector to target policies and activities. The institutional setting shall enable the state to

[2] It is expected that the recently established Maghreb Bank for Investment and Trade will play an active role in activating the regional cooperation in Maghreb. One of the priority projects that I suggest is to support the creation of a Maghreb Maritime Company.

[3] See Lederman and Maloney (2003) and de Ferranti et al. (2002) for the importance of export diversification in technology transfer and knowledge accumulation.

play its strategic role in accompanying the emergence of a vibrant private sector and the convergence of the economy to a high-income level. This will not be possible without sustained technological and organizational innovations. In this context, the development of clusters in textile, electronics, agrifood, pharmaceutical, IT and IT-based industries shall be considered as one of the priority axes of Tunisia's industrial policy. Clusters offer the framework of fruitful cooperation between companies, universities and financial and state institutions. They are particularly important in developing SMEs, supporting their technological progress, catalyzing synergies to overcome the constraints related to their small size and giving them the opportunity to joint effort when responding to national and international market needs.

### 7.1.2 Facilitating the Integration of SMEs in the Global Value Chains

*What Role Shall SMEs Play in Improving Tunisia's Integration in the Global Economy?*

One of the drivers for a successful integration of Tunisia into the global economy is to improve the participation of its firms in the global production networks or the Global Value Chains (GVCs). The GVCs offer the Tunisian firms new trade opportunities, especially in connection with multinationals from emerging economies. Indeed, it is expected that the latter will become the main anchors of global value chains (ITC, 2014). According to Kowalski et al. (2015), Tunisia could improve its participation in GVC by at least 15% in case of more liberalized trade policies. More importantly, there must be an increase in the intensity of participation through high-value-added activities that would translate into higher export intensity for intermediates goods.[4] As already noted in Chap. 2, Tunisia improved its productive knowledge capabilities. Its average position (out of 120 countries) according to the Economic Complexity Index passed from 63.5 in 2000–2005 to 46 during 2011–2014, positioning the Tunisian economy capabilities near the production space of the Malaysian economy (31.3) and the Turkish economy (42.3). Nevertheless, like many

[4] Kowalski et al. (2015) find that MENA and WCA (Western and Central Africa) have less than 20% of export intensities for intermediate goods, much lower than the approximately 50% across the world.

developing economies, *Tunisia shall rapidly reduce the transaction costs*[5] facing its private sector in order to catalyze the productivity gains and improve its competitiveness on the international markets. These costs include the inefficiency of the administrative processes in general and at the borders in particular, regulations, tariffs and non-tariff barriers, as well as the quality of the transit services, the costs of energy, financial services and telecommunications.

The state shall play a facilitating role by *subsidizing costly procedures for the SMEs*. It could be, for example, in the form of supporting firms in the process of certification and compliance with international standards and technical requirements. It is also important to enable domestic firms to supply goods and services to foreign firms hosted by the national economy. This requires naturally eliminating the barriers between the onshore and offshore sectors within the economy. As noted by Ahn et al. (2011), intermediaries play an important role in facilitating trade. In the case of China, for example, they accounted for around 20% of China's exports in 2005. The Tunisian government shall *encourage the emergence of modern and efficient intermediaries* in order to facilitate the exports of young Tunisian SMEs without exposing them directly to the costly exporting processes. In relation to the ICT services, the access of SMEs to the Internet and social media platforms will allow small businesses to enter global markets, sometimes bypassing local markets (ITC, 2014). The Tunisian government shall therefore *increase the availability of digital technologies for SMEs*.

Another axis of government intervention is the *facilitation of access to trade finance*. The World Bank (2013) notes that 40% of the Tunisian enterprises consider that access to bank financing is a major constraint mainly after the financial crisis of 2008. Given the slow growth, the high trade deficit and the weak diversification of the Tunisian exports, I suggest the development of a credit-facilitating program targeting the exporting enterprises. *Access to trade finance* is an important factor in explaining SMEs' export performance (Jinjarak et al., 2014). A survey conducted by the Asian Development Bank in 2016 covering 337 responding banks from 114 countries estimated the global trade finance gap to be $1.6 tril-

[5]The trade transaction costs constitute the most important obstacle for developing countries to benefit from the opportunities available to them at the international level (Wilson et al., 2003).

lion. It shows that 56% of the SMEs' trade finance proposals are rejected, a rate which is much higher than the rejection rates of large corporate (34%) and multinational firms (10%). More interestingly, the surveyed firms affirm that 25% more trade finance would enable them to hire 20% more people (Di Caprio et al., 2016).[6]

## 7.2 Adopting a Prudent Approach to Capital Account Liberalization

*Is Capital Account Liberalization Beneficial to Developing Countries?*
In the early 1990s, many economists advocated rapid capital account liberalization (CAL) emphasizing its positive effects on the financial sector (Guitián, 1996). At that time, the IMF advised the "big-bang" approach of capital account liberalization while recognizing the necessity of a prior domestic financial liberalization. The financial crises that hit many developing countries[7] consequently to the rapid openness of their capital account reduced the credibility of the "big-bang" approach. By 1999, the IMF's dominant thinking about CAL had become more focused on caution (IMF, 2005). DeLong (1998) acknowledges that CAL enabled some emerging economies to fasten their productivity levels and living standards but blames the free flow of financial capital for causing one major international financial crisis every two years. Panagariya (1998) argues that most of the benefits of capital mobility can be channeled via partial mobility,

[6] During the "*OIC High Level Forum on Trade Facilitation*" organized by the Committee for Economic and Commercial Cooperation (COMCEC) of the OIC in Morocco in February 2013, I distributed with my colleague Abdelkader Chachi a questionnaire in order to identify the most constraining factors to the intra-OIC trade. We distributed the questionnaire to the participants (customs administration (6), Ministry of Trade and public administration (14), Single Window Operator (2)) belonging to 17 countries (from GCC and Arab countries, WCA, South and South East Asia). The top constraining factor that emerged was the "inadequate transport and logistics services" followed by "access to trade finance and export credit or insurance". Therefore, it is not surprising that the 5th OIC Consultative Group Meeting on enhancing intra-OIC trade that took place on the same occasion recommended the establishment of Trade Finance Support Schemes, as one of the driving factors to accelerate the dynamic of the intra-OIC trade.

[7] Among the financial crises that hit middle-income countries during the 1990s one could cite the Mexican crisis of 1994–1995, the Turkish crisis of 1994 and the East Asian crisis of 1997–1998.

targeting equity and FDI. Aizenman et al. (2010) analyze the choices of developing countries with respect to the trilemma (exchange rate flexibility, monetary independence and capital account openness). They find a common trend of convergence toward a "middle ground" with medium levels of capital account openness and monetary independence as well as managed exchange rate flexibility (which requires holding sizable international reserves).[8] Progressively, a wide consensus among economists (e.g. Obstfeld, 2009; Yu, 2008) emerged about the prerequisites and sequencing of the capital account liberalization. It is becoming recognized that the minimal prerequisites for successful financial opening are greater trade account openness, a relatively stable macroeconomic environment, a viable and robust exchange rate arrangement and an effective regulatory framework, especially in relation with banking supervision (Obstfeld, 2009).

### 7.2.1 The Sequencing and Rapidity of Capital Account Liberalization

The sequencing of CAL is important in determining macroeconomic performance. It is now accepted that it should begin with the liberalization of FDI inflows. The second step is the liberalization of portfolio equity inflows taking into account the development level of the domestic financial market. The domestic financial system should be able to develop appropriate strategies to manage the risks arising from increased volatility of interest rates and/or exchange rates which affect not only the financial institutions but also non-financial companies and individual consumers (Gibson et al., 2006). At this stage, a sufficiently deep bond market particularly for government securities shall be developed to enable an efficient sterilization of the financial flows. The next step concerns the liberalization of debt flows. It should begin with long-term debt flows and be followed by short-maturity flows. The following step is the liberalization of capital outflows that shall be realized successively for corporate entities, institutional investors and individuals.

[8] In Nabi and Diop (2011), we show that under an "adjusted" inflation-targeting regime (where the inflation target is adjusted for temporary exchange rate movement) lower capital mobility reduces the volatility of the central bank's primary objective (output or inflation).

*How Rapidly Should these Steps be Fulfilled and What Kind of Optimal Path Should be Followed?*

The advocates of the gradual approach argue that CAL is not an end in itself and should be implemented in parallel or after building up the economic institutions and strengthening the financial markets (Prasad and Rajan, 2008; Kim and Yong, 2008). The empirical studies reveal that for its benefits to be realized, financial openness shall be implemented according to sequenced strategy in the presence of strong external balances and reserve position, and, if necessary, in phase with macroeconomic stabilization reforms (Obstfeld, 2009). Yet, sustainable stability and growth in developing countries require a strong institutional infrastructure. Therefore, these countries are exposed to a difficult trade-off. On the one hand, without external financial liberalization, the process of building strong institutions may take far longer. On the other hand, financial openness within an underdeveloped institutional environment will not materialize its benefits and might even incur costs (Prasad and Rajan, 2008). It is clear that a CAL faster than the rest of the policy reforms exposes a country to a financial crisis driven by sudden shifts in international investor sentiment. Meanwhile, one should be cautious about a too slow gradual approach of CAL (Prasad and Rajan, 2008). Indeed, a gradual approach may be inappropriate if it could create resistance from vested interests or if the existing economic system is so complex that a piecemeal reform generates significant distortions (Prasad, 2009).

### *7.2.2 The Capital Account Liberalization in Tunisia*

*What is the Current Stage of Tunisia in Relation to the Capital Account Liberalization Process, and What Are the Next Steps to Fulfill?*

Since the beginning of the 1990s Tunisia began a process of gradual liberalization of its capital account. Its strategy involved a three-phase approach. The first phase, which is almost completed, involves removing all restrictions on FDI by nonresidents and allowing nonresident investment in local currency financial securities. It is expected that the second phase will concern liberalizing outward FDI and portfolio investment in foreign markets by domestic institutional investors. The third and final phase concerns the full currency convertibility in parallel with the liberalization of domestic portfolio investment abroad and loans by residents to nonresidents. It is clear that the current situation of the Tunisian economy is not opportune for progressing further in the capital account liberalization strategy. Indeed, Tunisia should stabilize its macroeconomic fundamentals and accelerate the required structural reforms, modernize its financial sector and strengthen the financial soundness of its banking system, adopt a new monetary policy framework (inflation targeting), reduce the level of external indebtedness and reach a strong balance-of-payments position.[9]

## References

Ahn, J., A. K. Khandelwal and S.-J. Wei (2011) "The role of intermediaries in facilitating trade," Journal of International Economics, Elsevier, Vol. 84, No. 1, 73–85.

Aizenman, J., M. Chinn and H. Ito (2010) "The Financial crisis, rethinking of the global financial architecture, and the trilemma," ADBI Working Papers 213, Asian Development Bank Institute.

De Ferranti, D., G. E. Perry, D. Lederman and W. E. Maloney (2002) "From natural resources to the knowledge economy: Trade and job quality," World Bank Publications, The World Bank, number 14040, October.

DeLong, J.-B. (1998) "What's wrong with our bloody economies?" Los Angeles Times, 1998.

Di Caprio, A., S. Beck, Y. Yao and F. Khan (2016) "2016 trade finance gaps, growth, and jobs survey," ADB briefs No. 64, August 2016.

Fanelli, A. (2014) "Competitiveness and Structural Change," OCDE.

Gibson, H. D., N. T. Tsaveas and T. Vlassopoulos (2006) "Capital flows, capital account liberalization and the Mediterranean countries," Working Papers 33, Bank of Greece.

Guitián, M. (1996) "The Issue of Capital Account Convertibility: A Gap Between Norms and Reality," in "Currency Convertibility in the Middle East and North Africa," Edited by Saleh M. Nsouli and Manuel Guitián, IMF, Washington.

IMF (2005) "The IMF's approach to capital account liberalization," Evaluation Report, IMF, Washington, DC.

Ishii, S., K.-F. Habermeier and J.-I. Canales-Kriljenko (2002) "Capital account liberalization and financial sector stability," Occasional paper (International Monetary Fund), 211, International Monetary Fund, Washington, DC.

ITC (2014) "50 Years of unlocking SME competitiveness: Lessons for the future," International Trade Centre, Geneva.

[9] Ishii et al. (2002) argue that the CAL shall be part of an "integrated" approach including economic reforms and financial system-strengthening policies, taking into account the potential risks affecting financial and macroeconomic stability.

Jinjarak, Y., P. J. Mutuc and G. Wignaraja (2014) "Does finance really matter for the participation of SMEs in international trade? Evidence from 8,080 East Asian Firms," ADBI Working Paper Series, No. 470, March 2014.

Kim, S. and Y.-D. Yong (2008) "The impact of capital inflows on emerging East Asian economies: Is too much money chasing too little good?" Working Papers on Regional Economic Integration 15, Asian Development Bank.

Kowalski, P., J. Lopez Gonzalez, A. Ragoussis and C. Ugarte (2015) "The Participation of developing countries in Global Value Chains: Implications for trade and trade-related policies," OECD Trade Policy Paper No. 179.

Kwan, C. H. (2002) "The rise of China and Asia's Flying-Geese pattern of economic development: An empirical analysis based on US import statistics," NRI Papers, No. 52.

Lederman, D. and W. Maloney (2003) "Trade structure and growth," Policy Research Working Paper Series 3025, The World Bank.

Nabi, M. S. and N. Diop (2011) "Capital mobility and the optimal monetary policy rule: A Tunisian case study," in "Inflation targeting in MENA Countries," Edited by David Cobham and Mongi Boughzala, Palgrave Macmillan, August.

Nabi, M. S., R. Abdelkafi, I. Drine and S. Al-Suwailem (2015) "Enhancing Intra-Trade in OIC member countries through T-SDRs," Islamic Economic Studies, Vol. 23, No. 1, 101–124.

Obstfeld, M. (2009) "International finance and growth in developing countries: What have we learned?" NBER Working Papers 14691, National Bureau of Economic Research, Inc.

Panagariya, A. (1998) "Full convertibility: Must we have it?" The Economic Times, 26 October.

Prasad, E. (2009) "India's approach to capital account liberalization," IZA Discussion Papers 3927, Institute for the Study of Labor (IZA).

Prasad, E. and R. G. Rajan (2008) "A pragmatic approach to capital account liberalization," IZA Discussion Papers 3475, Institute for the Study of Labor (IZA).

Wilson, J. S., C. L. Mann and T. Otsuki (2003) "Trade facilitation and economic development: New approach to quantifying the impact," The World Bank Economic Review, Vol. 17, No. 13, 367–389.

World Bank (2013) "Projet de développement de la compétitivité et des exportations: Document d'information du projet (Pid) phase d'évaluation," Report N° 78503.

Yu, Y. (2008) "Managing capital flows: The case of the People's Republic of China," Finance Working Papers 2008.10, East Asian Bureau of Economic Research.

CHAPTER 8

# Moving Toward a Knowledge-Based Economy

## 8.1 Knowledge Management by a "Creative State"

*What role shall the Tunisian state play in knowledge management in order to transform Tunisia into a knowledge-based economy?*

Tunisia's development strategy shall set as its vision to be "*a knowledge-based economy*" by 2030. In this regard, the state has to play an active role in concretizing this vision. It shall catalyze the drivers of a deep socioeconomic transformation placing knowledge and innovation at the heart of the society. Such a transformation cannot be led by the private sector and markets solely. There is a room for intensive public investment to build the required ecosystem (institutions, incentives, infrastructure, national programs, etc.) I noted in Chap. 2, when diagnosing the Tunisian economy, that the country improved its productive knowledge capabilities passing from an average position of 63.5 in 2000–2005 to 46 out of 120 countries during 2011–2014.[1] However, the economy is still far from the technological frontier. Indeed, Tunisia has the potential to become a regional champion in innovation and entrepreneurship if it empowers its young aspiring businesswomen and businessmen (World Bank, 2014).

In order for the country to unleash its technological potential, the state has to play a critical role in spurring innovation by creating and shaping new markets. Indeed, as noted by Mazzucato (2016) the state has played

[1] According to Hausmann et al.'s (2014) ranking.



M. S. Nabi, *Making the Tunisian Resurgence*,
https://doi.org/10.1007/978-981-13-3771-0_8

a key entrepreneurial role in the world's most famous innovation hubs. It has designed and financed the creation of several new fields (ICT, biotech, nanotech and green tech). She recalls the central role played by public investment in the emergence of many high-tech innovations (the Internet, Global Positioning System (GPS), touch screens and the advances in voice recognition underlying Siri) and currently in the green technology. These successful experiences suggest that the Tunisian state shall be creative in the above-described manner. It shall build a prospective vision about the necessary public investments to drive future economic growth by betting on diversified innovative choices.

The speed of transforming Tunisia into a knowledge-based economy will depend on the effectiveness of the state's strategy in positioning knowledge at the core of the socioeconomic dynamic of Tunisia. It is expected that a successful transformation will pass through an intermediary stage focusing on improving the efficiency of the existing production system (mainly in the low knowledge-intensive sectors) while promoting the existing knowledge-based companies and encouraging the emergence of innovative ones in various sectors. Tunisia shall focus on promoting innovation capital in priority sectors like renewable energy, desalination of water and agriculture, in addition to traditional sectors (e.g. agri-food, pharmaceuticals, ICT, textile, mechanics and electronics). Given its scarce financial resources, the state shall encourage partnerships with international companies endowed with technology know-how and benefiting from wide access to Global Value Chains.

The active role of the state also requires the engineering of new financial mechanisms in order to support public investment in high-risk innovation. Mazzucato (2016) suggests the creation of a public innovation fund for the management of profits and losses, which are inherent to the risky investment in new technologies. She argues that creating such a fund could overcome the shortcomings of the current public financing mechanism which socializes the risks and privatizes the rewards.[2] Other financial mechanisms (like PPP) were suggested in Chap. 6.

[2] Inspired by this idea, I suggested in the context of an advisory mission for the Tunisian Ministry of ICT the creation of an R&D national fund financed by the telecom operators to finance R&D projects conducted by joint research teams from Tunisian engineering schools and the telecom operators.

## 8.2 What Are the Drivers of a Knowledge Economy?

The creation of wealth is a complex process requiring the conjunction of a multitude of factors: physical capital (K), labor (L), human capital (H), knowledge, R&D, organizational aspects of the production and marketing processes, networks and so on. Economists often reduce this complexity, especially when explaining economic growth by focusing on the accumulation of the production factors (K, L and H) and improving the total factor productivity (TFP). The growth of the TFP, which encompasses all the residual factors, results from the technological progress and/or higher productive efficiency.[3]

In recent years, digital capital is identified as an additional important driver of economic growth. Digital capital includes three dimensions: (1) ICT infrastructure (servers, routers, online-purchasing platforms and basic Internet software); (2) digital data and databases, R&D and intellectual propriety rights and (3) digital technical skills (Dimick, 2014). The first dimension includes tangible assets, whereas the two other dimensions consist of intangible digital assets. A recent estimation by Accenture (2016) shows that digital capital is the source of approximately one-third of global GDP growth, with two-thirds contribution from intangible assets and one-third from tangible assets.[4] The study adopts a larger definition of digital GDP going beyond measuring technology infrastructure, IT and communications sector, e-commerce and broadband penetration rates. Instead, it includes in the calculation of the digital GDP, how digital capital is adding value to the entire economic activities taking into account the use of digital skills, equipment and intermediate goods and services in the production of all goods and services.

[3] The technological progress pushes the production frontier upward and widens the set of production possibilities. However, higher productive efficiency occurs when the economy improves the way it uses the available resources, reducing waste and adopting (through learning and knowledge dissemination and absorption) the best available management practices and technologies.

[4] The study shows that digital capital is generating economic growth through accelerated impact on labor productivity in addition to the channel of capital deepening. It observes that the time lag that characterized the positive impact of digital capital on labor productivity is about 15 years. This time lag is shorter than the 80 years of steam engines, the 40 years of electricity and the 20 years of conventional ICT.

Therefore, it is clear that digital capital is becoming an important driver of economic growth in developed countries. McKinsey (2014) notes that the digital GDP of France increased by 5% annually during the period 2010–2013. Meanwhile, the global GDP increased with only 2% on average per year. It also observes that the average annual investment in digital capital is about 3% of GDP in the 40 most advanced countries. The investments in digital intangible assets are twice higher than those of tangible assets. Bughin and Manyika (2013) note that intangible digital capital is an important driver of innovation accounting for around 60% of innovation capital, alongside human capital[5] (24%) and tangible digital capital (16%). Hence, it is clear that for a developing country like Tunisia aiming to catch up with the developed countries, the only way is to speed up the accumulation of the innovation capital. The role of the state is crucial in activating the dynamic of innovation-capital accumulation. It is particularly important to develop an ICT-based strategy for the country in order to accelerate the accumulation of digital and innovation capitals.

## 8.3 Adopting an ICT-Based Strategy for Digital Capital Accumulation

Many countries have already developed their national ICT strategy. The Singaporean journey toward a Smart Nation is based on the development of capabilities in infrastructure, ICT and ICT-based industry and talents, as well as governance. IDA Singapore (2015) argues that Singapore is building the world's first Smart Nation aiming to improve the quality of life for individuals and enterprises. In order to serve and anticipate their needs, the government is moving to an anticipatory approach expanding the use of technologies to live, work and play. This approach is enabled through an agile process for building a Smart Nation Platform anchored around connectivity, data collection and efficient sharing and production of relevant insights.

The successive Tunisian governments have been aware of the importance to improve the contribution of digital capital to the economy. The ICT has been considered as an important catalyst of an inclusive economic growth progressively based on higher value-added economic activities.

[5] Including investments in tertiary Science, Technology, Engineering and Mathematics (STEM) education and training programs.

Digital Tunisia was launched in 2014 as a participatory roadmap toward a national plan aiming to make Tunisia an international place of digital technologies, and to develop the ICT sector as a driver of socioeconomic development. *Smart Tunisia*, the leading national program in the form of a PPP, is part of this plan.[6] The vision for Tunisia channeled through Smart Tunisia 2020 is "to become an international digital reference and make the ICT an important driver of socioeconomic development". The "e-transform Tunisia" reflects the vision of the public authorities about the role of ICT in transforming the Tunisian economy. It aims to improve the competitiveness of the enterprises in all sectors through investing in ICT and promoting the creation of ICT-based activities. In order to materialize these objectives, the country is preparing, through the *Tunisian Ministry of ICT and Digital Economy*, the Digital Code which encompasses many pillars. I had the occasion to motivate the importance to embed in the digital code principles and values as well as institutional mechanisms guaranteeing its sustainability and smooth evolution.[7] In cooperation with other colleagues, I identified the following axis within the socioeconomic pillars: (1) enabling ICT as cross-cutting enablers of sustainable development; (2) E-literacy, capacity building and R&D; (3) investment and entrepreneurship; (4) infrastructure, universal service and digital divide and (5) labor market and specific empowerment mechanisms.[8]

After analyzing the ninth and tenth pillars of "The Global Information Technology Report (GITR) 2016: Innovating in the Digital Economy", I suggested additional recommendations to include into the Tunisian Digital code. In relation to the item "PCT ICT patent applications", I recommended that the Tunisian authorities encourage and subsidize the application to patents at the international level. In relation to the "Impact of ICT on access to basic services" (e.g. health, education, financial services), I suggested conceiving specific coordination mechanisms between the various ministries and the telecom operators in order to generate such impacts. For

[6] Endowed with a budget of 500 million euros, its ambition is to create 50,000 jobs in five years in the areas of off-shoring, near-shoring and colocation. In June 2017, 30 off-shoring companies have already adhered to the program and planned to hire 3000 university graduates over a five-year period.

[7] I have had the opportunity to contribute to the development of the socioeconomic pillars of the digital code on the occasion of an advisory mission.

[8] Approximately 100 measures were suggested within those axes. I will not detail them here and invite the reader to consult the digital code of Tunisia.

example, it would be beneficial to develop a national foundation to fund innovative projects targeting access to health services in the rural regions. For the "Internet access in schools", it is important to set as objective the connectivity of all Tunisian public schools to the Internet by the year 2025 and the launching of a national initiative encouraging the development of pedagogical applications based on the national education curriculum.

In order to enhance "ICT use and government efficiency", it is important to fix as objective the facilitation of all the bureaucracy processes according to a five-year roadmap detailing the engagement of the various stakeholders. It is also important to improve the ranking of Tunisia in relation to the "e-Participation Index", which measures the quality, relevance and usefulness of government websites in providing online information and participatory tools and services to their citizens. To that end, I suggested the creation of an independent agency in charge of supervising and monitoring the digitalization of the administrative procedures and the measurement of the citizens' satisfaction using a quarterly barometer ranking the various administrative services as well as the services provided online through their websites. Applying a Total Quality Management approach, favoring competition and setting incentives for the public administrations and agencies will be very helpful in that regard.

In the study "Tunisia in transformation: The Digital Imperative" (IACE, 2016), conducted in cooperation with other colleagues, we recommended (1) providing financial, tax and technical incentives to support the digital transformation of the enterprises; (2) reinforcing the connection of the enterprises to their ecosystem and facilitating the mobility of the employees within the private sector and to the public sector (in order to generate positive externalities related to the dissemination of intangible digital skills); (3) creating an "ICT Academy" to build the digital skills of the employees in the private and public sectors; (4) adjusting the labor regulation in order to take into account the impact of digitalization on the status of employees and their relationship with the employers; (5) guaranteeing the security of the e-contracts and setting a framework ensuring digital trust; (6) defining the responsibilities of the various stakeholders on the cyberspace in relation to the privacy of private information; (7) conceiving an adequate institutional regulation of the cyberspace through independent regulators guaranteeing freedom and fairness of the competition as well as trust of the public, and ethics of the practitioners in various sectors, and (8) enforcing the intellectual property rights in general, and those related to the illicit utilization of databases and software in particular.

## 8.4 Improving the Ecosystem of Education, Innovation and Research

As noted when diagnosing the Tunisian economy (Chap. 2), improving the quality of education shall be one of the country's top priorities. I think that the reform of the public education institutions shall be governed by the same principles as the reform of the public sector in general: adopting modern mechanisms of governance including the right incentives and accountability mechanisms. The ministries in charge of education and research shall develop a governance framework embedding the adequate mechanisms to improve efficiency and performance of schools and institutions.[9] It shall also develop financial mechanisms that enable channeling/raising funds to/by schools and higher education and research institutions according to their performance and efficiency scores.

The assessment methodology of the schoolchild, the college students and the university students shall be modernized encouraging team working, critical thinking and creativity as well as openness to the multidimensional aspects of science and humanities. Students shall no more be obliged to memorize lessons but to observe, identify, learn to conceptualize problems, imagine and look for creative solutions, be challenged and improve their learning abilities progressively. Updating the pedagogical methods is crucial to endow the students with dynamism. Phelps (2014) notes that young people shall be exposed to literature, philosophy and history to catalyze their creativity and innovative contribution to society. He particularly advocates reviving the relationship of individuals with humanities to help them achieve fulfilling and productive lives.[10] Moreover, he argues that the lack of innovation spirit nowadays is due to insufficient development of soft skills including the ability to think imaginatively, develop creative solutions to complex challenges and adjust to the changing environment. The innovation spirit and the dynamism of the Tunisian population would benefit from attracting and partnering with the Tunisian

[9] Including but not limited to a nation-wide ranking in order to increase competition and improve the quality of education, research as well as the connection with the socioeconomic environment.

[10] He recalls the importance of the population's dynamism (desire, capacity and latitude to create) in catalyzing innovation in the UK and the US in the beginning of the 1800s and in Germany and France later in the nineteenth century.

brilliant brains shining across the globe and encouraging the dissemination of their know-how.

The relatively good performance of Tunisia in scientific research[11] is tempered by the inefficiency of Tunisia in terms of innovation due to the lack of an adequate and modern ecosystem that favors innovation and university/industry collaboration. Despite the multiple agencies and national programs to promote innovation, the economic sectors are not knowledge-related and ties with universities and research centers are rare. In October 2017, the *Ministry of Higher Education and Research* published a guide of the priorities, futures trends and initiatives in research for the period 2017–2022. It identifies six priorities on a broad research axis: (1) energy, water and food security; (2) education, culture and youth; (3) health; (4) digitalization and industry 4.0; (5) governance and decentralization and (6) circular economy. This guide has also briefly described the principles of a new governance framework announcing the creation of an *Instance of Scientific Research and Innovation* in charge of the coordination between the multiple stakeholders and developing modern governance mechanism. It seems a first good step that shall be materialized on the ground rapidly. However, Tunisia has not yet developed a clear research and innovation strategy and the existing system is fragmented and poorly governed. The report of Whiteshield Partners (2012) identifies this coordination failure between the private sector, the researchers and the research centers in Tunisia. It recommends stronger alignment between public R&D and private sector demand through efficient clusters and technological parks. It also calls for the establishment of solid intellectual property protection rights and enforcement as well as a functional financial support system to boost innovation.

The poor governance of the innovation system and its fragmentation are common issues in developing countries where most of the innovation initiatives are hi-tech oriented without an impact on the poor and the marginalized (Brito, 2013). In line with Brito's (2013) recommendations for developing countries, Tunisia's innovation policy shall be focused on the sustainable development axis targeting food security, energy access,[12]

[11] Particularly, in regard to the ratio of citable scientific documents per habitant as well as by the citations per document and the h-index (for more details see Chap. 2).

[12] Among the innovation axes recommended by Natarajan (2013) for India, clean energy (in particular solar energy) that can respond to the increasing demand of global energy is

water, job creation and poverty reduction.[13] Tunisian policy makers shall elaborate a more focused national innovation policy to promote social inclusion, generate job opportunities for the youth while improving the technological capital of the country in order to boost economic growth and improve competitiveness. Contrary to the existing systems, Brito (2013) notes that a pro-poor innovation system shall be based on a social learning process encompassing multi-stakeholders, generating new knowledge, putting it to use and expanding the capabilities and opportunities of the poor.

There are positive but insufficient signals revealing the emergence of technological venture capital firms in Tunisia. The state shall encourage the development of such financial firms to promote innovations that fulfill the national innovation agenda. It is also important to encourage academic entrepreneurship by enabling academicians to launch their innovative start-ups to be hosted by dedicated incubators in their universities and research centers. Garcia-Martinez (2014) notes that many universities across the world are supporting academic entrepreneurs through ad hoc courses and access to technology transfer offices, business incubators and innovation parks. The current law does not enable Tunisian academicians to undertake an entrepreneurial activity in parallel to their scientific and education activities. It is a paradoxical constraint as the Tunisian university suffers from disconnection with its socioeconomic environment. Meanwhile, its main actors, who are the academicians, are not sufficiently incentivized to develop such enabling activity. In addition to the encouragement of registering patents at the international level, it is important to enable academicians who want to transform their scientific research potential into marketable product, software or service. Enabling academicians to develop their start-ups within dedicated incubators in their universities would favor the emergent dynamism of start-ups in Tunisia.[14]

expected to rise by over 36% in the period up to 2030. He notes the importance of setting a strong connect between industry and academia as well as the launching of government initiatives in addition to improving India's climate.

[13] In this regard, Brito (2013) emphasizes the importance of capacity building in Genomics and Bioinformatics to improve food and agriculture productivity and quality of health care, increase income and reduce poverty. She also motivates the importance of using mathematical models and simulations to generate solid recommendations to policy makers.

[14] See Moreau (2016) for a description of the emergent dynamism of start-ups in Tunisia.

## 8.5 Benefiting from the Global Opportunities in the IT-Enabled Services and Data Science Fields

In developing countries like India, China, Mexico and the Philippines, as well as in developed one like Canada and Ireland, the industries of IT and IT-enabled services (ITES) are very dynamic. They are creating jobs, contributing to raising incomes and increasing exports and GDP.[15] Others countries from Central and Eastern Europe (like the Czech Republic, Hungary, Poland, Romania and the Russian Federation) are trying to catch up by developing their capacities in these industries (Sudan et al., 2010). Salela (2010) notes that the demand for Business Process Outsourcing (BPO) outpaced the demand for IT services in recent years. As a consequence, the revenues generated by the BPO services increased globally by 9% per year between 2004 and 2014 for only 7% for the IT services.[16] Salela (2010) recalls that BPO is considered a priority sector in South Africa since 2003, when the government identified the potential of this sector to create up to 100,000 jobs by the end of the seventh year. In order to exploit that opportunity, it was necessary for South Africa to quickly overcome the impeding constraints, namely its high costs relative to other BPO destinations, the insufficient skills and the lack of investors' support and marketing.

Tunisia has a huge economic growth potential if it can make ICT a driver of transformation of its economic system and benefit from the global opportunities in the IT-enabled services (ITES). For this to materialize it shall improve many dimensions of the ICT sector ecosystem. In particular, Tunisia shall not only support the developing of digital skills but also focus on the data science arena to satisfy the national demand and to tap into the rising global demand for that profile of experts. Natarajan (2013) notes that, until 2013, almost 90% of the world's data was created between 2011 and 2012. McKinsey (2016) recalls that demand for data scientists will continue to outstrip supply despite the increasing offers by universities of data science courses and training programs. The report esti-

[15] Sudan et al. (2010) note that the IT services and ITES industries are directly employing 2.3 million people in India, paying them 50–100% more than comparable industries. The authors recall the important spillover effects. Each new job in IT and ITES has led to the creation of three to four new jobs in other sectors in India.

[16] Considering the offshore activities, the difference between the growth rates becomes wider, with 25% for the BPO offshore and 18% for the IT services.

mates the potential shortfall of data scientists by approximately 250,000. This estimation is supported by the growth projection of graduates from data science programs by 7% per year, much lower than the high-case projection scenario of demand growth by 12% annually. The report notes also the importance of the business translator profile who interfaces between the data scientist and the practitioner in the organization. McKinsey (2016) estimates the demand for business translators between two million and four million in the US alone over the next decade.

Tunisia shall inspire from the rapid move of India that has developed a vibrant ecosystem and launched many governmental initiatives putting it at a favorable position to lead innovation in the big data arena.[17]

## 8.6 Accelerating the Digitalization of the Economy

Sachs (2015) emphasizes the importance for governments to benefit from the digital revolution to improve the quality of public services, fight corruption, free the economy and ensure equal access to the economic opportunities. Symmetrically, the accountability of governments and businesses becomes easier through modern information systems that publicly highlight the problems and their origins (Sachs, 2015). ADB et al. (2015) note the importance of evidence-based policymaking, noting that Asian and Pacific countries need to extend the benefits of technology to all citizens, to mobilize the necessary financial resources and to build statistical systems that can monitor the progress of the poorest groups in order to insure inclusive growth and the achievement of the Sustainable Development Goals.

In the Tunisian case, it is expected that the e-government program led by the Ministry of ICT and digital economy will encompass these modernization axes. The new technologies coupled with effective mechanisms of open governance shall enable the positive disruption of the public sector in Tunisia. This requires continuous measurement of the public services quality through multiple channels including the satisfaction of

[17] Natarajan (2013) cites Aadhar, the world's biggest big data experiment and the 'Right to Information Act' providing transparency in governance and performance. He also notes the presence of top big companies in India including hardware and software, and the top ten most funded Big Data start-ups.

citizens throughout the country. It also requires rewarding performance and setting incentives through modern management mechanisms. However, Tunisia has to develop the ICT infrastructure to fully benefit from the ICT as a driver of its digital transformation.[18]

The state shall encourage Tunisian firms to improve their competitiveness through digitalization by adapting their business models, adjusting their organizational structure, investing in digital skills and unleashing their innovation potential. In the IACE's (2016) report, we identified the main obstacles facing the digitalization of the Tunisian firms. The inexistence of an integrated digitalization strategy and the lack of digital skills constitute the main obstacles. Besides, digitalization is costly as the progress of one unit on a scale of 10 (corresponding to full digitalization) represents 6.25% of the turnover. Our estimations show that progress in digitalizing the Tunisian firms by one unit on a scale of 10 generates a potential growth of GDP (at constant price) varying from 1.63% to 2.09%. A strategy of full digitalization of the Tunisian firms over the period 2017–2024 would provide an additional GDP of at least 20,370.6 million dinars over the period 2018–2021 or equivalently 1.57 points of additional annual GDP growth.

## References

Accenture (2016) "Digital disruption: The growth multiplier" prepared by M. Knickrehm, Berthon and P. Daugherty, Accenture.

ADB, ESCAP and UNDP (2015) "Making it happen: Technology, finance and statistics for sustainable development in Asia and the Pacific," Asian Development Bank, May 2015.

Brito, L. (2013) "Innovation, science & technology: Drivers for sustainable development?" Presented on the occasion of the International Conference on Entrepreneurship and Innovation: Making Things Work Better Dubrovnik, Croatia, 23 May 2013.

[18] McKinsey (2010) classifies Tunisia among an intermediary group (Group 2) in terms of maturity of the telecommunication services. This group comprises transition economies with high mobile penetration. The report recommends public policies that increase the broadband penetration by encouraging investment in fixed networks and setting financial and regulatory incentives. In the Tunisian case, the financial incentives shall also be tailored to reduce the geographical digital divide in terms of the ICT infrastructure.

Bughin, J. and J. Manyika (2013) "Measuring the full impact of digital capital," McKinsey, July 2013.

Dimick, S. (2014) "Adopting digital technologies: The path for SMEs," Ottawa: The Conference Board of Canada.

Garcia-Martinez, J. (2014) "The third way: Becoming an academic entrepreneur," www.sciencemag.org, 20 March 2014.

Hausmann, R., C. A. Hidalgo, S. Bustos, M. Coscia, A. Simoes and M. A. Yildirim (2014) "The Atlas of Economic Complexity: Mapping Paths to Prosperity," MIT Press.

IACE (2016) "La Tunisie en Transformation: L'impératif digital," www.iace.tn.

IDA Singapore (2015) "Smart nation platform," Media Factsheet, Annex A, April 2015.

Mazzucato, M. (2016) "The Creative state," Project Syndicate, 16 April 2015.

McKinsey (2010) "How to compete and grow: A sector guide to policy," The McKinsey Global Institute.

McKinsey (2014) "Accélérer la mutation numérique des entreprises: un gisement de croissance et de compétitivité pour la France," September 2014.

McKinsey (2016) "The age of analytics: Competing in a Data-driven World," McKinsey Global Institute, December 2016.

Moreau, M. (2016) "Tunisia is becoming MENA's next Startup hub," 11 February 2016, www.techcrunch.com.

Natarajan, P. (2013) "Unlocking India's innovation potential," The Times of India, 31 August 2013.

Phelps, E. (2014) "Why teaching humanities improves innovation," Project Syndicates, Edmund S. Phelps, 4 September 2014.

Sachs, J. D. (2015) "Data for development," Project Syndicate, 6 May 2015.

Salela, P. (2010) "Building an ITeS country programme: Lessons from South Africa," A presentation during the World Bank Institute Training, "Financial and ICT/A Training of Trainers and Executive Course for MENA Countries," Vienna Joint Institute, 28 June–2 July 2010.

Sudan, R., S. Ayers, P. Dongier, A. Muente-Kunigami and C. Zhen-Wei Qiang (2010) "The global opportunity in IT-based services," World Bank.

Whiteshield Partners (2012) "Knowledge economy assessment of Tunisia: Identifying and addressing capability and innovation gaps in the Southern and Eastern Mediterranean region (SEMED)".

World Bank (2014) "Tunisia: Breaking the barriers to youth inclusion," World Bank, Report No. 89233-TN.

CHAPTER 9

# Appendix: Aspects from the History of Tunisia

## 9.1 Some Aspects from Tunisia's Contribution to Human Civilization

Tunisia occupies an area of 163,610 km$^2$ on the Mediterranean coast of North Africa with 1300 km of coastline. Its population increased from 3.605 million in 1950 to 11.254 million in 2015 (United Nations, 2015). The Sahara Desert constitutes around 40% of the country and the rest of the territory is fertile soil. It has 965 km of frontier with Algeria in the west and 459 km of south-eastern border with Libya (Fig. 9.1). The official language is Arabic and Islam is the religion of the quasi-totality of Tunisians.

### 9.1.1 *The Carthaginian Tunisia and Hannibal*

Tunisia was across history at the crossroads of many civilizations. The city of *Carthage* was the capital of a large empire which dominated the East Mediterranean trade by the end of the sixth century BC. The classical texts redeem its settlement in 814 BC to the Phoenician Queen *Elissa* (*Dido*) who was ousted from power in Tyre (in Lebanon) (Fantar, 1998). After losing the two Punic wars against Rome (264–241 BC and 218–201 BC), Carthage became the Africa Province (*Ifriqiyya*) or the bread basket of the Roman Empire. Following the second Punic war, Carthage was characterized by steep economic growth and increased



M. S. Nabi, *Making the Tunisian Resurgence*,
https://doi.org/10.1007/978-981-13-3771-0_9

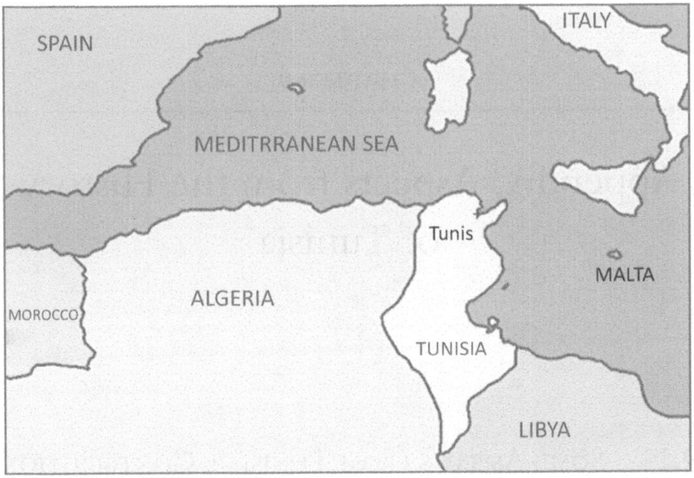


**Fig. 9.1** Geographic position of Tunisia

wealth (Bonde, n.d.).[1] It was famous for its seaport and was endowed with a well-governed state. Aristotle noted in his *Polities* that stability, absence of serious civil troubles and tyrants in Carthage were the result of its constitution (Newman, 2010). In 146 BC, Carthage was conquered, destroyed and rebuilt by the Romans. The vandals captured the city in 439 and held it until it became part of the Byzantine empire in 534. The warrior *Hannibal Barca* (247 BC–183 BC) who was given the command of the Carthaginian army at the age of 26 is one of the famous military strategists in history.[2] As a Statesman, Hannibal instituted elections for military judges and limited the terms of office from life to two years.

### *9.1.2 Some Prominent Tunisian Figures During the Golden Age of the Muslim World*

The Battle of *Carthage* of 698 marked the rising of the Islamic Empire over the Byzantine Empire despite the subsequent combats by the native Berbers (led by *Kusalah* and the female leader *Kahina*). In 670, *Oqba Ibn*

[1] "*Carthage was indeed destroyed*" accessed on www.media-progress.net.

[2] Hannibal is particularly known for leading an army (more than 100,000 troops) and nearly 40 war elephants through the Pyrenees toward Gaul (southern France) and sweeping across southern Europe and through the Alps Mountains. Carthage was able to inflict heavy losses on the Roman army in the battles of Trebbia, Trasimene and Cannae.

*Nafii* founded the city of *Al Qayrawan* (today *Kairouan* situated approximately 160 km south of modern Tunis), which emerged as the third most important center for Sunni Islamic scholarship after *Mecca* and *Medina*. During the *Aghlabid* dynasty (800–909) the *Great Mosque* (*Oqba Ibn Nafii*) was a center of knowledge not only in Islamic thought but also in secular sciences (Knapp and Barbour, 1977, 404).[3] One of *Qayrawan*'s influential physicians was *Ibn al-Jazzār* (895–979), who wrote a medical encyclopedia in seven volumes titled *Zād al-musafir wa-qut al-hadir* (Provisions for the Traveler and Nourishment for the Sedentary). This therapeutic guide was very influential in Europe where several medieval translations were produced. Many of his books were recently edited and translated into English (US National Library of Medicine).

The *Aghlabid* dynasty was granted a relative independence by the fifth Abbasid Caliph *Harun al-Rashid*. The *Abbasid* "*functioned autonomously, amassing wealth through the exploitation of trans-Saharan trade*" (Kreutz, 1996, 48).[4] The Aghlabid Basins in the city of *Kairouan* witnessed the ingenuity and the technical expertise at the time. These hydraulic installations, considered to have been the largest during the Middle Ages, have impressive dimensions. They were part of an ingenious system of drainage, established 60 years or so after the establishment of the city, in order to face the scarcity of water supply due to the semi-arid climate. This system enabled the collection and transport of rainwater and the overflow of the tributaries of the neighboring Merguellil River (Benhamida, 2015). The Aghlabid paid great attention to the fleet, developed the naval base of Tunis and planned to acquire Sicily (UNESCO, 2001). In 831, its capital Palermo fell, and Sicily passed in 909 under the control of the Fatimid dynasty (909–1171) (as Ifriqiya itself) until the Norman Conquest in 1061–1091. It is considered that Sicily played during that time a bridge of knowledge transmission to the Occident, as it was the case for Andalusia in Spain. In particular, Salerno had been, from the early Middle Ages onward, a center of medical study, from where Greco-Arabic knowledge was transmitted to the West (Houben, 2002).[5] Further dynasties

[3] Henri Saladin (1908, 118) compares its role to the one played by the University of Paris in the Middle Ages.

[4] Trade played a key role in the development and technological progress of the Muslim World during the golden age (eighth to thirteenth centuries) (Findlay and O'Rourke, 2007).

[5] Even under the Normans, many Muslim scholars continued their scientific activities. The geography expert Mohamed al-Idrissi drew for Roger II (1130–1154) the map of the world and wrote the book Nuzhat al-Mushtaq fi ikhtiraq al-afaq (the journey of those aspiring to penetrate the horizons) to describe it. It seems that Al-Idrissi was preferred by Roger II to all

(Almohad, 1171–1229; Hafsid, 1229–1573) ruled Tunisia until the sixteenth century.

Starting from 1204, Tunis became the capital of *Ifriqiya* under *Almohad* and *Hafsid* rule. This shift from *Kairouan* to *Tunis* improved the position of *al-Zituna Mosque* (built a few years after the *Great Mosque* of *Oqba Ibn Nafii*) and helped *al-Zituna* University to flourish and to become one of the major centers of Islamic learning. During that period, other Tunisian intellectuals contributed to advancing knowledge in various fields. *Ibn Abi al-Rijal* (?–1037) was an astrologer and astronomer famous for his treatise *Kitāb al-bāri' fi ahkām an-nujūm* (complete book on the judgment of the stars). This treaty was among the Arabic books translated into Latin and Castilian Spanish during the reign of Alfonso X of Castile (1252–1284). Its Latin translation *De Judiciis Astrorum* was published in Venice in 1485 and became an important source in Renaissance Europe for the understanding of medieval astrology (World Digital Library). Ibn Chabbat (1221–1285) was a scholar and mathematician born in Tozeur who wrote many books in literature and history but is mostly famous by his treaties in engineering (Boudhina, 1992). He developed an open-surface-canal system for the management and distribution of water in Tozeur's oasis.[6]

Tunisia is also proud of *Abd ur-Rahman Ibn Khaldun* (1332–1406), whose family had been forced to migrate from Spain to Tunis after the fall of Seville in 1248. He received classical Islamic education in *al-Zituna* until the age of 16. By the arrival of the Algerian mathematician and philosopher *Al-Abili* to Tunis in 1347, *Ibn Khaldun* was introduced to mathematics, logic and philosophy during three years (Nassif, 1964). He saw the rise and fall of various governments and interacted with many rulers (in Tunis, Morocco, Egypt and Spain) in various capacities (teacher, adviser, minister, ambassador and judge). *Ibn Khaldun* is considered as the father of modern sociology. His analytical method is a perennial contribution to the analysis of social dynamics, in advance by many centuries from the European Middle-aged thinking (Giovanni, 2010; Lacoste, 1984). According to Barnes (1963), the importance of Ibn Khaldun's

others experts to such an extent that the rumor arose that the ruler was going to convert to Islam (Houben, 2002).

[6]The system is still in use in several oases in southern Tunisia. It distributes a volume of water to each garden, during a given time, according to its size and the nature of its activity/production (Benhamida, 2015).

thinking lies on his ability to rationalize the subject of history and analyze its methods and purposes. He notes that Ibn Khaldun's analysis revealed the interconnected roles of psychic and environmental factors in the evolution of civilizations. His book *al-Muqaddima* (the Introduction) is a treasury of many sciences where he criticized the omnipotence of the state, denunciated the high fiscal charging and exalted freedom. It made him a precursor of modern political science and classical liberalism (Giovanni, 2010).

*Ibn Khaldun*'s theory of taxation is one of his most important contributions to economics thought. In the *Muqaddimah*, he recommends low tax rates to incentivize working and to encourage entrepreneurship through higher profits to the entrepreneurs. Islahi (2015) recalls the tax-curve finding of Ibn Khaldun characterized by a first stage during which the government relies on low taxes. This low taxation increases the number and size of firms and results in the growth of the tax base, tax revenue and governmental surplus. Therefore, *Ibn Khaldun* is rightly considered as the precursor of modern recommendations regarding the optimal choice of taxation in order to expand the tax base (which he already relates to the productive public spending, private investment and economic activity in general).

### *9.1.3 Abbas Bahri: A Prominent Contemporary Tunisian Mathematician*

Tunisia's contribution to advancing science and technology in recent times is still modest but fortunately marked by some brilliant figures. *Abbas Bahri* is considered as the supreme contemporary scientific personality of Tunisia in mathematics. *Abbas Bahri* was born in 1955 into a Tunisian family. After primary and secondary studies in Tunisia, he enrolled at the age of 17 in a French preparatory school in order to prepare for the French National Exam to enter engineering schools. In 1974, he was the first Tunisian to enter the most prestigious one, the *Ecole Normale Supérieure, Ulm* in Mathematics. *Paul Rabinowitz* from the University of Wisconsin describes him as an extremely original mathematician with great insight (Collectif d'auteurs, 2016, 18). He was Professor of Mathematics at Rutgers University since 1988. In 1989, he won the Fermat Prize and the Langevin Prize in mathematics. In 1990, he received Rutgers's highest honor for outstanding Research (the Board of Trustees Award for Excellence). His students and friends describe him as a mathematician, a philosopher and a nationalist anchored in the Arab-Muslim civilization.

Abbas Bahri introduced the method of the critical points at infinity which was a breakthrough in the calculus of variations. His colleague Professor Brezis qualifies him as a great speaker who charms his students by his talent to "create" mathematics in front of their eyes. He also pinpoints his moral qualities reflected in encouraging, caring and supporting young researchers from Rutgers and from all over the world (Collectif d'auteurs, 2016, 18).

## 9.2 The Political Reform Attempt of the Nineteenth Century

In 1574, the Othman Empire conquered Tunis and replaced the *Hafsids* by Ottoman governors (*Beys*). The first economic modernization tentative was launched by Hammuda Pasha Bey (NA–1666) who realized many architectural achievements (Boularès, 2017). In 1705, *Husain ibn Ali Al-Turki* founded the *Hussainid* dynasty which remained until 1957. By the beginning of the nineteenth century, Tunisia lost its brightness. The quality of its educational system deteriorated and became centered on teaching advanced religious courses with no place to pure sciences and technical education. Agriculture was the main economic activity using ancient methods (Islahi, 2015).

The economic crisis pushed toward a political reform movement beginning from 1859, when *Mohammed al-Sadok Bey* promulgated the Fundamental Act (*Ahd El Amen*) stipulating the equality before the law of all citizens regardless of their religion, as well as the freedom of trade. This reform was implemented in the presence of a corrupted institutional environment. As a consequence, some corrupted senior officials, like Prime Minister *Mustapha Khaznadar*, had the opportunity to self-enrich and to misappropriate considerable amount of public funds that they diverted to Europe (Fenina, 2003). This period was also marked by an increased influence of the reformer *Khayr al-Din Pasha* (1810–1890), who played a major role in the adoption of the first Tunisian constitution in 1861 under the rule of *al-Sadok Bey*. This constitution transformed the political system to a constitutional monarchy with the separation of powers.[7] In practice,

[7] The executive was assigned to the Bey and his ministers. A Supreme Council headed by Khayr al-Din had the legislature and was mandated to control the executive. The judiciary was the responsibility of civic courts.

the functioning of the new political system was disrupted by the reluctance of the executive, namely Prime Minister *Mustapha Khaznadar*. The political crisis culminated in 1862 with the resignation of *Khayr al-Din* and six members of the Supreme Council. The economic situation of the country deteriorated, namely due to weak management of public funds, corruption of senior officials and overindebtedness of the state.[8] The constitution was suspended in 1864 due to the discordance between the executive and the Supreme Council in relation to increasing taxes to face the financial crisis.

In 1864, *Ali Ben Ghdahem* led an uprising against the Bey's regime in the Sahel and the southwest regions. The rebels called for the abolition of the oppressive fiscal system and for better treatment from the political regime. The rebellion was crushed and the oppression of the population increased. In addition, the economic and financial crises continued and the overindebtedness of the country generated its bankruptcy in 1869. At that year, under the pressure of the creditor countries (Italy, France and Britain) an international debt commission was established and presided over by Khayr al-Din. In 1873, the latter was nominated prime minister and succeeded in implementing a package of reforms.

As a prime minister, *Khayr al-Din* reformed public institutions and courts, strived to limit corruption, to restructure the economic activities and to restore peace and confidence in the political system in all the regions of the country. He founded a modern education institution, the *Sadiqi* College in 1875, combining Islamic studies, humanities, mathematics and scientific knowledge. He tried to revive *al-Zituna* University by restructuring the regime of studies and establishing a public library nearby. He encouraged farmers and reformed the charges they bear which led to increased cultivated land from 60,000 to 700,000 ha in 1877. He reformed the customs system to protect handicraft and other Tunisian industries, and to promote exports. He launched public projects such as paving the streets of Tunis. Moreover, he canceled the tax increases and stopped its military collection. Despite these reforms, the economic conditions worsened primarily because of the dryness of 1876 and 1877. The decline of agriculture production contributed to the deterioration of public receipts and stressed the public budget which was already under the burden of a huge external debt. In addition to these economic factors, *Kayr al-Din*

[8] The government contracted two loans from France in 1863 and 1865.

faced a political maneuver from his Minister *Mustafa Ben Ismail* and the councils of France, Italy and Britain. In the absence of political support from the Bey, *Khayr al-Din* resigned from the premiership in July 1877. This resignation took place against a backdrop of economic and financial crises, which were exacerbated after the canceling of *Khayr al-Din*'s major reforms.

## 9.3 From the French "Protectorate" to Independence

At the Congress of Berlin in 1878, France and Britain came to an agreement putting Tunisia under France's colonization. This agreement materialized in May 1881 and June 1883 with the signature of the treaty of *Bardo* and *La Marsa* Convention respectively. Under the colonization, the authority of the Bey was limited and the sovereignty on main public policies including the monetary policy was transferred to the General Residency of France. During the protectorate the Tunisian economy was dual. French-owned companies, European landowners and French building contractors benefited from the best economic opportunities. They made huge investments in infrastructure, in agricultural sector, in olive and oil production, in the exploitation of phosphate and so on. At the opposite, the economic conditions of Tunisians (who were in majority occupied by agricultural activities and denied from working in public administration) deteriorated, unemployment rose and poverty increased.

The dissatisfaction of Tunisians was initially elitist and started among educated people who channeled their opinions through various platforms (associations, newspapers, meetings). This intellectual movement gave way to the emergence in 1907 of the *Tunisian Youth Movement*. In 1920, *Abdelaziz Thaalbi* (1876–1944) led the creation of the *Constitutionalist Party* (*Destour*) calling for the implementation of political reforms in the spirit of the 1861 constitution, but without direct and straightforward opposition to the French Protectorate status. In 1934, the *Neo-Destour* party was created by a new group of young leaders[9] with the ambition of creating a new constitution and a democratic government that would pave the way to independence. *Habib Bourguiba* and *Salah Ben Youssef* were

[9] The majority received secondary education in the *Sadiqi* College and postbaccalaureate studies in French universities.

among the young leaders who played important roles in the development of the *Neo-Destour*, and led its national and international outreach. After a first tentative negotiation process beginning in 1950 with the government of *Mohammed Shanniq*, in January 1952 the French authorities arrested the major nationalist leaders (except *Ben Youssef* who escaped the French net and exiled to Egypt). The torch of the Nationalist movement passed to the *Tunisian General Union of Labor* (UGTT, created in January 1946) through labor strikes and population protests that intensified after the assassination of the nationalist leader *Farhat Hached* in December 1952.

After a first period of cooperation, a conflict between the two leaders *Bourguiba* and *Ben Youssef* emerged in June 1955 on the occasion of the internal autonomy agreements. *Ben Youssef* declared his unshakable support to full independence within a regional independence project including Algeria. Despite his participation in 1950 in the first aborted negotiations (as minister of justice), *Ben Youssef* considered the internal autonomy agreement as treason to the national movement. At the opposite, *Bourguiba* defended a gradual approach toward full independence. This conflict divided the Tunisian society mainly when, in November 1955, *Ben Youssef* was removed from the *Neo-Destour*.[10] Following independence on 20 March 1956, *Bourguiba* assumed the responsibility of Prime Minister of *Al-Amin Bey* until the declaration of the Republic on 25 July 1957, when he became the first president of Tunisia.

## 9.4 The Political System and Place of Religion After the Independence

### *9.4.1 Evolution of the Political System*

In March 1956, the National Constituent Assembly (NCA) was elected and mandated to draw up the constitution of June 1959. The 1959 constitution developed the basis of a modern democracy with the separation

[10] As testified by Béchir Ben Yahmed, Salah Ben Youssef has reacted by planning a rebellion of the Tunisian South, acting from Libya as the Higher Commander of a Tunisian National Liberation Army. Having failed in overthrowing the authority of Bourguiba and his government he tried to assassinate him. *Ben Youssef* was sentenced to death in January 1957 and November 1958. He was assassinated in August 1961 in Frankfort by those he initially commissioned to assassinate Bourguiba (Leaders, 2016).

of powers and the guarantee of fundamental human rights (Boubakri, 2015). However, few years after the adoption of the new constitution the political system deviated to a one-party system taking the form of an authoritarian presidential model. In January 1966, the militant Ahmed Tlili[11] sent an open letter to president Bourguiba criticizing the political regime and recommending urgent and feasible political reforms (Fondation Ahmed Tlili, 2011). Unfortunately, hopes about the emergence of democracy in the country vanished in June 1975 when Bourguiba was assigned presidency for life. The political and social atmosphere degenerated and led to the general strike of January 1978 (coordinated by UGTT) and to the uprising of January 1984.

Bourguiba was evicted in November 1987 in a bloodless coup by his Prime Minister Ben Ali, who initiated, upon coming to power, a dialogue with the opposition parties. The parliamentary elections of 1989 witnessed large participation from a wide array of the political movement. Even the Islamic party al-Nahdha participated through independent candidates and obtained 15% of votes. However, the pluralistic political environment vanished by the beginning of the 1990s. The regime reneged on its promises to initiate a democratic process. The constitution, which limited the presidential mandates to three, was amended several times in order to renew the presidential mandate of Ben Ali until 14 January 2011. The opposition and human rights activists were harassed, and restrictions on journalists and media increased. By the end of the 1990s, the democratic resistance revived. The National Council of Freedoms in Tunisia (Conseil National des Libertés en Tunisie) was founded in December 1998. Meanwhile, the Tunisian Human Rights League resurged and was accompanied by the lawyer activism, the stirrings within the judiciary and the increased determination of the opposition parties (Hibou, 2011).

The authoritarian deviation of the regime was also reflected in the systematic repression of the Islamist party al-Nahdha.[12] The militant Sadri Khiari considers that the slogan "no freedom for the enemies of freedom" allowed Ben Ali to benefit from passive complicity on the part of the majority of the Tunisian democratic movement, and the major Western

[11] Cofounder of the *Tunisian General Union of Labor* (UGTT) and member of the political office of the *Neo-Destour* from 1954 to 1963.

[12] In 1991, the government blamed *al-Nahdha* for being responsible of an attack on the office of the ruling party.

powers (Hibou, 2011). For Marks (2014), the repression of al-Nahdha might be due to its perception as a threat to the existing political system. The dictatorial policy of the regime resulted in an unexpected effect culminating on 18 October 2005, when the secularist and Islamist components of the opposition adopted a joint resolution and created a common front against the dictatorship (Ben Achour, 2012).

### *9.4.2 Bourguiba's Modernization Approach*

Bourguiba belongs to the Tunisian elite resulting from the nineteenth century's reforming cycle. His modernization approach of Tunisia was inspired from the civilizational trajectory of the West and distanced from the Pan-Arabism and Political Islamic ideologies. Under his leadership, Tunisia was endowed with the basic pillars of a modern state: universal education and health, women empowerment and family planning. These reforms were embedded not just in the Tunisian legislation but more importantly in people's mentalities (Dhif, 2015). Although secular, his approach tried to avoid antagonism with Islam. In 1955, the religious authority[13] severely opposed the secularity approach promoted by the emerging political elite. They opposed the separation between the state and the religion in line with the French political system and feared the replication of the Kamel Ataturk experience in Turkey (Nouira Ben Daaya, 2001). Finally, the political elite reached a balanced approach reflected in the first Article of the 1957 constitution. This Article states that Tunisia's "religion is Islam, its language is Arabic, and its political regime is the Republic".[14] It is important to shed light on Bourguiba's perception of the religious authority. This could be inferred from the letter he sent in May 1951 to Salah Ben Youssef.[15] He clearly expressed his fear from the potential influence of *al-Zituna's* scholars on the Tunisian political arena. This position might not be an opposition to the Islamic religion per se, as some

[13] Represented by the *Mufti Cheikh Jaïet.*

[14] This article was maintained in the new constitution of 2014. According to Charfi (2005), it is understandable in the sense that Tunisians are in majority Muslims, and the state doesn't ignore this sociological fact and takes charge of the management of the mosques and the religious education.

[15] Letter released in 2012 by the ex-prime minister Rachid Sfar: http://www.tunivisions.net/35432/224/149/lettre-de-bourguiba-adressee-a-salah-ben-youssef-le-25-mai-1951.html.

of his opponents think, but rather skepticism toward the religious scholars' willingness to adhere to a postindependence modernization project. In that letter, Bourguiba argues that "there is—among the heads, among the pontiffs—the obvious awareness of the danger to which they will be exposed, if the leaders of the Neo-Destour—with western schooling and progressive mind-access to power".[16] In order to avoid antagonism with the scholars, Bourguiba advocated dissipating their fears while maintaining contact with the *al-Zituna* students and involving them in the independence movement. In the same letter Bourguiba suggested the renewal of the attempt to "neutralize" the influential scholar Mohamed al-Fadhel Ben Achour in order to "deprive the religious clan from the unique thinking and active mind he has in Tunisia".[17] This letter informs that, before the triggering of the conflict in 1955, Bourguiba intended to build with Ben Youssef[18] a common vision of the postindependence project. The latter had more tight relationship with the religious elite and the leaders of the old political party The Destour. After the emergence of the conflict between Bourguiba and Ben Youssef in 1955, the latter received great support from the religious sphere and the leaders of *The Destour*. Hence, even if the conflict between Bourguiba and Ben Youssef were about the leadership of the New Destour, it was certainly tinted with the religious support received by Ben Youssef in opposition to the modernization approach advocated by Bourguiba.[19] This conflict continues to polarize large spectrums of the Tunisians.

### *9.4.3 Rise of Political Islam*

After the independence, the religious sphere (symbols, norms, morality, cultic practices, language, etc.) was placed under the political regime auspice, serving its policies even with those hostile to the religious majority

[16] Ibid.

[17] Ibid.

[18] Ben Youssef would have played an important role in the meeting of January 1946 which led to the creation of the *Tunisian General Union of Labour* (UGTT). During that founding meeting, the religious scholar al-Fadhel Ben Achour was elected the president and Farhat Hached the Secretary-General.

[19] Interviews of the militant Ali Ben Salem and Mohamed Dhifallah. "*Salah Ben Youssef: A Crime of state*", Aljazeera Documentary Channel, 2012.

(Yadh Ben Achour, 2012).[20] The emphasis of Bourguiba on the coherence between modernity and Islam contributed to soothing the fears from the dilution of the Islamic identity. Frégosi and Zeghal (2005) note that even the most audacious acts of reform, like the Personal Status Code (PSC), have been accompanied by justifications from a liberal interpretation of the religious law. However, the increasing secularization of the society was accompanied by the marginalization of the religious elite (namely the scholars of *al-Zituna*). Mohamed Talbi, one of the founders of the Tunisian University, relates this fact to the failure to revive *al-Zituna*,[21] which would have developed in the manner of many ancient Western universities like the Sorbonne in France (Talbi, 2006).[22]

I think that the state control over the religious authority has certainly facilitated the rapid implementation of several reforms. However, it might have discredited the religious scholars in the eyes of many Tunisians, especially in the context of a sociopolitical crisis combined with the feeling of an identity dilution. These factors along with the rise of the Islamic movements in many countries paved the way to the emergence of the Islamic Tendency Movement in the beginning of the 1970s by a group of young Tunisians aged between 22 and 32 (Enneifer, 2011). The founding statement of the Islamic party in 1981[23] was heavy on references to a moral and cultural renewal (Enneifer, 2011). Marks (2015) notes that this new political comer gathered together conservative Tunisians who felt disappointed and excluded from the secular orientation of the political regime (Marks, 2015).[24] The fact that the conflict between Bourguiba and Ben Youssef was tinted with religious affinity, and the opposition of the religious elite to the modernization approach of the former would have played a catalyzing factor in the emergence of the Islamic Tendency Movement.[25]

[20] In February 1957, the function of Mufti (the higher religious authority) was created. In January 1988, the Higher Islamic Council was created and placed under the auspice of the prime ministry.

[21] Considered as the oldest university in the Arab-Muslim world, where teaching of religious sciences began in the year 737 (www.uz.rnu.tn).

[22] Marks (2015) note that many leaders of the Islamic party al-Nahdha consider that the decline of *al-Zituna* and the weakness of the religious education in public schools are among the major factors that contributed to the vulnerability of the youth to the Salafi literalism.

[23] The political pluralism was officially recognized in that year.

[24] This thesis is coherent with François Burgat's explanation of the Islamist movement's emergence. Indeed, he argues that it remounts to the reaction to the "cultural deficit" of the postindependence elite, and the revival of the religious referential, rather than its sacred character (Valiadis, 2011).

[25] The in-depth analysis of this assumption by specialists is worthwhile to be analyzed.

## References

Barnes, H. E. (1963) "A history of historical writing," New York: Dover Publishing.

Ben Achour, Y. (2012) "Religion, revolution, and constitution: The case of Tunisia," Lecture at the Center for Middle Eastern Studies, Harvard University, 17 September 2012.

Benhamida, K. (2015) "The story of water in three major sites in Tunisia," in Proceedings of Water Views: Caring and Daring – Waterwheel World Water Day Symposium 2014 – 3WDS14, Edited by Suzon Fuks, Australia.

Boubakri, A. (2015) "Interpreting the Tunisian revolution: Beyond Bou'azizi" in "Routledge Handbook of the Arab Spring," Edited by Larbi Sadiki, Routledge, New York.

Boudhina, M. (1992) "Machahîr Al Tûnusiyyîn (Tunisiens célèbres)," éd. Cérès, Tunis, 1992.

Boularès, H. (2017) "Histoire de la Tunisie," Cèrès Editions.

Charfi, M. (2005) "Islam and liberty: The historical misunderstanding," Albin Michel, Paris, 1998, Zed Books, London and New York.

Dhif, K. (2015) "'Tunisian exception' teaches democratic lessons" interview of Yadh Ben Achour, www.swissinfo.ch/eng/global-forum-in-tunis_-tunisian-exception%2D%2Dteaches-democratic-lessons/41426492?ns_mchannel=rss.

Enneifer, E. (2011) "A testimony on the founding years," in "From the control of Ben Ali to the Jasmin revolution: The political Islam in Tunisia" (in Arab), Almesbar Studies and Research Centre, Dubai, UAE.

Fantar, M. H. (1998) "Carthage: Approche d'une civilisation," Tome I–II, Alif – Les éditions de la Méditerranée, Tunis, 1998.

Fenina, A. (2003) "Les monnaies de la régence de Tunis sous les H'usaynides," Faculté des Sciences Humaines et Sociales de Tunis.

Findlay, R. and K. H. O'Rourke (2007) "Power and plenty: Trade, War, and the world economy in the second millennium," Princeton University Press.

Fondation Ahmed Tlili (2011) "Lettre à Bourguiba: Janvier 1966," Fondation Ahmed Tlili, Tunis, 2011.

Frégosi, F. and M. Zeghal (2005) "Religion et politique au Maghreb: les exemples tunisien et marocain," Policy Paper No. 11, Institut français des relations internationales.

Giovanni, P. (2010) "A Medieval Approach to Social Sciences: The Philosophy of Ibn Khaldun – Some Historical Notes and Actual Reflections," Journal of Markets & Morality, Vol. 13, No. 1 (Spring 2010), 175–188.

Hibou, B. (2011) "The Tunisian Revolution did not come out of nowhere," Interview with Sadri Khiari, April 2011, www.pambazuka.net/en/category.php/features/73574.

Houben, H. (2002) “Roger II of Sicily: A ruler between East and West,” Cambridge University Press, 231.
Islahi, A. A. (2015) “The economic ideas of two Tunisian statesmen: Khayr al-Din al-Tunisi and Bayram al-Khamis” in “Economic Thinking of Arab Muslim Writers During the Nineteenth Century,” Palgrave Studies in the History of Economic Thought Series, 78–105.
Knapp, W. and N. Barbour (1977) “North West Africa: A political and economic survey,” Editions Oxford University Press, Oxford.
Kreutz, B. M. (1996) “Before the Normans: Southern Italy in the ninth and tenth centuries,” University of Pennsylvania Press.
Lacoste, Y. (1984) “Ibn Khaldun: The birth of history and the past of the Third World,” Verso Editions, London.
Leaders (2016) “Le différend Bourguiba-Ben Youssef revisité par Béchir Ben Yahmed,” News, 16 March 2016, www.leaders.com.tn.
Marks, M. (2014) “Convince, coerce, or compromise? Ennahda’s approach to Tunisia’s constitution,” Brookings Doha Center Publications, Analysis Paper, No. 30, The Brookings Doha Center.
Marks, M. (2015) “Tunisia’s Ennahda: Rethinking Islamism in the context of ISIS and the Egyptian coup,” Working Paper, Rethinking Political Islam Series, Brookings.
Nassif, N. (1964) “Le Maitre d’Ibn Khaldūn: Al-Ābilī,” Maisonneuve & Larose, Studia Islamica, No. 20, 103–114.
Newman, W. L. (2010) Edited, “The politics of Aristotle,” Vol. 2, Cambridge Library Collection.
Nouira Ben Daaya, A. (2001) “Mufti of the Republic in Tunisia: The institution and the function” (in Arab), Cérès Edition, Tunis.
Saladin, H. (1908) “Tunis et Kairouan,” Editions Henri Laurens, Paris.
Talbi, M. (2006) “Eyel Allah,” Cérès edition 2006.
UNESCO (2001) “The Different aspects of Islamic culture,” Vol. IV, “Science and Technology in Islam,” Edited by A. Y. al-Hassan, M. Ahmed and A. Z. Iskandar, UNESCO Publishing, Paris, 2001.
United Nations (2015) “World population prospects: The 2015 revision,” Department of Economic and Social Affairs, Population Division.

### Other Sources

Collectif d’auteurs (2016) “Hommage au Professeur Abbas Bahri,” Bibliothèque Nationale Tahar Haddad.
Interviews of the militant Ali Ben Salem and Dr Mohamed Dhifallah. “Salah Ben Youssef: A crime of state,” Aljazeera Documentary Channel, 2012.
Valiadis, N. (2011) “Le mot “islamiste” ne veut plus dire grand-chose,” http://rue89.nouvelobs.com/2011/12/17/le-mot-islamiste-ne-veut-plus-dire-grand-chose-227603.

# References

Abdelhady, H. (2013) "Islamic finance as a mechanism for bolstering food security in the Middle East: Food security WAQF," Sustainable Development Law & Policy, Vol. 13, No. 1, 29–35.

Abdelkafi, R. and M. S. Nabi (2013) "A proposal for jobs creation based on Islamic microfinance and cooperatives," Sfax 2nd International Forum on Islamic Finance, 27–29 June 2013.

Abdelkafi, R. and M. S. Nabi (2017) "Integrating microfinance and cooperatives for jobs creation in Tunisia," IRTI Policy Paper Series No. PP/2017/02, Jeddah: Islamic Research and Training Institute.

Abdullah, A. K. (2011) "Overcoming the weaknesses in sukūk: Toward risk-sharing instruments in Islamic finance," Islam and Civilisational Renewal, Vol. 2, No. 4.

Accenture (2016) "Digital disruption: The growth multiplier" prepared by M. Knickrehm, Berthon and P. Daugherty, Accenture.

Acemoglu, D. (2006) "A Simple model of inefficient institutions," Scandinavian Journal of Economics, Vol. 108, No. 4, 515–546.

Acemoglu, D. and J. A. Robinson (2000) "Inequality, Growth and Development: Democratization or repression?" European Economic Review, Vol. 44, 683–693.

Acemoglu, D. and J. A. Robinson (2012) "Why nations fail: The origins of power, prosperity and poverty," New York: Crown Business.

Acemoglu, D. and J. A. Robinson (2013) "Economics versus politics: Pitfalls of policy advice," Journal of Economic Perspectives, Vol. 27, No. 2, 173–192.

Achy, L. (2011) "Tunisia's economic challenges," The Carnegie Papers, Carnegie Middle East Center, December 2011.



M. S. Nabi, *Making the Tunisian Resurgence*,
https://doi.org/10.1007/978-981-13-3771-0

ADB (2015) "Beyond the MDGs: Technology, finance and statistics to unlock sustainable development in Asia Pacific," News Release, 28 May 2015.

ADB, ESCAP and UNDP (2015) "Making it happen: Technology, finance and statistics for sustainable development in Asia and the Pacific," Asian Development Bank, May 2015.

African Union Commission, UNECA, AfDB and UNDP (2013) "Food security in Africa: Issues, challenges and lessons," MDG Report 2013. Assessing Progress in Africa toward the Millennium Development Goals.

Aghion, P. and P. Bolton (1997) "A Theory of trickle-down growth and development," Review of Economic Studies, Vol. 59, 151–172.

Ahn, J., A. K. Khandelwal and S.-J. Wei (2011) "The role of intermediaries in facilitating trade," Journal of International Economics, Elsevier, Vol. 84, No. 1, 73–85.

Aizenman, J., M. Chinn and H. Ito (2010) "The Financial crisis, rethinking of the global financial architecture, and the trilemma," ADBI Working Papers 213, Asian Development Bank Institute.

Alkebsi, A. and M. Malouche (2015) "It's time for Tunisians to take the next big step," Foreign Policy, 11 April 2015, http://foreignpolicy.com/2015/04/11/tunisians-next-big-step-arab-spring/.

Alm, J. (2015) "Analyzing and reforming Tunisia's tax system," CEQ Institute, Working paper No. 34.

Andrews, M., J. McConnell and A. Wescott (2010) "Development as leadership-led change – A report for the global leadership initiative and the World Bank Institute (WBI)," Harvard Kennedy School, Faculty Research Working Paper Series, RWP10-009.

Aoki, M. (2014) "Economic and political transitions from Pre-modern to modern states in the Meiji restoration and Xinhai revolution: A Strategic approach," ADBI Working Paper Series No. 486.

Arieff, A. (2012) "Political transition in Tunisia," Congressional Research Service.

Asonguab, S. A. and De Moora (2015) "Recent advances in finance for inclusive development: A survey," African Governance and Development Institute, Working Paper WP/15/005.

Ata, A., M. Shukla and M. Singh (2012) "Financing SME Supply Chains," SWIFT Institute Working Paper No. 2012-002.

Ayadi, L., N. Benjamin, S. Bensassi and G. Raballand (2013) "Estimating informal trade across Tunisia's land borders," Policy Research working paper No. WPS 6731, World Bank Group, Washington, DC.

Bagehot, W. (1873) "Lombard Street: A description of the money market," Homewood, IL: Richard D. Irwin, 1962 Edition. Boyd et Smith, 1997.

Barnes, H. E. (1963) "A history of historical writing," New York: Dover Publishing.

Barro, R. and J.-W. Lee (2013) "A New Data Set of Educational Attainment in the World, 1950–2010," Journal of Development Economics, Vol. 104, 184–198.

Behr, P. and R. H. Schmidt (2015) "The German banking system: Characteristics and Challenges," White Paper No. 32.

Ben Achour, Y. (2012) "Religion, revolution, and constitution: The case of Tunisia," Lecture at the Center for Middle Eastern Studies, Harvard University, 17 September 2012.

Ben Achour, Y. (2015) "La constitution tunisienne permet au musulman de sortir de sa religion!" Interview in www.espacemanager.com.

Ben Cheikh, N. (2013) "The extension of social protection to informal economy under the challenge of Tunisia's transition," Mai 2013 CRES. Centre de Recherches et d'Etudes Sociales.

Ben Miled, M. (1956) "Tunisia between the East and the West," lecture in April 11, 1956, Tunis. Tunisian Society of Art Printing.

Benhamida, K. (2015) "The story of water in three major sites in Tunisia," in Proceedings of Water Views: Caring and Daring – Waterwheel World Water Day Symposium 2014 – 3WDS14, Edited by Suzon Fuks, Australia.

Bensoussan, E., R. Ruparell and L. Taliento (2013) "Innovative development financing," McKinsey.

Berlemann, M. and J.-E. Wesselhöft (2014) "Estimating aggregate capital stocks using the perpetual inventory method: A survey of previous implementations and new empirical evidence for 103 countries," Review of Economics, Vol. 65, No. 1, 1–34.

Besley, T. (1994) "How do market failures justify interventions in rural credit markets?" The World Bank Research Observer, Vol. 9, No. 1, 27–47.

Bonde, B. N. (n.d.) "Carthage was indeed destroyed," accessed on www.media-progress.net.

Boubakri, A. (2015) "Interpreting the Tunisian revolution: Beyond Bou'azizi" in "Routledge Handbook of the Arab Spring," Edited by Larbi Sadiki, Routledge, New York.

Boudhina, M. (1992) "Machahîr Al Tûnusiyyîn (Tunisiens célèbres)," éd. Cérès, Tunis, 1992.

Boughzala, M. and S. Ben Romdhane (2015) "Transition from autocracy to democracy in Tunisia: Factors underlying the Tunisian uprising and the prospects for consolidating the transition to democracy," American University of Beirut Institute of Financial Economics, Lecture and Working Paper Series No. 3.

Boughzala, M. and M. T. Hamdi (2014) "Promoting inclusive growth in Arab countries rural and regional development and inequality in Tunisia," Global Economy & Development Working Paper N° 71.

Boukhars, A. (2015) "The reckoning Tunisia's perilous path to democratic stability," Carnegie Endowment for International Peace.

Boularès, H. (2017) "Histoire de la Tunisie," Cèrès Editions.

Boyd, J. H. and B. D. Smith (1996) "The co-evolution of the real and financial sectors in the growth process," World Bank Economic Review, Vol. 10, No. 371–396.

Bradlow, D. (2008) "An experiment in creative financing to promote South African reconciliation and development," in "Africa's finances: The contribution of remittances," Edited by R. Bardouille, M. Ndulo, and M. Grieco, Cambridge Scholars Publishing, 2008.

Brito, L. (2013) "Innovation, science & technology: Drivers for sustainable development?" Presented on the occasion of the International Conference on Entrepreneurship and Innovation: Making Things Work Better Dubrovnik, Croatia, 23 May 2013.

Buehn, A. and F. Schneider (2009) "Shadow economies and corruption all over the World: Revised estimates for 120 Countries," Economics: The Open-Access. Open-Assessment E-Journal, Vol. 1, No. 2007–9, 1–53 (Version 2).

Bughin, J. and J. Manyika (2013) "Measuring the full impact of digital capital," McKinsey, July 2013.

CGAP (2015) "Global landscape of innovations in digital finance," https://fr.slideshare.net/CGAP/the-global-landscape-of-digital-finance-innovations.

Chapra, M. U. (1983) "Monetary policy in an Islamic economy," in "Money and Banking in Islam," Edited by Ziauddin Ahmed, et al., International Centre for Research in Islamic Economics, Jeddah, KSA, 1983.

Chapra, M. U. (1985) "Towards a just monetary system," The Islamic Foundation, Leicester, UK.

Chapra, M. U. (2008) "Ibn Khaldun's theory of development: Does it help explain the low performance of the present-day Muslim world?" The Journal of Socioeconomics, Vol. 37, No. 2, 836–886.

Charfi, M. (2005) "Islam and liberty: The historical misunderstanding," Albin Michel, Paris, 1998, Zed Books, London and New York.

Cheng-Han, T., D. W. Puchniak and U. Varottil (2015) "State-owned enterprises in Singapore: Historical insights into a potential model for reform," LAW, National University of Singapore, Working Paper 2015/003.

Clappison, A. (2011) "Building new democracies: Norms shape practice not policies," ERF 17th Annual Conference, https://erfblog.org/category/erf-17th-annual-conference/.

Clarke, G., L. C. Xu and H.-F. Zou (2003) "Finance and income inequality: Test of alternative theories," Policy Research Working Paper Series 2984, The World Bank.

Cobanoglu, M. (2016) "Sukuk as an alternative instrument for public finance: The experience of Turkey," https://medium.com/@CASEresearch/sukuk-as-an-alternative-instrument-for-public-finance-the-experience-of-turkey-1878c6247694.

Cœuré, B. (2012) "SME financing – A euro area perspective," speech at the Conference on Small Business Financing, Frankfurt, 13 December 2012.

Coeuré, B. (2014) "Rethinking economics after the crisis," https://www.ecb.europa.eu/press/key/date/2014/html/sp140624.en.html.

Cressy, R. (2002) "Funding gaps: A symposium," The Economic Journal, Vol. 112, F1–F16.

De Ferranti, D., G. E. Perry, D. Lederman and W. E. Maloney (2002) "From natural resources to the knowledge economy: Trade and job quality," World Bank Publications, The World Bank, number 14040, October.

De Grauwe, P. (2009) "Lessons from the banking crisis: A return to narrow banking," CESifo DICE Report 2/2009.

De Soto, H. (2000) "The mystery of capital: Why capitalism triumphs in the West and fails everywhere else," Basic Books, New York.

De Soto, H. (2013a) "L'économie informelle. Comment y remédier. Une opportunité pour la Tunisie," Tunis, Cérès Editions.

De Soto, H. (2013b) "The Secret to reviving the Arab Spring's promise: Property rights," The Wall Street Journal, 26 February 2013.

DeLong, J.-B. (1998) "What's wrong with our bloody economies?" Los Angeles Times, 1998.

Dhif, K. (2015) "'Tunisian exception' teaches democratic lessons" interview of Yadh Ben Achour, www.swissinfo.ch/eng/global-forum-in-tunis_-tunisian-exception%2D%2Dteaches-democratic-lessons/41426492?ns_mchannel=rss.

Di Caprio, A., S. Beck, Y. Yao and F. Khan (2016) "2016 trade finance gaps, growth, and jobs survey," ADB briefs No. 64, August 2016.

Dimick, S. (2014) "Adopting digital technologies: The path for SMEs," Ottawa: The Conference Board of Canada.

Dow, S. (2016) "People have had enough of experts," the blog of the Institute for New Economic Thinking, https://www.ineteconomics.org/perspectives/blog/people-have-had-enough-of-experts.

Easterly, W., J. Ritzan and M. Woolcock (2006) "Social cohesion, institutions, and growth," Economics and Politics, Vol. 18, No. 2, July 2006, 103–120.

Enneifer, E. (2011) "A testimony on the founding years," in "From the control of Ben Ali to the Jasmin revolution: The political Islam in Tunisia" (in Arab), Almesbar Studies and Research Centre, Dubai, UAE.

Erdogan, R. T. (2013) "The Turkish economy meets EU entry criteria," huffingtonpost.com.

Fanelli, A. (2014) "Competitiveness and Structural Change," OCDE.

Fantar, M. H. (1998) "Carthage: Approche d'une civilisation," Tome I–II, Alif – Les éditions de la Méditerranée, Tunis, 1998.

FAO (2013) "Tunisie: Financement du secteur agricole," Centre d'investissement de la FAO, Zoom sur les Pays.

Fenina, A. (2003) "Les monnaies de la régence de Tunis sous les H'usaynides," Faculté des Sciences Humaines et Sociales de Tunis.

Findlay, R. and K. H. O'Rourke (2007) "Power and plenty: Trade, War, and the world economy in the second millennium," Princeton University Press.

Fondation Ahmed Tlili (2011) "Lettre à Bourguiba: Janvier 1966," Fondation Ahmed Tlili, Tunis, 2011.

Frégosi, F. and M. Zeghal (2005) "Religion et politique au Maghreb: les exemples tunisien et marocain," Policy Paper No. 11, Institut français des relations internationales.

Fullerton, J. (2015) "Regenerative capitalism: How universal principles and patterns will shape our new economy," Capital Institute.

Galal, A. and H. Selim (2012) "The elusive quest for Arab economic development," ERF Working Paper No. 722, November 2012.

Galor, O. and O. Moav (2004) "From physical to human capital accumulation: Inequality and the process of development," Review of Economic Studies, Vol. 71, No. 4, 1001–1026.

Garcia-Martinez, J. (2014) "The third way: Becoming an academic entrepreneur," www.sciencemag.org, 20 March 2014.

Gherib, B. (2012) "The political economy of the Tunisian revolution: Social groups versus crony capitalism," Revue Tiers Monde, No. 212, 2012/4.

Ghorbel, S. (2006) "Mokhtar Latiri," http://www.jeuneafrique.com/132277/archives-thematique/mokhtar-latiri/.

Gibson, H. D., N. T. Tsaveas and T. Vlassopoulos (2006) "Capital flows, capital account liberalization and the Mediterranean countries," Working Papers 33, Bank of Greece.

Giovanni, P. (2010) "A Medieval Approach to Social Sciences: The Philosophy of Ibn Khaldun – Some Historical Notes and Actual Reflections," Journal of Markets & Morality, Vol. 13, No. 1 (Spring 2010), 175–188.

Griffith-Jones, S. and K. Sharma (2009) "GDP-Indexed Bonds: Making It Happen," in "Innovative Financing for Development," Edited by S. Ketkar and D. Ratha, The World Bank, ISBN: 978-0-8213-7685-0, 79–98.

Guerrero, I., L. Felipe, L. Calva and M. Walton (2009) "The Inequality Trap and Its Links to Low Growth in Mexico," in "No Growth Without Equity? Inequality, Interests, and Competition in Mexico," Edited by Santiago Levy and Michael Walton, A co-publication of The World Bank and Palgrave Macmillan.

Guitián, M. (1996) "The Issue of Capital Account Convertibility: A Gap Between Norms and Reality," in "Currency Convertibility in the Middle East and North Africa," Edited by Saleh M. Nsouli and Manuel Guitián, IMF, Washington.

Haddad, M. (2011) "Political Islam in Tunisia after the Jasmin Revolution," in "From the Control of Ben Ali to the Jasmin Revolution: The Political Islam in Tunisia" (in Arab), Almesbar Studies and Research Centre, Dubai, UAE.

Hanushek, E. A. and L. Woessmann (2012) "Do Better Schools Lead to More Growth? Cognitive Skills, Economic Outcomes and Causation," Journal of Economic Growth, Vol. 17, No. 4, 267–321.

Hassan, Z. (2011) "Scarcity, self-interest and maximization from Islamic angle," MPRA Paper 29414, University Library of Munich, Germany.

Hausmann, R., C. A. Hidalgo, S. Bustos, M. Coscia, A. Simoes and M. A. Yildirim (2014) "The Atlas of Economic Complexity: Mapping Paths to Prosperity," MIT Press.

Helbitz, A., R. R. Lotan, J. Newman, G. C. Sims, A. Zaroulis (2016) "Social impact bonds: The early years," Social Finance.

Hibou, B. (2011) "The Tunisian Revolution did not come out of nowhere," Interview with Sadri Khiari, April 2011, www.pambazuka.net/en/category.php/features/73574.

Hicks, J. (1969) "A theory of economic history," Oxford: Clarendon Press.

Houben, H. (2002) "Roger II of Sicily: A ruler between East and West," Cambridge University Press, 231.

Hu, Z. and M. Khan (1997) "Why is China Growing so Fast?" International Monetary Fund, Economic Issues No. 8.

IACE (2016) "La Tunisie en Transformation: L'impératif digital," www.iace.tn.

IACE (2017) http://www.iace.tn/communique-de-presse-26-05-2017-lutte-contre-corruption-menee-gouvernement-communique-de-soutien-de-liace/.

IBM Belgium (2010) "Etude sur le marché de la microfinance en Tunisie: Contexte réglementaire, offre, demande et conditions de développement".

Ibn Khaldun, A. (1377) "The Muqaddimah" translated by Franz Rosentha, http://asadullahali.files.wordpress.com/2012/10/ibn_khaldun-al_muqaddimah.pdf.

ICC (2013) "Tunisia's Borders: Jihadism and contraband," Middle East/North Africa Report N° 148. International Crisis Group.

IDA Singapore (2015) "Smart nation platform," Media Factsheet, Annex A, April 2015.

IFAD (2006) "Diaspora Investment in Agriculture (DIA) initiative," Financing Facility for Remittances, www.ifad.org/remittances/pub/dia.pdf.

IFAD (2017) "Sending money home: Contributing to the SDGs, one family at a time," IFAD, June 2017.

ILO (2011) "Tunisia: A new social contract for fair and equitable growth," Studies on Growth with Equity, ILO.

ILO (2015) "Background note for the panel on "Transition from the informal to the formal economy in Africa: The way forward". AFRM-13-D4-Note-informal-economy".

IMF (2005) "The IMF's approach to capital account liberalization," Evaluation Report, IMF, Washington, DC.

IMF (2015) "Tunisia 2015 article IV consultation, sixth review under the stand-by arrangement, and request for rephasing," press release; staff report; and statement by the executive director for Tunisia.

IMF (2016) "Tunisia: Program note," August 2016, https://www.imf.org/external/np/country/notes/pdf/tunisia.pdf.

InfoDev (2013) "Crowdfunding's potential for the developing world," Finance and Private Sector Development Department, World Bank, Washington, DC.

INS (2012) "Mesure de la pauvreté, des inégalités et de la polarisation en Tunisie 2000–2010," Institut National de la Statistique.

IsDB (2013) "Member country partnership strategy for Tunisia," Country programs Department, Islamic Development Bank Group, June 2013.

Ishii, S., K.-F. Habermeier and J.-I. Canales-Kriljenko (2002) "Capital account liberalization and financial sector stability," Occasional paper (International Monetary Fund), 211, International Monetary Fund, Washington, DC.

Islahi, A. A. (2015a) "The economic ideas of two Tunisian statesmen: Khayr al-Din al-Tunisi and Bayram al-Khamis" in "Economic Thinking of Arab Muslim Writers During the Nineteenth Century," Palgrave Studies in the History of Economic Thought Series, 78–105.

Islahi, A. A. (2015b) "Ibn Khaldun's theory of taxation and its relevance," Turkish Journal of Islamic Economics, Vol. 2, No. 2.

ITC (2014) "50 Years of unlocking SME competitiveness: Lessons for the future," International Trade Centre, Geneva.

ITCEQ (2016) "Rapport sur l'économie du savoir," Février 2016. N° 6.

Jinjarak, Y., P. J. Mutuc and G. Wignaraja (2014) "Does finance really matter for the participation of SMEs in international trade? Evidence from 8,080 East Asian Firms," ADBI Working Paper Series, No. 470, March 2014.

Kaplan, S. and M. Freeman (2015) "Inclusive transitions framework," Institute for Integrated Transitions, July 2015.

Ketkar, S. and D. Ratha (2009a) "Future-flow securitization for development finance," in "Innovative Financing for Development," Edited by S. Ketkar and D. Ratha, The World Bank, ISBN: 978-0-8213-7685-0, 79–98.

Ketkar, S. and D. Ratha (2009b) "Development finance via Diaspora Bonds," in "Innovative Financing for Development," Edited by S. Ketkar and D. Ratha, The World Bank, ISBN: 978-0-8213-7685-0, 79–98.

Khan, M. (1987) "Islamic interest-free banking: A theoretical analysis," in "Theoretical studies in Islamic banking and finance," Edited by Mohsin Khan and Abbas Mirakhor, The Institute of Islamic Studies, 15–36.

Kim, S. and Y.-D. Yong (2008) "The impact of capital inflows on emerging East Asian economies: Is too much money chasing too little good?" Working Papers on Regional Economic Integration 15, Asian Development Bank.

Knapp, W. and N. Barbour (1977) "North West Africa: A political and economic survey," Editions Oxford University Press, Oxford.

Kouki, M. (2017) "Efficacité des services publics," IACE.

Kowalski, P., J. Lopez Gonzalez, A. Ragoussis and C. Ugarte (2015) "The Participation of developing countries in Global Value Chains: Implications for trade and trade-related policies," OECD Trade Policy Paper No. 179.

KPMG (2017) "Baromètre du Crowdfunding, 2016" Financement Participatif France.

Kreutz, B. M. (1996) "Before the Normans: Southern Italy in the ninth and tenth centuries," University of Pennsylvania Press.

Kuznets, S. (1955) "Economic growth and income inequality," American Economic Review, Vol. 49, 1–28.

Kwan, C. H. (2002) "The rise of China and Asia's Flying-Geese pattern of economic development: An empirical analysis based on US import statistics," NRI Papers, No. 52.

Lacoste, Y. (1984) "Ibn Khaldun: The birth of history and the past of the Third World," Verso Editions, London.

Lederman, D. and W. Maloney (2003) "Trade structure and growth," Policy Research Working Paper Series 3025, The World Bank.

Leigland, J. (2018) "Public-Private Partnerships in developing countries: The emerging evidence-based critique," World Bank Research Observer, Vol. 33, No. 1, February 2018, 103–134.

Levine, R. (1997) "Financial development and economic growth: Views and agenda," Journal of Economic Literature, Vol. XXXV, 688–726.

Levine, R. (2011) "Finance, regulation and inclusive growth," paper presented at the OECD and World Bank Conference on "Challenges and policies for inclusive growth," Paris, 24–25 March.

Lewis, B. (1996) "The Middle East: 2000 years of history from the rise of Christianity to the present day," Weidenfell and Nicholson, London.

Lilischkis, S., M. Janssen and F. Barjak (2013) "Policies in support of high-growth innovative enterprises," Revised Draft Final Policy Brief 2, Version 1.6, November 2013.

Malitza, M. (1976) "L'intégration de la culture dans le nouvel ordre" in La culture est inséparable du processus de développement économique et social, Cultures, Vol. III, N° 4, 101–110.

Marks, M. (2014) "Convince, coerce, or compromise? Ennahda's approach to Tunisia's constitution," Brookings Doha Center Publications, Analysis Paper, No. 30, The Brookings Doha Center.

Marks, M. (2015) "Tunisia's Ennahda: Rethinking Islamism in the context of ISIS and the Egyptian coup," Working Paper, Rethinking Political Islam Series, Brookings.

Mau, S. (2003) Moral Economy of Welfare States. Routledge, 74, ISBN: 978-1-134-37055-9.

Maxwell, J. (1996) "Social dimensions of economic growth," Eric John Hanson Memorial Lecture Series, Vol. 8, University of Alberta.

Mazzucato, M. (2016) "The Creative state," Project Syndicate, 16 April 2015.

McKinsey (2010) "How to compete and grow: A sector guide to policy," The McKinsey Global Institute.

McKinsey (2014) "Accélérer la mutation numérique des entreprises: un gisement de croissance et de compétitivité pour la France," September 2014.

McKinsey (2016) "The age of analytics: Competing in a Data-driven World," McKinsey Global Institute, December 2016.

Meddeb, R. (2013) "Les Sukuks au secours de l'économie tunisienne: mythe ou réalité?" Leaders, opinions, 19 July 2013, http://www.leaders.com.tn/article/11874-les-sukuks-au-secours-de-l-economie-tunisienne-mythe-ou-realite.

Meddeb, M. (2016) "Dans quelles conditions l'armée nationale peut-elle contribuer à réduire le chômage?" Leaders, 9 February 2016.

Mestiri, M. (2017) "Immersion au cœur de la fuite des cerveaux," Nawwat.org, 27 March 2017.

Milovanovitch, M. (2014) "Trust and institutional corruption: The case of education in Tunisia," Edmond J. Safra Working Papers, No. 44, Harvard University.

Mohieldin et al. (2012) "The role of Islamic finance in enhancing financial inclusion in Organization of Islamic Cooperation (OIC) Countries," Islamic Economic Studies, Vol. 20, No. 2.

Monaldi, F., R. A. González de Pacheco, R. Obuchi and M. Penfold (2006) "Political institutions, policymaking processes, and policy outcomes in Venezuela," Research Network Working Paper No. R-507.

Moreau, M. (2016) "Tunisia is becoming MENA's next Startup hub," 11 February 2016, www.techcrunch.com.

Morsay, H., A. Giamouridis and R. Selim (2017) "Rethinking the role of the state in Tunisia," European Bank for Reconstruction and Development, https://www.ebrd.com/news/2017/rethinking-the-role-of-the-state-in-tunisia.html.

Nabi, M. S. (1998) "Productivité globale des facteurs et politique salariale de l'entreprise," projet de fin d'études, Ecole Polytechnique de Tunisie, juin 1998.

Nabi, M. S. (2009) "Financial imperfections, inequality and capital accumulation," Economics Bulletin, Vol. 29, No. 3, 2400–2415.

Nabi, M. S. (2011a) "Moins d'ambiguïté, plus d'optimisme et de cohésion pour une reprise rapide de l'économie tunisienne," Leaders, 31 May 2011.

Nabi, M. S. (2011b) "L'intelligence des Tunisiens, leur lucidité et leur solidarité leur permettront d'inventer leur propre chemin démocratique," Leaders.com, opinions, 25 February 2011.

Nabi, M. S. (2015a) "Equity-financing, income inequality and capital accumulation," Economic Modelling, Vol. 46, April 2015, 322–333.

Nabi, M. S. (2015b) "Une piste pour débloquer les négociations sociales et une proposition d'un "Tunisian Development Institute,"" Espace Manager, 16 November 2015.

Nabi, M. S. (2016a) "L'exigence d'un leadership institutionnel pour la réussite de la transition économique," Leaders, 22 February 2016.

Nabi, M. S. (2016b) "Politique monétaire En Tunisie, Osons un Targeted Quantitative Easing !" 10 November 2016, http://www.investir-en-tunisie.net/fr/index.php/2016/11/10/politique-monetaire-en-tunisie-osons-un-targeted-quantitative-easing/.

Nabi, M. S. (2016c) "Revisiting equity and debt: Access to finance and economic inefficiency," International Review of Economics, December 2016, Vol. 63, No. 4, 393–429.

Nabi, M. S. (2016d) "La titrisation au secours du budget de l'Etat tunisien? Quelques propositions!" 3 November 2016, https://www.espacemanager.com/la-titrisation-au-secours-du-budget-de-letat-tunisien-quelques-propositions.html.

Nabi, M. S. and M. Boughzala (2009) "Chiffrer le coût social du chômage en Tunisie?" Etude préparée pour la 24ème Session des Journées de l'Entreprise (11–12 Décembre 2009) organisées par l'Institut Arabe des Chefs d'Entreprises.

Nabi, M. S. and N. Diop (2011) "Capital mobility and the optimal monetary policy rule: A Tunisian case study," in "Inflation targeting in MENA Countries," Edited by David Cobham and Mongi Boughzala, Palgrave Macmillan, August.

Nabi, M. S. and T. Rajhi (2013) "Banking emergence, contract enforcement and endogenous growth," International Review of Economics, Vol. 60, No. 1, 83–100.

Nabi, M. S. and O. Suliman (2009) "Institutions, banking development, and economic growth," The Developing Economies, Vol. 47, No. 4.

Nabi, M. S., R. Abdelkafi, I. Drine and S. Al-Suwailem (2015) "Enhancing Intra-Trade in OIC member countries through T-SDRs," Islamic Economic Studies, Vol. 23, No. 1, 101–124.

Nassif, N. (1964) "Le Maitre d'Ibn Khaldūn: Al-Ābilī," Maisonneuve & Larose, Studia Islamica, No. 20, 103–114.

Natarajan, P. (2013) "Unlocking India's innovation potential," The Times of India, 31 August 2013.

Newman, W. L. (2010) Edited, "The politics of Aristotle," Vol. 2, Cambridge Library Collection.

North, D. C. (1990) "Institutions, Institutional change and Economic Performance," Cambridge: Cambridge University Press.

North, D. C. and R. P. Thomas (1973) "The Rise of the Western World: A New Economic History," Cambridge: Cambridge University Press.

Nouira Ben Daaya, A. (2001) "Mufti of the Republic in Tunisia: The institution and the function" (in Arab), Cérès Edition, Tunis.

Nucifora, A., E. Churchill and B. Rijkers (2015) "Cronyism, corruption, and the Arab Spring: The case of Tunisia," Chapter 4 in 2015 Index of Economic Freedom: Promoting Economic Opportunity and Prosperity, The Heritage Foundation.

Obstfeld, M. (2009) "International finance and growth in developing countries: What have we learned?" NBER Working Papers 14691, National Bureau of Economic Research, Inc.

OCDE (2014) "Un nouveau virage à prendre: les grands enjeux des 50 prochaines années," Notes de politique économique du Département des Affaires Économiques, No. 24, Juillet 2014.

OECD/DAC (2007) "The principles for good international engagement in fragile states and situations," OECD, Paris.

OECD/DAC (2008) "Concepts and dilemmas of state building in fragile situations: From fragility to resilience," Discussion Paper, OECD, Paris.

Oláh, D. (2017) "The amazing Arab scholar who beat Adam Smith by half a millennium," http://evonomics.com/amazing-north-african-scholar-beat-adam-smith-half-millennium/.

Panagariya, A. (1998) "Full convertibility: Must we have it?" The Economic Times, 26 October.

Parra, C. and F. Moulaert (2011) "La nature de la durabilité sociale: vers une lecture socioculturelle du développement territorial durable," Développement durable et territoires Vol. 2, No. 2, "Culture et développement durable: vers quel ordre social?".

Patriarca, G. (2010) "A medieval approach to social sciences: The philosophy of Ibn Khaldun – Some historical notes and actual reflections," Journal of Markets & Morality, Vol. 13, No. 1, 175–188.

Pattillo, C., H. Poirson and L. Ricci (2002) "External debt and growth," IMF Working Paper WP/02/69, IMF, Washington, DC.

Pattillo, C., H. Poirson and L. Ricci (2004) "What are the channels through which external debt affects growth?" IMF Working Paper WP/04/15, IMF, Washington, DC.

Pettus, S. (2013) "Social impact bonds," Harvard Magazine, 11–12, July–August 2013.

Phelps, E. (2011) "For a successful Arab revolution," http://web.stanford.edu/~johntayl/PHELPS LeMonde On G8 Proposal 2011-5-20.pdf.

Phelps, E. (2014) "Why teaching humanities improves innovation," Project Syndicates, Edmund S. Phelps, 4 September 2014.

Piketty, T. (2013) "Capital in the twenty-first century," Éditions du Seuil, Harvard University Press, Vol. 63, No. 4, 393–429.

Pisani-Ferry, J. (2015) "Reengineering government," Project Syndicate, 30 April 2015.

Pittman, R. (2009) "Restructuring in times of crisis," Network Industries Quarterly, Vol. 11, No. 4.

Pofeldt, E. (2012) "An untapped source of entrepreneurial financing," https://www.forbes.com/sites/elainepofeldt/2012/08/30/an-untapped-source-of-financing-for-job-creation/#36252d4b435e.

Polychroniou, C. J. (2016) "Socialism for the rich, capitalism for the poor: An interview with Noam Chomsky," Truthout, 11 December 2016.

Porter, M. (2015) "Why social progress matters," Project Syndicate, 9 April 2015.

Prasad, E. (2009) "India's approach to capital account liberalization," IZA Discussion Papers 3927, Institute for the Study of Labor (IZA).

Prasad, E. and R. G. Rajan (2008) "A pragmatic approach to capital account liberalization," IZA Discussion Papers 3475, Institute for the Study of Labor (IZA).

Prizzon, A., R. Greenhill and S. Mustapha (2016) "An age of choice for development finance: Evidence from country case studies," The Overseas Development Institute, Research reports and studies April 2016.

Reich, R. (2015) "What happened to the moral center of American capitalism?" robertreich.org/post/128336881225FRIDAY, 4 September 2015.

Robalino, D., A. Kuddo, and D. F. Angel-Urdinola (2015) "Policy recommendations" Chapter 4 in "Labor Policy to Promote Good Jobs in Tunisia: Revisiting Labor Regulation, Social Security, and Active Labor Market Programs," Edited by Diego F. Angel-Urdinola. Antonio Nucifora, and David Robalino, World Bank Group.

Roded, R. (1994) "Women in Islamic bibliographical collections from Ibn Sa'ad to who's who," Lynne Rienner Publishers, Boulder and London.

Rousseau, J.-J. (1962) "Du contrat social, ou principes du droit politique" in Collection complète des oeuvres, Genève, 1780–1789, Vol. 1, in-4° édition en ligne www.rousseauonline.ch version du 7 octobre 2012, http://www.rousseauonline.ch/Text/du-contrat-social-ou-principes-du-droit-politique.php.

Sachs, J. D. (2015) "Data for development," Project Syndicate, 6 May 2015.

Saladin, H. (1908) "Tunis et Kairouan," Editions Henri Laurens, Paris.

Salela, P. (2010) "Building an ITeS country programme: Lessons from South Africa," A presentation during the World Bank Institute Training, "Financial and ICT/A Training of Trainers and Executive Course for MENA Countries," Vienna Joint Institute, 28 June–2 July 2010.

Schwab, K. (2015) "How can we achieve growth for the many, not just the few?" World Economic Forum.

Shiller, Robert J. (2014) "Creativity, corporatism, and crowds," Project Syndicate, 18 November 2014.

Shirazi, N. S. and M. F. Bin Amin (2009) "Providing for the resource shortfall for poverty elimination through potential zakat collection in OIC-member countries: Reappraised," The Pakistan Development Review, Vol. 48, No. 4, 739–754.

Sitorus, D. (2013) "Smart policy: Why Islamic banks matter in Indonesia," CGAP Blog, http://www.cgap.org/blog/smart-policy-why-islamic-banks-matter-indonesia.

Spence, M. (2016) "Economic decline is leading to political instability. What's the solution?," World Economic Forum and Project Syndicate, 24 March 2016.

Stiglitz (NETI), http://ineteconomics.org/institute-blog/joseph-stiglitz-economics-has-come-terms-wealth-and-income-inequality.

Stiglitz, J. E. (1998) "Towards a new paradigm for development: Strategies, policies, and processes," Prebisch Lecture at UNCTAD, Geneva, 19 October 1998.

Stiglitz, J. E. (2002) "Globalization and its discontents," W. W. Norton & Company, United States.

Stiglitz, J. E. (2011) "The Tunisian catalyst," Project Syndicate, 4 February 2011.

Stiglitz, J. E. (2014) "Capitalism needs new rules to restore the growth and stability of postwar era," The Guardian, 2 September 2014, https://www.theguardian.com/business/2014/sep/02/joseph-stiglitz-capitalism-new-rules-growth-stability.

Stiglitz, J. E. (2015a) "Rewriting the rules of the American economy: An agenda for shared prosperity" Roosevelt Institute.

Stiglitz, J. E. (2015b) "A Greek morality tale," Project Syndicate, 3 February 2015, https://www.project-syndicate.org/commentary/greece-eurozone-austerity-reform-by-joseph-e%2D%2Dstiglitz-2015-02.

Stiglitz, J. E. and H. Rashid (2016) "What's holding back the World economy?" Project Syndicate, 8 February 2016, https://www.project-syndicate.org/commentary/whats-holding-back-the-global-economy-by-joseph-e%2D%2Dstiglitz-and-hamid-rashid-2016-02?barrier=accessreg.

Sudan, R., S. Ayers, P. Dongier, A. Muente-Kunigami and C. Zhen-Wei Qiang (2010) "The global opportunity in IT-based services," World Bank.

Syed Ali, S., N. S. Shirazi and M. S. Nabi (2013) "Role of Islamic finance for the development of IDB-member countries: A case study of Kyrgyz Republic and Tajikistan," IRTI Occasional Paper No. 14.

Talbi, M. (2006) "Eyel Allah," Cérès edition 2006.

Thomson Reuters (2017) "Sukuk perceptions & forecast Study 2017".

Tong, G. C. (2007) "Opening Speech, Singapore International WAQF Conference 2007," Integration of AWQAF (Islamic Endowment) in the Islamic Financial Sector, 6 March 2007.

Trabelsi, K. (2014) "Current state of the informal economy in Tunisia as seen through its stakeholders: Facts and alternative," Solidarity Center, solidarity-center.org.

Tsang, J. C. (2016) "The 2016–17 Budget," Speech on Wednesday 24 February 2016.

UNDP (2006) "Report on the meeting on "GDP-indexed bonds: An idea whose time has come," Washington, DC, 21 April 2006.

UNDP (2010) "A Guide to UNDP democratic governance practice," http://www.undp.org.

UNDP (2015) "UNDP and governance: Experiences and lessons learned," UNDP.

UNESCO (2001) "The Different aspects of Islamic culture," Vol. IV, "Science and Technology in Islam," Edited by A. Y. al-Hassan, M. Ahmed and A. Z. Iskandar, UNESCO Publishing, Paris, 2001.

United Nations (2015) "World population prospects: The 2015 revision," Department of Economic and Social Affairs, Population Division.

Verhelst T. (2000) "Mondialisation, culture et spiritualité," Cultures et Développement.

Whiteshield Partners (2012) "Knowledge economy assessment of Tunisia: Identifying and addressing capability and innovation gaps in the Southern and Eastern Mediterranean region (SEMED)".

Wilson, R. (2004) "Innovation in the structuring of Islamic sukuk securities," Humanomics, Vol. 24, No. 3, 170–181.

Wilson, J. S., C. L. Mann and T. Otsuki (2003) "Trade facilitation and economic development: New approach to quantifying the impact," The World Bank Economic Review, Vol. 17, No. 13, 367–389.

World Bank (1999) "Knowledge for development," World Development Report, published for the World Bank by Oxford University Press.

World Bank (2008) "Tunisia's global integration: Second generation of reforms to boost growth and employment," World Bank Country Studies, The World Bank, Washington DC.

World Bank (2010) "Republic of Tunisia development policy review: Towards innovation-driven growth," Development Policy Review, January 2010, Report No. 50847-TN.

World Bank (2013) "Projet de développement de la compétitivité et des exportations: Document d'information du projet (Pid) phase d'évaluation," Report N° 78503.

World Bank (2014a) "The unfinished revolution: Bringing opportunity. Good jobs and greater wealth to all Tunisians," Development Policy Review, May 2014, Report No. 86179-TN.

World Bank (2014b) "Tunisia: Breaking the barriers to youth inclusion," World Bank, Report No. 89233-TN.

World Bank (2014c) "The opportunities of digitizing payments," A report by L. Klapper and D. Singer, World Bank Development Research Group of the World Bank, 28 August 2014.

World Bank (2016) "Poverty has fallen in the Maghreb, but inequality persists," Feature Story, 17 October 2016.

World Bank, the Better Than Cash Alliance, and the Bill & Melinda Gates Foundation (2014) "The opportunities of digitizing payments,"| http://www.gpfi.org/publications/opportunities-digitizing-payments.

World Economic Forum (2012a) "Redefining the emerging market opportunity: Driving growth through financial services innovation".

World Economic Forum (2012b) "The financial development report 2012," http://www.weforum.org/reports/financial-development-report-2012.

Yu, Y. (2008) "Managing capital flows: The case of the People's Republic of China," Finance Working Papers 2008.10, East Asian Bureau of Economic Research.

## Other Sources

Abdessalem, T., R. Bordier and J. Nussbaumer (2015) "Révolution à l'École Polytechnique," La Jaune et la Rouge, N° 705, Mai 2015.

Biography.com Editors, "Hannibal biography" www.biography.com/people/hannibal-9327767, Access Date: 28 January 2016.

Collectif d'auteurs (2016) "Hommage au Professeur Abbas Bahri," Bibliothèque Nationale Tahar Haddad.

Government of Tunisia (2018) "Livre Blanc: Rapport de synthèse sur la réforme des entreprises publiques en Tunisie," Mars 2018, www.reformes.gov.tn.

Letter released in 2012 by the ex-prime Minister Rachid Sfar: http://www.tunivisions.net/35432/224/149/lettre-de-bourguiba-adressee-a-salah-ben-youssef-le-25-mai-1951.html.

IMF (2017) https://www.imf.org/en/News/Articles/2017/06/12/pr17217-imf-executive-board-completes-first-review-under-eff-arrangement-with-tunisia.

Interviews of the militant Ali Ben Salem and Dr Mohamed Dhifallah. "Salah Ben Youssef: A crime of state," Aljazeera Documentary Channel, 2012.

Leaders (2016a) "69 universitaires, experts et dirigeants appellent à la réforme de l'Ecole Polytechnique de Tunisie," Leaders.com.tn, News, 19 January 2016.

Leaders (2016b) "Le différend Bourguiba-Ben Youssef revisité par Béchir Ben Yahmed," News, 16 March 2016, www.leaders.com.tn.

Leaders News (2011a) "Les grèves et les sit in: la médication de Mohamed Ennaceur" Leaders NEWS, 9 December 2011.

Leaders News (2011b) "Mohamed Ennaceur: Pourquoi continuer à aligner les rémunérations sur celles des moins productifs?," 11 April 2011.

Nabi, M. S. et al. (2014) "Libérer le potentiel de l'EPT: L'exigence d'une réforme," Ecole Polytechnique de Tunisie, https://goo.gl/bNFBWo.

Nobel Prize press release, https://www.nobelprize.org/nobel_prizes/peace/laureates/2015/tndq-facts.

U.S. National Library of Medicine, https://www.nlm.nih.gov/hmd/arabic/bioI.html.

Valiadis, N. (2011) "Le mot "islamiste" ne veut plus dire grand-chose," http://rue89.nouvelobs.com/2011/12/17/le-mot-islamiste-ne-veut-plus-dire-grand-chose-227603.

World Digital Library, https://www.wdl.org/en/item/7387/.

# Index[1]



[1] Note: Page numbers followed by 'n' refer to notes.


M. S. Nabi, *Making the Tunisian Resurgence*,
https://doi.org/10.1007/978-981-13-3771-0

## C



## D

The manufacturer's authorised representative in the EU is Springer
Nature Customer Service Centre GmbH, Europaplatz 3, 69115 Heidelberg,
Germany. If you have any concerns regarding our products, please
contact ProductSafety@springernature.com

Printed and bound by CPI Group (UK) Ltd, Croydon, CR0 4YY
25/09/2026
02222897-0005